T0355050

...AND THE DEVIL IS DEFEATED!

WINNING THE WAR AGAINST SATAN!

KARI QUIJAS

WESTBOW
PRESS®
A DIVISION OF THOMAS NELSON
& ZONDERVAN

WestBow Press books may be ordered through booksellers or by contacting:

WestBow Press
A Division of Thomas Nelson & Zondervan
1663 Liberty Drive
Bloomington, IN 47403
www.westbowpress.com
844-714-3454

Scripture taken from the King James Version of the Bible.

ISBN: 978-1-6642-3624-0 (sc)
ISBN: 978-1-6642-3625-7 (hc)
ISBN: 978-1-6642-3623-3 (e)

Library of Congress Control Number: 2021911188

Print information available on the last page.

WestBow Press rev. date: 06/25/2021

CONTENTS

DEDICATION

This book is lovingly dedicated to Sister Claudette Walker, from (Faith Apostolic Church of Troy, Michigan).

Thank you, Sister Claudette Walker, thank you for your prayers in Ladies Ministries; thank you for sharing your faith, your personal experiences, your abundant testimonies of the goodness and faithfulness of God; thank you for sharing your amazing victories and your honest struggles. Thank you for boldly reminding me and other women around the world of the power of our great God! But even more so, thank you for teaching us how to be successful in the Spirit. Your testimonies and training in conferences or YouTube videos have lifted multitudes.

I know that they have strengthened me, and helped me to face the medical field I work in. As I x-rayed one COVID positive patient after another, worked around a staff that was fearful of getting sick and dying, I remembered your words! I had the courage to rebuke Satan, to rebuke sickness and disease, and to firmly declare, we will see better days, we will get through this! The fear left and I could face 2020-2021 with great hope in Jesus Christ.

— Sister Kari Quijas,
NEW LIFE CHURCH Morgan Hill

A MESSAGE FROM THE LATE REV. BILLY COLE

From the words of the late Rev. Billy Cole, *"The Power of Speaking the Word of Faith"* - 1993 Landmark Conference, Christian Life Church, Stockton, California.

"I love to fight the devil! He paused and smiled. Then continued, *Because I always win!* And then he laughed heartily. And he got serious and looked at the congregation and declared, *"That is not arrogance, that is knowledge."* He continued, *"Someone once said, Brother Cole, aren't you afraid to attack the devil?"* He stood tall and said, *"Absolutely not!"* And he yelled out, *"The devil is scared to death of me! That is not arrogance, that is knowledge of the Word of God."* And Rev. Cole quoted scripture, *"Because He who is within me, is greater than he that is in the world!"* He looked around; his eyes twinkled at the congregation and he spoke. *I was sitting on the platform one day at a conference. The song service worship was just about over, and a lady walked through the doors and the pastor leaned over to me and said, "That woman is full of the devil!"* He laughed and said, *"Well, good!"* Rev. Cole smiled, *If she's full of the devil, we can take care of her in ten seconds. We won't even have to touch her, but* he said cautiously, *If it's flesh, it will take you twenty years to straighten her out."*

> —From the words of the late Rev. Billy Cole,
> "The Power of Speaking the Word of Faith"
> 1993 Landmark Conference,
> Christian Life Church, Stockton, California.

PART ONE

PART ONE

CHAPTER ONE

THE LORD GAVE ME A DREAM

I laid my head down and dreamed a dream.

I saw my ex-boyfriend, Jim, laying on a concrete floor. Somehow, I knew that he had been in a terrible fight and he had lost. The battle was now over and the only thing left was for Jim to succumb to his injuries, lay his head back, and draw his last breath. Yes, Jim was dying. But who did he fight? No one was around him. His face had been beaten black and blue, his left eye swollen shut. Jim had always been so strong, tall, and muscular, but now he was utterly destroyed. In his youth, Jim was the epitome of masculine strength. To see him so overpowered and ravaged was more than unsettling. He lay there flat on his back and I stood over him examining the damage to his body. An angel stood by my side, or maybe it was the Lord. I sensed a heavenly presence yet I could not see Him, but there we both were staring down at Jim; it was finished. Then the angel took me in a second to another young man, Mark, Jim's younger brother; Jim's more attractive brother. He was standing upright, but his neck had been broken in twelve places; his arm hung down to his side, but his eyes glared at me. Mark was still alive; however, he could not touch me. He seemed mad at me, ruthlessly glaring at me. He looked at me as though I had caused his calamity. I didn't know how I could have been responsible for it, yet I sensed I had been. I asked the LORD, what does this mean? It was all unspoken, but I felt the LORD share with me, *"Jim represents your past.*

Your past is dead. Mark represents the things of this world that you were attracted to, I have broken his neck." And I awoke from my dream.

It was January 2005. I had this dream after my first 21-day fast, but my initial conversion to Christianity was in the Summer of 1998: seven years earlier. This event confirmed for me that the Christian disciplines such as prayer and fasting opened the door to the supernatural – they complemented each other *like fire to explosive dynamite!* Strongholds were broken by them. By my own strength, I could not *"will"* the memories of my past away – nor the shattered self-esteem that accompanied it. I had held on to my past, with the thought, *"That must be who I am – that is what others said I was."* But, all the LORD needed was for me to die out to my flesh through a 21-day time of holy consecration. Psalm 23 speaks of a Great Shepherd of the sheep who diligently and carefully watches over His fold. The LORD's rod and staff was about to take care some nagging problems in my life I wasn't even aware of. I mean, I knew they existed, (under the surface), but I reasoned, it just was, what it was – present with me. The LORD God destroyed the Satanic stronghold in our mind.

The amazing thing about all of this was that I didn't even know that God was going to do that for me. He had a special gift to give me. He honored my obedience to my Pastor. I had participated in the corporate fast even though, at the time, I didn't believe I had any pressing needs. But in the end, the LORD gave me a clean slate and my complete freedom in Jesus Christ.

WE ARE NOT OUR PAST!

The idea that we are our past seems so childish now, especially in the light of my long relationship with Jesus. I have lovingly served him for over 22 years in my Christian Pentecostal faith. In 2005, I had to ask myself, *What things was I attracted to in the world? What things warranted my loving Father to intervene on my behalf?* I cannot answer that question and my Father never told me; He didn't give me a reason for His decision. This event was my first time that I recognized the idea of belonging in His loving fold and that I could trust Him for my wellbeing. Also, that it was okay to not have all the answers, but to just be thankful.

> "That Christ may dwell in your hearts by faith; that ye, being rooted and grounded in love, may be able to comprehend with all saints what is the breadth, and length, and depth, and height; and to know the love of Christ, which passeth knowledge, that ye might be filled with all the fulness of God. Now unto him that is able to do exceeding abundantly above all that we ask or think, according to the power that worketh in us, Unto him be glory in the church by Christ Jesus throughout all ages, world without end. Amen."
>
> — The Apostle Paul, (Ephesians 3:17-21)

THE BEAUTY OF OUR CHRISTIAN FAITH

My *God-dream* was an example of the beauty of our Christian faith in action! It is when *God steps in, has a pastor lead his flock into a dedicated time of corporate fasting, and uses the power of the church praying in one accord, in order to enable the weaker congregants to obtain their spiritual breakthrough they so desperately need.*

Many times, Christian believers have a miraculous conversion, just as I did in the Summer of 1998, yet still feel haunted by their past. For me, it was as if it was just over my shoulder trying to reach me, or always threatening to take me out. The memories of my past bossed me around and reminded me of my faults. (Interesting, it acted towards me in the very same way that my dysfunctional relationships treated me). Yes, I will say, Satanic strongholds manifest in our relationships, (person to person), but human beings really don't realize where it is coming from. Remember, all Satan needs is an avenue to channel through. Somehow, the mark of God is upon us, (as Believers), yet, it is only seen in the spiritual realm. Satan's job is to destroy you before you realize who you are in Christ, and what your purpose is.

Today, my identity is found in my Savior, but when I just came out of the world, it was right there in front of me. In August of 1998, I was a new babe in Jesus Christ; I had renounced all sin from my life and I most certainly was not my old self. I was no longer living the way I used to live, or behaving in the way of a sinner. I was doing it all the right way, but my process was still in the early stages.

Beautiful child of God, sometimes those fiery darts of the enemy get in. There are just little insecurities that are hidden in the shadows. We internalize that we feel less valuable than others. We feel that our past will always represent our future. It's not true. Just as I am no longer a 16-year-old young girl, but a 53-year-old woman; wife, mother, and grandmother.

After the dream He gave me in 2005, I felt that I was God's beautiful daughter and that He felt that I was worth saving. The fast had broken the curse! (Mindset stronghold). I want to share with every new person, *we are not our past mistakes! We are not who we once were out in the world. We are not an unregenerated sinner, but a redeemed precious child of God.*

> "Who is a God like unto thee, that pardoneth iniquity, and passeth by the transgression of the remnant of his heritage? he retaineth not his anger forever, because he delighteth in mercy. He will turn again; he will have compassion upon us; he will subdue our iniquities; and thou wilt cast all their sins into the depths of the sea. Thou wilt perform the truth to Jacob, and the mercy to Abraham, which thou hast sworn unto our fathers from the days of old."
>
> — Micah 7:18-20

I love that passage of scripture! The LORD had helped me to remove the old garments of yesteryear and He, (God Almighty), gently helped me to turn the page to a new chapter in my life called *"living a life in Jesus Christ."* That new life contained unlimited potential and great rewards! My fresh start was bright, cheerful, and filled with all God's blessings and goodness. I was given hope and God instructed me lovingly to walk forward in His promises! The new course, or new journey carried these instructions: *"Don't look back."* I would learn through time, that I was who God said I was in scripture. He gave me a *"yes,"* in my spirit! Living in your past is like re-reading a chapter over and over. *"My past, my past, my past."* How horrible is that? and many live there. This is called a satanic stronghold.

I'm here to tell you, *"Satanic strongholds can be broken!"*

We can live in the peace of God and abide in His presence. You will discover that being alone with God, is not lonely, but brings a greater satisfaction in life than our earthly relationships. And in a course of time, our loving Father will bring to you brand new friends; ones that will help you and be there for you. We can move forward into a new day, a new year, and a new life! God does not want you to live in regret, unfulfilled dreams, or disappointment. Here we can learn to dream again and live in hope. And neither does God want us to go back to the world He just drew us out from. The question that I have for you is this, *"Will you allow God, (through His Son), to bury your old man in order for Him to resurrect a new one: body, mind, soul, and spirit?*

> "Brethren, I count not myself to have apprehended: but this one thing I do, forgetting those things which are behind, and reaching forth unto those things which are before, I press toward the mark for the prize of the high calling of God in Christ Jesus. Let us therefore, as many as be perfect, be thus minded: and if in anything ye be otherwise minded, God shall reveal even this unto you."
> — Philippians 3:13-15

INTIMACY IN RELATIONSHIPS IS BIRTHED IN THE TIME YOU SPEND TOGETHER WITH ONE ANOTHER.

It is conceived through a quiet time of prayer, Bible reading, and journaling.

"And he arose and came to his father. But when he was yet a great way off, his father saw him, and had compassion, and ran, and fell on his neck, and kissed him. And the son said unto him, Father, I have sinned against heaven, and in thy sight, and am no more worthy to be called thy son.

But the father said to his servants, Bring forth the best robe, and put it on him; and put a ring on his hand, and shoes on his feet: And bring hither the fatted calf, and kill it; and let us eat, and be merry: For this my son was dead, and is alive again; he was lost, and is found. And they began to be merry."

— Luke 15:20-24
The Prodigal Son Returns

Look at the above story again. *"The Father had compassion and ran to him. He fell upon the child's neck and kissed him!"* As the child may his way home, the Father ran! He had an immediate response – and that was to gather him into His arms! What does the prodigal begin to say to the Father? His confession: *"Father, I have sinned against heaven and in Your sight, and am no more worthy to be called your son."* What happened next? The Father doesn't even address what the son said to Him; He only gladly recognized that his dead son was now alive and safely back home in his arms! Now read the parable and make it literal. It was the Father, (the LORD God), that said to the servants, (His angels), *bring forth the best robe and put it on him.* (Or her!) The best robe is Jesus Christ! And it was the Father that said, *"Let us eat and be merry!"* (Rejoice together). *"For this child was dead and is alive again. My son, (or daughter) was lost and is now found!"*

God still speaks to His children!

CHAPTER TWO

THEY OVERCAME HIM BY THE BLOOD OF THE LAMB

"And they overcame him by the blood of the Lamb, and by the word of their testimony, and they loved not their lives unto the death. Therefore rejoice, ye heavens, and ye that dwell in them. Woe to the inhabiters of the earth and of the sea! for the devil is come down unto you, having great wrath, because he knoweth that he hath but a short time."
— The Revelation of Jesus Christ, to our Beloved John, Revelations 12:11-12

Let me ask you this question, in the above scripture reference, who is the *"him"* Jesus is referring to? The Bible says, *"...they overcame him by the blood of the Lamb and by the word of their testimony?"*

THE INTRODUCTION TO OUR NATURAL ENEMY

The *"him,"* is Satan, himself.

"And they overcame ...SATAN... by the blood of the Lamb, and by the word of their testimony," is just that! The sinless blood of the Lamb was Jesus Christ's blood which was poured out on Calvary's Cross over two thousand

years ago in Jerusalem, in our first century, A.D. (Anno Domini – the year of our LORD.)

The Word of their Testimony refers to the saints of God's conversion story. It's our eyewitness account of deliverance; then our eagerness and boldness to share our faith with others: *"Jesus Christ indeed has risen and has the power to save!"* An example of a recorded testimony can be found in Psalm 78. It's a beautiful chapter – it's their history! (It is their eye witness account). *The Word of our Testimony* is the story of how Jesus Christ delivered us from the curse of sin: death, hell, and the grave. (Revelation 1:18). The word of our personal Testimony is the redemptive love story that has been gifted to us. Each believer has a *"conversion story"* and it is as unique and special as we are. As our fingerprints elaborate the story of our amazing DNA, as the snowflake proclaims the formation of God's ingenuity, so our stories are to humanity! Proof! We are a living eye witnesses of God's profound supernatural mercy and glorious grace, as well as the moving of the power of the Holy Ghost, today.

The 21ˢᵗ Century Christian believer is the walking miracle and testimony of the resurrected Christ!

The next sentence from Revelation 12, which is often missed or glossed over: *"...and they loved not their lives unto death."* The early church was severely persecuted for their faith in Jesus Christ; each of the twelve disciples of our LORD faced harsh persecution for the furtherance of the Gospel. Eventually, one by one, all of the Apostles of Jesus Christ were killed for their faith, except John. It is the beloved John who pens these words for us in the book of Revelation. The Apostle John had been tried for his faith in Christ Jesus, beaten, and then boiled alive in oil. (Revelation 1:9). When he survived his immense torture, our faithful disciple was banished, (exiled) to the Isle of Patmos to live out his days, and there he died. But understand this point, before our last Apostle drew his last breath, he recorded, *"I was in the Spirit on the Lord's day, and heard behind me a great voice as of a trumpet!"* (Revelation 1:10).

TO DIE FOR LOVE!

Have you ever heard this saying, *"No person willingly dies or sustains torture for a lie?"* (Paraphrased from the movie, *Case for Christ*, Lee Strobel's interview with Dr. Craig Blomberg). The Christian believer's willingness to suffer and die for their faith destroys the argument that Jesus Christ wasn't the Messiah. He obviously was the Messiah! And His Holy Spirit boldened the believers to proclaim it's truth – without fear of man! Jesus Christ is the Risen King! When it is our moment in human history to die for our Savior, we have confidence that we will lay down our lives for Him! A life lived in Jesus Christ, is a life well lived. And our Savior will not abandon us in our hour of need. If our Father desires for us to die for Him then He will make a a way for us to endure the suffering – through a heavenly anointing, (or empowerment). Our love is secure in Him, so overwhelming real that it literally brings with it the greatest honor given to us, to lay our lives down for Him! It's all about love! *Perfect love casts out fear!* God says,

> "There is no fear in love; but perfect love casteth out fear: because fear hath torment. He that feareth is not made perfect in love."
>
> — I John 4:18

God imparts to every believer extraordinary FAITH and joy replaces fear! It's, *"supernatural."* Remember, it is not natural for human beings to give up their life; (Romans 5:6-9), but when God is in it, it happens effortlessly! To God be the glory!

When we become physical or emotional martyrs for Christ, our blood, tears, and anguish mixes with His blood and a testimony is developed from it. It then helps to strengthen the hands of others who will come after us. *"Emotional and Psychological spiritual warfare – martyrdom."* You may question the wording of that particular phrase, but for those of us who have lost our immediate families or so-called friends because they learned of our Christian conversions, the pain is very real: *isolation, rejection, and cruel mocking.* For those of us who have encountered real emotional psychological abuse on the job for our faith in Jesus Christ, we know profoundly: ***Martyrdom in the United States is very real; Constitution, and First Amendment clause or not.***

Interestingly, Revelation twelve tells of a spectacular battle in the physical and spiritual realm, yet it seems to be in the past tense. Today, we are experiencing the difficulties of Christianity, (in sharing Jesus Christ) to the present world we live in, but the Bible tells us that we've already won the battle! Nevertheless, Revelation twelve sounds the warning for us all today, *"Woe to the inhabitants of the earth and of the sea!"* (Using an exclamation point to stress the importance of what He's saying to them,

> "The devil is come down unto you, having great wrath because he knows that he has but a short time."
> — Revelation 12:12 (b)

Note: *Satan knows that his time is short - he is running out of time!*

WHAT TIME IS IT!

Mankind has been given the element of time on earth. Our lives are ordered meticulously in time segments: seconds, minutes, hours, days, weeks, months, and years. Then seasons, Summer, Fall, Winter and Spring. We use time as a point of reference. (Ezekiel 30:3; Daniel 2:31-45; Daniel 7:21-27; John 10:9; Acts 14:27, I Corinthians 16:9; II Corinthians 2:12; and Revelation 3:8).

> "The day is thine, the night also is thine: thou hast prepared the light and the sun. Thou hast set all the borders of the earth: thou hast made summer and winter. Remember this, that the enemy hath reproached, O Lord, and that the foolish people have blasphemed thy name."
> — Psalm 74:15-18

A dispensation is a period of time. The dispensation to the Gentiles and Jewish Christian believers is ending. (Isaiah 17:7; Isaiah 62:11-12; Luke 13:22-30; Romans 11:25-26; Revelation 11:2; Revelation 19:17-19).

For me, Revelation twelves sentence structure demonstrates man's timeline with the imagery of a simple hourglass. Sand granules slowly emptying down, down, down the narrow passageway dropping gracefully into the center between the two sections of glass. It's all captured at the bottom of the foundation spilling with velocity, yet effortlessly landing on top of each other to build a mountain of time in sand granules, until there is nothing left on top of the hourglass. The process ends. Time stops when all the sand complete their mission, resting gracefully at the bottom of the base. Naturally our eyes dart from the top of the glass to the very bottom. The drawing force of gravity seems to make it speed past us. The response in observing an hourglass is to ask the question, *how much time is left?*

Now understand that the hourglass is on Satan's dashboard before his eyes and there is no getting around it! I would even say that the revelation of time consumes him. God tells me that Satan is aware of the season we are living in. The last book of the Bible is coming to pass before our eyes and Satan judgement is inevitable. That reality is pressing him every day and he is scared. Satan knows his determined fate and he's working under a tight time restraint. Allow me to prove that thought. Let's look at Mark 1, where devils cry out, *"It's not our time yet!"*

Mark 1:22-28

> "And they were astonished at his doctrine: for he taught them as one that had authority, and not as the scribes. And there was in their synagogue a man with an unclean spirit; and he cried out, Saying, Let us alone; what have we to do with thee, thou Jesus of Nazareth? art thou come to destroy us? I know thee who thou art, the Holy One of God.

And Jesus rebuked him, saying, Hold thy peace, and come out of him. And when the unclean spirit had torn him, and cried with a loud voice, he came out of him.

And they were all amazed, insomuch that they questioned among themselves, saying, What thing is this? what new doctrine is this? for with authority commandeth he even the unclean spirits, and they do obey him. And immediately his fame spread abroad throughout all the region round about Galilee."

— Mark 1:22-28

This is just one account, there were dozens just like this one. (Matthew 8:28-31; Mark 5:9; Mark 5:12; Luke 8:27-30; James 2:19). They, (the spiritual realm and creatures), knew Jesus Christ was the Son of God. Meaning: God Himself manifested in a human form walking amongst them. The demons cried out in terror. *"...Saying, let us alone; what have we to do with thee, thou Jesus of Nazareth?* (Paraphrased from Mark 1:22-28).

Christian believer, you need to understand that Satan is not ready for this great event in human history and it's coming upon us all fast! Can you, (personally), not sense the demonic activity that we are going through today? It's tangible and we know it's evil. The Church is so used to being on defensive maneuvers with Satan that we miss that our very existence bothers him and puts him on the defense. And during all of this, the body of Christ, called the Church, makes every effort to reach the dying, lost world around them – to save them from a devil's hell: only to be mocked, spurned and ridiculed by that same world for the Christian's efforts. It's more than ironic, it's tragic!

SATAN'S MISSION

"The thief cometh not, but for to steal, and to kill, and to destroy: I am come that they might have life, and that they might have it more abundantly. I am the good shepherd: the good shepherd giveth his life for the sheep."

— John 10:9-11

According to the Bible, this is Satan's mission: *to steal, to kill, and to destroy mankind.* He's after your spouse, your marriage, children, and grandchildren. He's after your coworkers, your neighbors, your community, and your nation! My question for you is this, *Will you fight for your loved ones, family, and your friends?*

"Thou believest that there is one God; thou doest well: the devils also believe, and tremble."

— The Apostle, James 2:19

THE ORIGINS OF THE BATTLE BETWEEN SATAN AND MAN

It began in a garden!

"Now the serpent was more subtil than any beast of the field which the Lord God had made. And he said unto the woman, Yea, hath God said, Ye shall not eat of every tree of the garden? And the woman said unto the serpent, We may eat of the fruit of the trees of the garden: But of the fruit of the tree which is in the midst of the garden, God hath said, Ye shall not eat of it, neither shall ye touch it, lest ye die.

And the serpent said unto the woman, Ye shall not surely die: For God doth know that in the day ye eat thereof, then your eyes shall be opened, and ye shall be as gods, knowing good and evil.

And when the woman saw that the tree was good for food, and that it was pleasant to the eyes, and a tree to be desired to make one wise, she took of the fruit thereof, and did eat, and gave also unto her husband with her; and he did eat. And the eyes of them both were opened, and they knew that they were naked; and they sewed fig leaves together, and made themselves aprons."

— Genesis 3:1-7

In Genesis three, God tells us certain things about the fall in the garden of Eden which brought it all together.

1. Satan is cursed for his part in our fall. Upon thy belly shalt thou go, and dust shalt thou eat all the days of your life. So, there must have been a time the serpent had legs; or certainly had a different shape. (Genesis 3:14b).

2. Genesis 3:15, God shall put enmity between Satan and the woman. Enmity is a Hebrew word that means extreme hatred or hostility. God naturally placed in the Garden a rival (an enemy): particularly to the woman - not just *"hate"* us but will be *"hostile"* to/towards us.

So, how do we combat this dark force? By understanding spiritual truths in the Holy Bible and learning to defend ourselves against his vicious attacks.

3. Genesis three tells us that the battle will not just rage against the woman alone, but it will come against her children.

Two camps are drawn: The demonic world and humanity. Good and evil and light and dark. It would be between God's children (children of the Day), and Satan's children, (children of the night.) It will continue until Satan is thrown forever into outer darkness!

4. God would raise up a Savior from the woman, (a child). We know Him to be our Messiah, the Christ. It was foretold in the Garden of Eden the child, (Jesus Christ of Nazareth) would bruise Satan's head, where Satan would strike at his heel. (Genesis 3:15). The Cross of Calvary.

Now, in saying that, it would make sense for the next generation to carefully listen to those who came before them and ask the question, *how did they overcome the enemies' temptations and schemes?*

- They knew who their God was, and how to serve Him faithfully.
- They knew who they were, (beloved sons and daughters of God, in Jesus Christ) and they knew how to behave themselves accordingly.
- And lastly, they knew who their enemy was and how to resist him, to fight back spiritually (lawfully) through the word of God, and how to cast Satan out if it came to that, by the very power of God!

CHAPTER THREE

IF MY PEOPLE WHICH ARE CALLED BY MY NAME

THE CALL AND MISSION TO WITHSTAND SATAN!

As a Christian woman, I wanted Satan and his influence out of my life; out of the life of my family, out of my nation, and out of the world around me! After 2020, the American people wanted America free again, we just didn't know how to get it all back again!

It was time to petition the LORD for His counsel and help from above! Immediately! If you are waiting for the *"Liberty"* bell to sound the alarm, this is it!

It is time to stand up for yourself, for your family, and your country. It is time to shove back hard with a force that will knock this enemy on his butt. I'm sorry, but bullies will not just go away. They thrive on the energy they create through fear and intimidation. Bullies don't shrink in time, (if left unchecked); no, they grow in power. Yes, Believer, we shall have our crosses to bear, but not everything is your cross! This was a true satanic attack against humanity! Know this: We do not have to live in fear or live beneath God's best for our life.

2020 was my breaking point! When I declared, *"ENOUGH!"*

LET US BEGIN...

Since what America has lost is spiritual, then our Christian faith leads us back to God. We must humble ourselves and ask for forgiveness. (II Chronicles 7:14). We need to ask our Father for help! He only is the Omnipotent (all-powerful) God that can stop it. Where do we begin again? Jesus Christ, (is our Savior and Deliverer), His Holy Word, (as our sourcebook), His Ten Commandments, (rules of conduct), God's precepts, ordinances, statutes, judgments, and laws, (were for our direction and instruction in righteousness.).

Righteousness, means, Right Standing with God!

If you truly want God's intervention and help, then we must ask Him to help you. We, as a nation need to invite Him back into our lives. I've never in my life heard so many Christians quoting II Chronicles 7:14. Christians had memorized it and meant it. Let's look at it.

> "If my people, which are called by my name, shall humble themselves, and pray, and seek my face, and turn from their wicked ways; then will I hear from heaven, and will forgive their sin, and will heal their land."
> — II Chronicles 7:14

THE HISTORY BEHIND II CHRONICLES 7:14

In 2020, and 2021 the Christian nation was waking up to find that we had fallen short of our responsibilities to God. Now, the history behind II Chronicles 7:14: It was recorded by King Solomon. It was God who was speaking to Solomon in a dream. The time frame, was that the King, or leader had successfully completed God's house and the building of his own house. (I Kings 7).

II Chronicles 7 comes in during Israel's dedication or consecration service. It was Israel's Great Awakening! The nation was joyfully turning back to

God in a grand celebration! The event was filled with song and worship and corporate prayer.

> "It came even to pass, as the trumpeters and singers were as one, to make one sound to be heard in praising and thanking the Lord; and when they lifted up their voice with the trumpets and cymbals and instruments of music, and praised the Lord, saying, For he is good; for his mercy endureth for ever: that then the house was filled with a cloud, even the house of the Lord; so that the priests could not stand to minister by reason of the cloud: for the glory of the Lord had filled the house of God."
>
> — II Chronicles 5:13-14

The entire nation of Israel had been there for over seven days offering to God thanksgiving and praise. Thousands of oxen and beasts were offered upon the altar of sacrifice that could not be numbered! Thousands! This was the time of animal sacrifices! The blood poured out; fires came down from heaven and licked up the offering! God was very pleased with them. The Shekinah glory came down from heaven and filled the temple! (As it were smoke).

I'm going to make this point, before II Chronicles 7, there was much preparation involved with the celebration – and every citizen was participating. Solomon prayed publicly, (in front of the congregation of thousands), leading them with his hands lifted high to God. Israel's king was on his knees in humility! Think about a world leader engaging in these types of events. (II Chronicles 6.) Many can quote II Chronicles 7:14 but miss the very promises and sacrifices that lead up to God responding to them.

Let's look at King Solomon's prayer in II Chronicles 6 and ask yourself are you ready to commit to God, like Solomon was?

> "And said, O Lord God of Israel, there is no God like thee in the heaven, nor in the earth; which keepest covenant, and shewest mercy unto thy servants, that walk before

thee with all their hearts: Thou which hast kept with thy servant David my father that which thou hast promised him; and spakest with thy mouth, and hast fulfilled it with thine hand, as it is this day.

Now therefore, O Lord God of Israel, keep with thy servant David my father that which thou hast promised him, saying, There shall not fail thee a man in my sight to sit upon the throne of Israel; yet so that thy children take heed to their way to walk in my law, as thou hast walked before me.

Now then, O Lord God of Israel, let thy word be verified, which thou hast spoken unto thy servant David. But will God in every deed dwell with men on the earth? behold, heaven and the heaven of heavens cannot contain thee; how much less this house which I have built! Have respect therefore to the prayer of thy servant, and to his supplication, O Lord my God, to hearken unto the cry and the prayer which thy servant prayeth before thee:

That thine eyes may be open upon this house day and night, upon the place whereof thou hast said that thou wouldest put thy name there; to hearken unto the prayer which thy servant prayeth toward this place.

Hearken therefore unto the supplications of thy servant, and of thy people Israel, which they shall make toward this place: hear thou from thy dwelling place, even from heaven; and when thou hearest, forgive.

If a man sin against his neighbour, and an oath be laid upon him to make him swear, and the oath come before thine altar in this house; then hear thou from heaven, and do, and judge thy servants, by requiting the wicked, by recompensing his way upon his own

head; and by justifying the righteous, by giving him according to his righteousness.

And if thy people Israel be put to the worse before the enemy, because they have sinned against thee; and shall return and confess thy name, and pray and make supplication before thee in this house; then hear thou from the heavens, and forgive the sin of thy people Israel, and bring them again unto the land which thou gavest to them and to their fathers.

When the heaven is shut up, and there is no rain, because they have sinned against thee; yet if they pray toward this place, and confess thy name, and turn from their sin, when thou dost afflict them; then hear thou from heaven, and forgive the sin of thy servants, and of thy people Israel, when thou hast taught them the good way, wherein they should walk; and send rain upon thy land, which thou hast given unto thy people for an inheritance.

If there be dearth in the land, if there be pestilence, if there be blasting, or mildew, locusts, or caterpillers; if their enemies besiege them in the cities of their land; whatsoever sore or whatsoever sickness there be: then what prayer or what supplication soever shall be made of any man, or of all thy people Israel, when everyone shall know his own sore and his own grief, and shall spread forth his hands in this house:

Then hear thou from heaven thy dwelling place, and forgive, **and render unto every man according unto all his ways, whose heart thou knowest; (for thou only knowest the hearts of the children of men:)** That they may fear thee, to walk in thy ways, so long as they live in the land which thou gavest unto our fathers.

Moreover concerning the stranger, which is not of thy people Israel, but is come from a far country for thy great name's sake, and thy mighty hand, and thy stretched out arm; **if they come and pray in this house; then hear thou from the heavens, even from thy dwelling place, and do according to all that the stranger calleth to thee for; that all people of the earth may know thy name, and fear thee,** as doth thy people Israel, and may know that this house which I have built is called by thy name.

If thy people go out to war against their enemies by the way that thou shalt send them, and they pray unto thee toward this city which thou hast chosen, and the house which I have built for thy name; then hear thou from the heavens their prayer and their supplication, and maintain their cause.

If they sin against thee, (for there is no man which sinneth not,) and thou be angry with them, and deliver them over before their enemies, and they carry them away captives unto a land far off or near; yet if they bethink themselves in the land whither they are carried captive, and turn and pray unto thee in the land of their captivity, saying, We have sinned, we have done amiss, and have dealt wickedly;

If they return to thee with all their heart and with all their soul in the land of their captivity, whither they have carried them captives, and pray toward their land, which thou gavest unto their fathers, and toward the city which thou hast chosen, and toward the house which I have built for thy name: then hear thou from the heavens, even from thy dwelling place, their prayer and their supplications, and maintain their cause, and forgive thy people which have sinned against thee.

Now, my God, let, I beseech thee, thine eyes be open, and let thine ears be attend unto the prayer that is made in this place.

Now therefore arise, O Lord God, into thy resting place, thou, and the ark of thy strength: let thy priests, O Lord God, be clothed with salvation, and let thy saints rejoice in goodness. O Lord God, turn not away the face of thine anointed: remember the mercies of David thy servant."

> — King Solomon, with the entire Nation
> of Israel, II Chronicles 6:14-42

So, God is asking the American Christian, do you really know what you are asking for?

Do you really want the terms to II Chronicles 7:14? Do you want a Covenant relationship with God? Do you know the contract agreement you signing?

Because it comes with blessings for obedience and curses for disobedience. Or do you just want the blessings of God without the relationship? Once you have committed to God, there are serious consequences towards willful disobedience to a holy God. Will you do your part so those plagues and enemies don't come upon you for your own disobedience or rebellion? The entire nation of Israel had all dedicated their lives back to God in a solemn oath. II Chronicles 5 describes the holy vessels being brought into the sanctuary and the Ark of God finding its resting place in the holies. II Chronicles 4 describes all the provision, riches, and details that King David had set for Solomon were being laid out. David spent years, (probably the last fifteen years of his life), preparing for this moment, but he never lived to see the day. Build anyway!

"And others had trial of cruel mockings and scourgings, yea, moreover of bonds and imprisonment: They were stoned, they were sawn asunder, were tempted, were slain with the sword: they wandered about in sheepskins and goatskins; being destitute, afflicted, tormented; (Of whom the world was not worthy:) they wandered in deserts, and in mountains, and in dens and caves of the earth. And these all, having obtained a good report through faith, received not the promise: God having provided some better thing for us, that they without us should not be made perfect."

— Hebrews 11:36-40

The promise of God came to a spectacular fruition - even though King David never got to see his dreams of God's glorious resting place among the nation. All glory, honor, and praise to God Almighty. His mercy endures forever to a thousand generations! David had the heart of God. Every piece of furniture, every sacrificial offering, every hand selected tapestry, every piece of the best timber purchased, every slab of precious marble housed in a warehouse for that moment of completion - when it all came together! Oh, how David wanted to see it all!

The point of the above story is for us to check in with God. Where do we stand before Him?

Are we really rebuilding to consecrate our lives back to him, or are we quoting scriptures and willfully continuing in disobedience? Because that is the only way to defeat Satan. So, let me ask you, *How's your prayer life?* Or ask yourself, *"Am I doing everything I know to do? Am I walking in the perfect will of God for my life? Am I partnered with Christ; or what the Bible refers to as "yoked" with Him?"* Look at Moses' letter in Deuteronomy 6 to the Nation of Israel. Take note of when God mentions to the people, *"Be careful that you do not forget me, or forget the great things that I have done for your Nation, in deliverance, in provision, care, and protection."*

"Now these are the commandments, the statutes, and the judgments, which the Lord your God commanded to teach you, that ye might do them in the land whither ye go to possess it: that thou mightest fear the Lord thy God, to keep all his statutes and his commandments, which I command thee, thou, and thy son, and thy son's son, all the days of thy life; and that thy days may be prolonged.

Hear therefore, O Israel, and observe to do it; that it may be well with thee, and that ye may increase mightily, as the Lord God of thy fathers hath promised thee, in the land that floweth with milk and honey.

Hear, O Israel: The Lord our God is one Lord: and thou shalt love the Lord thy God with all thine heart, and with all thy soul, and with all thy might. And these words, which I command thee this day, shall be in thine heart: and thou shalt teach them diligently unto thy children, and shalt talk of them when thou sittest in thine house, and when thou walkest by the way, and when thou liest down, and when thou risest up.

And thou shalt bind them for a sign upon thine hand, and they shall be as frontlets between thine eyes. And thou shalt write them upon the posts of thy house, and on thy gates.

And it shall be, when the Lord thy God shall have brought thee into the land which he sware unto thy fathers, to Abraham, to Isaac, and to Jacob, to give thee great and goodly cities, which thou buildedst not, and houses full of all good things, which thou filledst not, and wells digged, which thou diggedst not, vineyards and olive trees, which thou plantedst not; when thou shalt have eaten and be full;

Then beware lest thou forget the Lord, which brought thee forth out of the land of Egypt, from the house of bondage.

Thou shalt fear the Lord thy God, and serve him, and shalt swear by his name. Ye shall not go after other gods, of the gods of the people which are round about you; (For the Lord thy God is a jealous God among you) lest the anger of the Lord thy God be kindled against thee, and destroy thee from off the face of the earth.

Ye shall not tempt the Lord your God, as ye tempted him in Massah. Ye shall diligently keep the commandments of the Lord your God, and his testimonies, and his statutes, which he hath commanded thee.

And thou shalt do that which is right and good in the sight of the Lord: that it may be well with thee, and that thou mayest go in and possess the good land which the Lord sware unto thy fathers. To cast out all thine enemies from before thee, as the Lord hath spoken.

And when thy son asketh thee in time to come, saying, What mean the testimonies, and the statutes, and the judgments, which the Lord our God hath commanded you? Then thou shalt say unto thy son, We were Pharaoh's bondmen in Egypt, and the Lord brought us out of Egypt with a mighty hand: and the Lord shewed signs and wonders, great and sore, upon Egypt, upon Pharaoh, and upon all his household, before our eyes:

And he brought us out from thence, that he might bring us in, to give us the land which he sware unto our fathers. And the Lord commanded us to do all these statutes, to fear the Lord our God, for our good always, that he might preserve us alive, as it is at this day. And it shall be our righteousness if we observe to do all these commandments before the Lord our God, as he hath commanded us."

— Moses, (Deuteronomy 6)

Note the relationship that Israel had with the God of Abraham, Isaac, and Jacob. At this moment, ask yourself, *What is the order of God for my life and for my family?* There is a sacred, consecrated hierarchical structure in

Christianity. It has always existed. Those Christian *"practices,"* carefully organized as ordinances, statutes, judgments, commandments, and precepts. They act as serious roadblocks that Satan, (himself), cannot pass without permission. The highest permission can only come from God! That's exciting. The *"anointed covering"* supernaturally works as a barrier - it will be our *Shield of Defense!*

TODAY'S BATTLE CAN BE WON IN THE SPIRITUAL DIMENSION!

II Chronicles 7:14 asks every believer to *"Humble themselves"*.

Question

1. Will you follow the Word of God to the "letter"?
2. Will you allow yourself to obey the voice of God?
3. Will you dig deeper? Truly spend quality time with Him?
4. Yes, will you kneel before the LORD? Will you allow Him to be Lord over your life?
5. Will you be governed by an authoritative figure in your life such as an elder or a Pastor? Will you allow them to speak into your life and especially in regards to being corrected by them?
6. Will you be held spiritually accountable to a body of believers?
7. Will you allow yourself to die out so that Christ may live in you?

PART TWO

PART TWO

CHAPTER FOUR

KNOW YOUR ENEMY - WHO IS SATAN?

"If you know the enemy and know yourself,
you need not fear the results of a hundred battles."
—Sun Tzu,
(Chinese General, Military Strategist, and Philosopher.
Credited for the Art of War)

Remember the bullet points from the previous chapter; those who came before us – knew how to overcome this world and to withstand Satanic attacks:

- They knew who their God was, and how to serve Him faithfully.
- They knew who they were, (beloved sons and daughters of God, in Jesus Christ) and they knew how to behave themselves accordingly.
- And lastly, they knew who their enemy was and how to resist him, to fight back spiritually (lawfully) through the word of God, and how to cast Satan out if it came to that, by the very power of God!

Ready:

1. Our enemy is SATAN, not each other! We don't fight man to man, or woman to woman; though it may feel like we are. No, it's the spirit behind them and that spirit's driving force. It's the invisible world of the demonic energies that stir up competition, suspicions,

jealousies, and quarrels and then sit back and watch us destroy each other. It's very similar to a reality T.V. show.

2. Next, it is our own unchecked fleshly appetites and our own disobedience working along with Satan. Galatians lists the works of the flesh as *"the flesh of man warring against the Spirit of God"*. (Paraphrased from Galatians 5:17). These are the physical acts inventoried in the Bible: *"...adultery, fornication, uncleanness, lasciviousness, idolatry, witchcraft, hatred, variance, emulations, wrath, strife, seditions, heresies, envying's, murders, drunkenness, reveling and such like."* (Galatians 5:19-21). All of the above are when mankind yields to the temptation of the god of this world. Note: lower case "g". (See II Corinthians 4:4 reference.) That means Satan. Yes, Satan is the god of this world. It is when we give in to the flesh – or lusts of the flesh.

II Corinthians 4:1-11

"Therefore seeing we have this ministry, as we have received mercy, we faint not; but have renounced the hidden things of dishonesty, not walking in craftiness, nor handling the word of God deceitfully; but by manifestation of the truth commending ourselves to every man's conscience in the sight of God.

But if our gospel be hid, it is hid to them that are lost: In whom the god of this world hath blinded the minds of them which believe not, lest the light of the glorious gospel of Christ, who is the image of God, should shine unto them. For we preach not ourselves, but Christ Jesus the Lord; and ourselves your servants for Jesus' sake.

For God, who commanded the light to shine out of darkness, hath shined in our hearts, to give the light of the knowledge of the glory of God in the face of Jesus Christ. But we have this treasure in earthen vessels, that the excellency of the power may be of God, and not of us.

We are troubled on every side, yet not distressed; we are perplexed, but not in despair; persecuted, but not forsaken; cast down, but not destroyed; Always bearing about in the body the dying of the Lord Jesus, that the life also of Jesus might be made manifest in our body.

For we which live are always delivered unto death for Jesus' sake, that the life also of Jesus might be made manifest in our mortal flesh."
— The Apostle Paul, (II Corinthians 4:1-11)
Paul wrote this second letter to the
congregation in Corinth.

Question: How do we know if it's Satan or our flesh?

Satan can bring a temptation to you. If you yield to it, it then becomes a work of the flesh. Meaning that a Christian believer has just bypassed their training and acted upon their desires of lust. You have to choose to resist the sin and walk away, or you can give in. One brings victory and the other defeat; accompanied with ruination and despair. You get to choose. As Christians, we know the story of Joseph and Potiphar's wife. Joseph chose to run away from her; even leaving his garments in her hand. So what's the lesson? Flee and resist the temptation! (Genesis 39:1-20).

FOUR LEVELS OF DEMONIC ENERGY

1. Infestation
2. Vexation
3. Oppression
4. And demon possession

If you are living a godly, holy life and you are finding yourself at odds with other people, and you cannot put your finger on the disruption in the room, that could very well be the Devil stirring things up.

I've experienced, in 1998, when I was in the presence of a certain manager, (we will call him Ed.) And I will also tell you that he has since passed away, so I will be careful how I write this out. This is just meant to be an example. He would begin to swear and cuss more; or even bring up sexual conquests; and he was our manager in the Radiology department. I wasn't the only one who noticed it, my supervisor and other colleagues did as well. Even asking me, *"Why does Ed act like that around you?"* I had no comment; he just did. I knew it was demonic, but what was I going to say? *The devil made him do it?* It was cringeworthy! It made my skin crawl; it made others uncomfortable. Ed said, *"I don't know what it is about you, but you bring out the devil in me?"*

There was times when God's Holy Spirit would nudge me, *"volunteer to go do a portable x-ray, leave the area."* Sometimes I listened to God and sometimes I didn't. I will say, that when I didn't, I regretted it because things heated up pretty fast. I had to make the conscious decision, every day, to avoid him, but I still had to work around him for seven years. If you find yourself in a place that for some reason, they do not like you, your very presence in the room bothers them, know there is something behind that.

Allow me to touch on this. If your finances are under attack; if your health is struggling, if you and your husband are fighting and your kids are running amok, you must check to see if there is an entry point in your life, that enabled Satan to attack it.

For example: finances. As Christian believers, we know that tithing is biblical. I believe tithing is 10% of my income, or more, so I tithe. Our family lives within a budget. Our finances are healthy and sound. If you make the choice to stop tithing and giving in offering, and discover that you cannot make ends meet, you might want to return to tithing again. I know it doesn't make sense – the natural man will not understand this, but it does work. It's God's accounting system and it is ALWAYS sound!

> "Bring ye all the tithes into the storehouse, that there may
> be meat in mine house, and prove me now herewith, saith
> the Lord of hosts, if I will not open you the windows of

heaven, and pour you out a blessing, that there shall not be room enough to receive it And I will rebuke the devourer for your sakes, and he shall not destroy the fruits of your ground; neither shall your vine cast her fruit before the time in the field, saith the Lord of hosts. And all nations shall call you blessed..."

— Malachi 3:10-12(b)

Next, if your health is struggling, ask yourself, *am I doing anything to contribute to my illness?* Somethings could be a trial of your faith: Cancers, or other serious concerns; especially if the outcome is bleak. However, others are not trials of faith, but the consequences for bad choices, or what we call sin. For example: Type II Diabetes. *Are you eating foods that you should not be eating?* Regarding family matters: fighting with your spouse, or your kids getting out of hand. *Have you neglected your disciplines of praying for your family? Or even spending time with them.* Many times we are too busy and our communication breaks down. That breakdown, or hiccup, or disruption leaves an opportunity for the enemy to enter those relationships. Here, we are not left alone to figure it all out. We can go to God and ask for help; yes, even wisdom on how to handle a situation. (James 1:5). God has your back!

BE ON GUARD! WE WATCHFUL!

When God asks us to be on guard, He really meant, *"As a military solider would guard his post, wall, area or jurisdiction – awake, alert and on guard!"*

II Corinthians 2:11(a) paraphrased says, *"Lest Satan should get an advantage of us: for we are not ignorant of his devices."* This scripture reference in II Corinthians 2:11, was in regards to forgiving others. I Corinthians 7:5 Paraphrased speaks about *not withholding marital relations, unless it's for a period of fasting and prayer.* But Paul was quick to say, *"only for a consent of time, but come back together, unless Satan tempt you for your inconstancy."*

We see the warning from the Apostle Paul, to safeguard our relationships. One scriptural reference was to be forgiving and let the offense go: to become peacemakers. The other was to be more physical and intimate in marriage so the partner is not tempted by Satan. We really need to become a friend to our spouse and children – be present in their lives. In 2021, it's easy to check out! But in Christ, we sincerely have to go the extra mile, (Matthew 5:41), and our flesh doesn't always want to. It's at that moment, that the demonic realm watches, evaluates us, and then endeavors to infiltrate. I will be honest, living for Christ is not for wimps. It takes patience and steadfast practices to walk a very straight and narrow course. (Matthew 7:14). That is why we need to be prayed through, and prayed up: not just on Sundays at Church, but every day! We need that holy anointing to get through life; and we need our LORD guidance. I will say this, *"my day is better when I put God first."*

Profound spiritual truth: Ephesians 6:12, paraphrased. *We do not wrestle against flesh and blood.*

Look at the full thought in Ephesians, chapter six.

> "Finally, my brethren, be strong in the Lord, and in the power of his might. Put on the whole armour of God, that ye may be able to stand against the wiles of the devil.
>
> For we wrestle not against flesh and blood, but against principalities, against powers, against the rulers of the darkness of this world, against spiritual wickedness in high places.
>
> Wherefore take unto you the whole armour of God, that ye may be able to withstand in the evil day, and having done all, to stand. Stand therefore, having your loins girt about with truth, and having on the breastplate of righteousness; and your feet shod with the preparation of the gospel of peace;
>
> Above all, taking the shield of faith, wherewith ye shall be able to quench all the fiery darts of the wicked. And take the helmet of salvation, and the sword of the Spirit, which is the word of God: Praying always with all prayer and

supplication in the Spirit, and watching thereunto with all perseverance and supplication for all saints."

— Apostle Paul, Ephesians 6:11-18

Every day before I leave my home, I recite this prayer. As a Sunday School teacher, I taught the children (ages 8-12), how to put on the armor of God and memorize the Word.

Material Point#1: Recite the prayer and put on your armor!

CHAPTER FIVE

WHAT THE BIBLE SAYS ABOUT SATAN

Originally, Satan was named Lucifer, or the son of morning. Today, he is no more the morning glory, but a slanderous, lying, deceiving demonic creature.

The name Satan occurs 56 times in our Christian Holy Bible. It is a Hebrew word, (masculine noun) meaning *Adversary,* (rival). He is one who withstands the authority and will of God. Our Bible also references him as the Devil. The word is found 61 times in a total of 57 scriptures references. The name has a Greek meaning: Diabolos. Obviously where we get our English word, (adjective), for diabolical.

Okay, so, let's understand this together. *We have (in existence, around us), an invisible demonic adversary that hates our guts!*

If you had a serial killer living next door to you, how would you act? If you knew the person next door was a child pedophile, how closely would you watch your children? If you knew that there was a person on the job that was secretly trying to get your spouse to fall into adultery, how would you prevent it? If you knew someone on the job was stealing from the company, what measures would you take to catch them?

SATAN IS NOT EQUAL WITH GOD!

Understand this tremendous spiritual truth, Satan is not, nor has ever been equal to God, not in brilliance, not in strength, nor in creativity. Every attack, every effort to make him better than he is, is a falsehood, lie, or error. Satan has always been a copycat rendition of God's powers. That which he saw God do, that is what he attempts to do. In fact, Satan has endeavored to destroy the work of God; to kill his children, (disfigure them or confuse them), and create a kingdom on earth where it is a living hell. Sound like 2020 to you? Satan is a twisted, perverted creature.

Do not despair, the book of Revelation gives us the end results: ***Satan is ETERNALLY DEFEATED!***

Ponder this next thought. If you were given the book of life; if you could see your origins, life, future, and end would you make the necessary changes to avoid disastrous pitfalls? Of course you would! We all would. Satan had this knowledge and still attempted to overthrow God and avoid the consequences for his actions. I would say, even try and make himself the victim, and God Almighty, unfair.

HOLLYWOOD'S LOVE AFFAIR WITH THE DEMONIC

Here Hollywood doesn't help society, also depicting God and the church in the same way. In 2014, they made a movie, *"a dark fantasy adventure film directed by Robert Stromberg"* according to Wikipedia. Angie Jolie played the lead, Maleficent. The movie came from the 1959 Walt Disney animated film, called Sleeping Beauty. Here, Hollywood flips the roles. Good becomes evil, and evil becomes good. And what does the Bible have to say about that?

> "Woe unto them that call evil good, and good evil; that put darkness for light, and light for darkness; that put bitter for sweet, and sweet for bitter!"
>
> — Isaiah 5:20

Let's start with the name of the movie: *Maleficent.* Dictionary meaning: Causing harm, destruction, especially by supernatural means. The word is a descriptive adjective. The preface, *Mal,* in Latin meaning bad, or malignant, (malicious). The Online visual thesaurus says, *"it is the opposite of beneficent."*

So, what does beneficent mean? Dictionary meaning: *(Of a person) generous or doing good. Charity; producing good. Kindness.* So, the audience is meant to see the slight that the King did unto poor Maleficent. The dark creature was hurt by the King; the wings of the angel severed off. I found the children's movie blasphemous. When people from my congregation asked me about it; I recommended that they not see it with their children. I spelled out the plot; compared it to the LORD God (our Father), the son in the movie, representing Jesus Christ, and of course, the dark creature as Satan. The movie attempts to gain your sympathy and support for the other side. Our children don't understand what this is really about, but an astute, Christian should have the spiritual maturity and discernment to recognize evil – and the danger in it. And we all should be vocal in our children's training, ***"That's not how the story goes; that creature is deceptive and evil."*** Then, shut the movie off! If you will not teach your children good from evil, Hollywood, and this upside-down culture will train them their way. Do you understand what I just said, ***Hollywood and the 21st Century Culture are trying to re-program your children to accept evil for good and good for evil.***

The point I'm making in the above paragraph is this: Satan made no adjustments to his distorted behavior, even knowing his fate was sealed in hell. That is, what I call, mental sickness; and yes, Satan is the origins of all mental disease. Let us look at what God records in scripture regarding Satan. (Revelation 20:10-15).

> "And the devil that deceived them was cast into the lake of fire and brimstone, where the beast and the false prophet are, and shall be tormented day and night for ever and ever. And I saw a great white throne, and him that sat on it, from whose face the earth and the heaven fled away; and there was found no place for them.

And I saw the dead, small and great, stand before God; and the books were opened: and another book was opened, which is the book of life: and the dead were judged out of those things which were written in the books, according to their works. And the sea gave up the dead which were in it; and death and hell delivered up the dead which were in them: and they were judged every man according to their works.

And death and hell were cast into the lake of fire. This is the second death. And whosoever was not found written in the book of life was cast into the lake of fire."

— Revelation 20:10-15

Even with this recorded account, many still will not believe it or listen to us.

PRINCE OF THE DEVILS – BEELZEBUB (LORD OF THE FLIES)

That's a precarious title: *Beelzebub, Lord of the flies.* Knowing in science flies follow death and decay; even a basic google search finds: *"Flies literally eat poop. They are scavengers consuming rotting organic matter."* (by Nikki Galovic, January 2, 2018). The worst insult to Jesus Christ was when the Pharisees proclaimed, *"He does great miracles of healing, helping, and restoring others through the powers of Satan.* Their accusations were utterly ridiculous! (References: Mark 3:22; Matthews 12:24-25). So, Jesus has to school the teachers of the Law. Here is His accurate theological lesson of the hidden kingdom mysteries, found in Mark 3.

Mark 3:22-30

And the scribes which came down from Jerusalem said, He hath Beelzebub, and by the prince of the devils casteth he out devils.

And he called them unto him, and said unto them in parables, How can Satan cast out Satan? And if a kingdom be divided against itself, that kingdom cannot stand. And if a house be divided against itself, that house cannot stand. And if Satan rise up against himself, and be divided, he cannot stand, but hath an end.

No man can enter into a strong man's house, and spoil his goods, except he will first bind the strong man; and then he will spoil his house. Verily I say unto you, All sins shall be forgiven unto the sons of men, and blasphemies wherewith soever they shall blaspheme: But he that shall blaspheme against the Holy Ghost hath never forgiveness, but is in danger of eternal damnation. Because they said, He hath an unclean spirit."

— Mark 3:22-30

Frequently, in the New Testament, we find the Pharisees, Sadducees, Scribes, and lawyers of the Mosaic law blaspheming God and declaring Christ's power from Beelzebub. This was very dangerous waters to be in for any person – in that century or this one. The Bible tells us all that there are some things that will not be forgiven: blaspheming the Holy Ghost is that one act. (Matthew 12:30-32) . Jesus is talking here:

"He that is not with me is against me; and he that gathereth not with me scattereth abroad. Wherefore I say unto you, All manner of sin and blasphemy shall be forgiven unto men: but the blasphemy against the Holy Ghost shall not be forgiven unto men. And whosoever speaketh a word against the Son of man, it shall be forgiven him: but whosoever speaketh against the Holy Ghost, it shall not be forgiven him, neither in this world, neither in the world to come."

— Jesus Christ, (Matthew 12:30-32)

THE ORIGINS OF SATAN

In a time frame, which I believe was the earliest formation of planet earth, a challenge took place in the heavenlies. It would be the very 1ˢᵗ mutiny! An angelic being was created for divine purpose: to glorify God, but instead rebelled against the Great Creator!

This historical character was different than all the other angels; Satan was called *"an anointed cherub of God."* Anointed is a significant word, with extraordinary privileges. Hebrew, *mimsah.* According to the Bible dictionary, it means the sense of expansion; outspread, (i.e. with outstretched wings), anointed!

Understand there are multitudes; thousands upon ten thousand of angels in heaven. It has been referred to as a host of angels or a legion of angels. The archangels, (God's special angels) are Gabriel; the messenger angel, and Michael, the great captain of the heavenly host that leads into battle. The Catholic Bible and some Jewish sources records another archangel as Raphael, but the Christian Bible does not reference him. I have excluded him for that purpose. As I have previously mentioned, Lucifer was an archangel, an anointed cherub. His name meant, *Son of the Morning.* We find a portion of the story in the book of Ezekiel, chapter twenty-eight. Let us look at the Prophet Ezekiel depiction of evil: Ezekiel 28:12-19. Though it names the king of Tyrus, make no mistake, Ezekiel is speaking of Satan. Let's look at the Bible's description and you will understand why I say that.

> "Son of man, take up a lamentation upon the king of Tyrus, and say unto him, Thus saith the Lord God; Thou sealest up the sum, full of wisdom, and perfect in beauty.
>
> Thou hast been in Eden the garden of God; every precious stone was thy covering, the sardius, topaz, and the diamond, the beryl, the onyx, and the jasper, the sapphire, the emerald, and the carbuncle, and gold: the workmanship of thy tabrets and of thy pipes was prepared in thee in the day that thou was created.

Thou art the anointed cherub that covereth; and I have set thee so: thou wast upon the holy mountain of God; thou hast walked up and down in the midst of the stones of fire. Thou wast perfect in thy ways from the day that thou wast created, till iniquity was found in thee.

By the multitude of thy merchandise they have filled the midst of thee with violence, and thou hast sinned: therefore I will cast thee as profane out of the mountain of God: and I will destroy thee, O covering cherub, from the midst of the stones of fire.

Thine heart was lifted up because of thy beauty, thou hast corrupted thy wisdom by reason of thy brightness: I will cast thee to the ground, I will lay thee before kings, that they may behold thee.

Thou hast defiled thy sanctuaries by the multitude of thine iniquities, by the iniquity of thy traffic; therefore will I bring forth a fire from the midst of thee, it shall devour thee, and I will bring thee to ashes upon the earth in the sight of all them that behold thee.

All they that know thee among the people shall be astonished at thee: thou shalt be a terror, and never shalt thou be any more."

— Ezekiel 28:12-19

He was majestic in design: "*full of wisdom and perfect in beauty*". So, what happened?

What transformed the son of morning into the archenemy of God and every living creature? What caused his fall? His iniquity (lawlessness) was found in two areas: his Pride and Coveting. Coveting is also known as lust: Full self-absorption and unbridled evil passions. Paul said this in Romans 7:7 (b), "*...for I had not known lust, except the law had said, Thou shalt not covet.*" Satan wanted more than he was given!

THE FALL OF SATAN – AND
THE SIN OF COVETING

The sin of coveting is often missed as a great sin, but mark my words, COVETING IS A GREAT SIN! It morphs into deadly actions as individuals will rob and steal to have what does not belong to them! You can never become what you meant to become in this world, (in potential, talent, or abilities), if your eyes are always on what others have. Coveting leaves humanity in a perpetual state of dissatisfaction - wanting more than what they have –yet never satisfied; never fulfilled, never happy nor thankful.

> "Little children, let no man deceive you: he that doeth righteousness is righteous, even as he is righteous. He that committeth sin is of the devil; for the devil sinneth from the beginning. For this purpose the Son of God was manifested, that he might destroy the works of the devil.
>
> Whosoever is born of God doth not commit sin; for his seed remaineth in him: and he cannot sin, because he is born of God. In this the children of God are manifest, and the children of the devil: whosoever doeth not righteousness is not of God, neither he that loveth not his brother.
>
> For this is the message that ye heard from the beginning, that we should love one another. Not as Cain, who was of that wicked one, and slew his brother. And wherefore slew he him? Because his own works were evil, and his brother's righteous."
>
> — I John 3:7-12

In the Garden of Eden, there was only one Commandment, *Do not eat from the tree of the knowledge of good and evil.* The only object that was forbidden to them in the garden was that which could hurt them. At the moment of their disobedience, sin is loosed into the world and mankind loses his full dominion and authority. Over two thousand years later a new nation is born. That nations is called Israel and God gives to His chosen people Ten Commandments, written by His own finger on top of Mount Sinai.

The Ten Commandments: The first four Commandments are all about God; His introduction to them, who He is, what He has done for them; what His name means, how to worship Him; He then gave them a day of rest. The fifth commandment is to honor our parents: that is would be, *"well with us."* It is considered the first commandment with promise. The last four commandments dealt with Israel's personal character and behaviors towards each other. Called the *"Thou shalt not Commandments."*

Let's look at Deuteronomy 5:4-24.

The Ten Commandments can also be found in the book of Exodus, chapter 20; however, I feel Deuteronomy gives to the readers more information and more details. Details that matter.

Remember, just because the ceremonial laws, (i.e. animal sacrifices or dietary restrictions) have been abolished by the Cross, the moral law of God has not been. It remains the same as the day it was written. Jesus summarized the Commandments perfectly in Matthew 22:36-40: to *love God and love each other.* You will discover the truth in what Jesus said; because If you sincerely and entirely loved God (with all your heart, soul, and strength), and if you genuinely and honestly loved your neighbor as yourself, the Law of God would naturally follow.

THE ORIGINAL TEN COMMANDMENTS OF GOD

> "The Lord talked with you face to face in the mount out of the midst of the fire, (I stood between the Lord and you at that time, to shew you the word of the Lord: for ye were afraid by reason of the fire, and went not up into the mount;) saying,

I am the Lord thy God, which brought thee out of the land of Egypt, from the house of bondage.

Thou shalt have none other gods before me. Thou shalt not make thee any graven image, or any likeness of anything that is in heaven above, or that is in the earth beneath, or that is in the waters beneath the earth: thou shalt not bow down thyself unto them, nor serve them: for I the Lord thy God am a jealous God, visiting the iniquity of the fathers upon the children unto the third and fourth generation of them that hate me, and shewing mercy unto thousands of them that love me and keep my commandments.

Thou shalt not take the name of the Lord thy God in vain: for the Lord will not hold him guiltless that taketh his name in vain.

Keep the sabbath day to sanctify it, as the Lord thy God hath commanded thee. Six days thou shalt labor, and do all thy work: But the seventh day is the sabbath of the Lord thy God: in it thou shalt not do any work, thou, nor thy son, nor thy daughter, nor thy manservant, nor thy maidservant, nor thine ox, nor thine ass, nor any of thy cattle, nor thy stranger that is within thy gates; that thy manservant and thy maidservant may rest as well as thou.

And remember that thou wast a servant in the land of Egypt, and that the Lord thy God brought thee out thence through a mighty hand and by a stretched-out arm: therefore the Lord thy God commanded thee to keep the sabbath day.

Honor thy father and thy mother, as the Lord thy God hath commanded thee; that thy days may be prolonged, and that it may go well with thee, in the land which the Lord thy God giveth thee.

Thou shalt not kill.

Neither shalt thou commit adultery.

Neither shalt thou steal.

Neither shalt thou bear false witness against thy neighbor.

Neither shalt thou desire thy neighbor's wife, neither shalt thou covet thy neighbor's house, his field, or his manservant, or his maidservant, his ox, or his ass, or anything that is thy neighbor's.

These words the Lord spake unto all your assembly in the mount out of the midst of the fire, of the cloud, and of the thick darkness, with a great voice: and he added no more. And he wrote them in two tables of stone, and delivered them unto me."

— Deuteronomy 5:2-22

It's all a matter of the human heart.

The focus here that I want to take you to is *the sin of coveting*. If people wanted to know what's happening in the world today? The core is the sin of coveting what others have been given, gifted or worked for. Unbridled lust, desiring what does not belong to them – so the culture attempts to steal, kill, and destroy for it. The idea: *I don't have it, I will take it from you!* In fact, *"I demand it!"* Does this not sound like the Summer of 2020 when our cities were burning down with protestors?

My question is, *why couldn't Satan be content to be what God created him to be?*

Satan coveted everything that came from God – but he wanted even more than that. Yes, he wanted to be God. Let's look again at his amazing description in our Bible – called his covering: The Covering Anointed Cherub.

"...every precious stone was thy covering, the sardius, topaz, and the diamond, the beryl, the onyx, and the jasper, the sapphire, the emerald, and the carbuncle, and gold: the workmanship of thy tabrets and of thy pipes was prepared in thee in the day that thou wast created." (13) b

We see a description of stones upon Satan. Question: How do stones sparkle?

Stones and gems sparkle from the light reflecting off of it. Where did this light come from? The light came from the absolute splendor and glory of God. Remember Satan's original name: It's the only time it's mentioned. *Lucifer: Light bearer.* A shiny one, and morning star. (Hebrew: helel – as in brightness. Isaiah 14:12).

TAKING WHAT WAS ORIGINALLY GIFTED TO LUCIFER, SON OF MORNING, AND GIVING IT TO THE CHURCH

Piece together what I have already shared with you, and you will begin to see why Satan hates humanity. We see that Satan has lost his position or placement in the heavens. We see that Satan has lost his wings. We see that Satan has lost his stones and gems. He has lost his ability to shine. He has become absolute darkness. We see that Satan has lost his special anointing. His name was changed to be a disfigured demonic creature. That's a huge hit! He was also defeated publicly in the heavens; so all eternity knows his fall!

Now, let's go back in time, over four thousand years ago, to the Middle East. An interesting event takes place in the wilderness when the nation of Israel were released from Pharaoh's bondage in Egypt. God designed a dwelling place for Israel to meet him and worship Him – His way. God's request, *"that my people would be free to serve me."* (Paraphrased from Exodus 7, 8, and 9). Israel, God's chosen people, had spent over 430 years in captivity (as slaves), surrounded by pagan gods and a false demonic worship. Our country has only been one for 244 years. I wanted to give you a perspective how long Israel was enslaved. Now, drawing His people out from the land of Ham, God was about to introduce Himself to His people and orchestrate a very detailed Tabernacle plan – one that matched the order in heaven. Exodus 36, through 40 was the correct way God asked Israel to come before Him to serve and worship. He sincerely spells it out to them. During this time, God manifested Himself in a huge flame from heaven, or pillar of cloud by day. Do you understand that? *Israel, physically saw the presence of God in their midst every day.*

In our society today we have places of worship called a Church. The Nation of Israel in Jerusalem called them Synagogues. But here the Jehovah Yahweh - I AM, calls His house a <u>Tabernacle, (tent)</u>. Even in the Muslim religion, they have Mosques. The word Mosque literally means, *"place of ritual prostration."* I find that definition very interesting. Words matter in the Bible; Sikhs and Buddhists have Temples. (Temples means a great house). Most of us in the United States know only English, but in other languages especially Hebrew and Greek, even Latin, have meaning behind the names – it's the heartbeat of what something is. Word study:

> Tabernacle: Hebrew (Strong's H4908) Miskan. A Residence. (Including a shepherd's hut, the lair of animals). God's dwelling place. A tent.

> Church: Greek (Strong's G1577) Ekklesia. A gathering of citizens called from their homes into some public place, an assembly.

> Synagogue: Greek (Strong's G4864) It is not pronounced "Sin-a-gogue", but "Soon-Ag-Go-gay" An assembly of persons, meeting place.

INSTRUCTIONS OF WORSHIP

Aaron, Moses brother became the first High Priest of the earthly tabernacle, (wilderness Church). What garments did God instruct Israel to make? It would have precious stones interwoven on the breast plate. Each stone was to represent each of the 12 sons of Jacob, or the 12 tribes of Israel. The High Priest would wear the mantle, interwoven with stones; in God's presence glorious light would emanate in brilliant colors, or reflect the light of God. In ministry, God's glory would shine upon humanity. (See: Exodus 25-30; Exodus 28:6-30; Leviticus 10:10-11; Leviticus 16:4).

During Israel's wilderness experience, Aarons' breastplate had an Urim and Thummin attached to it. (See: Exodus 28:30; Leviticus 8:8; Numbers 27:21, and Deuteronomy 33:8). I find this extremely fascinating. In the Old Testament, only the priest could offer sacrifices to God, done in a very organized way. Only the High Priest could wear the special garment, or mantle of God; he could enter the Holiest of Holies once a year – called the day of atonement. Now watch the transition after Jesus Christ was crucified upon the Cross of Calvary.

God transfers the role of priesthood to all born-again Christian believers.

> "Jesus, when he had cried again with a loud voice, yielded up the ghost.
>
> And, behold, the veil of the temple was rent in twain from the top to the bottom; and the earth did quake, and the rocks rent; and the graves were opened; and many bodies of the saints which slept arose, and came out of the graves after his resurrection, and went into the holy city, and appeared unto many. Now when the centurion, and they that were with him, watching Jesus, saw the earthquake, and those things that were done, they feared greatly, saying, Truly this was the Son of God."
>
> — Matthew 27:50-54

The earth did quake; darkness was upon the land; (Mark 15:33), the veil in the Temple, (Synagogue), was torn in two in a special way that was significant: from the very top to the bottom, and done by the very hand of God Himself! Wow!

In the New Testament, (under a new dispensation – called the Church age), we are all called to be priests of God, ministering to our LORD. (I Peter 2:9). Not just one tribe, the Levitical tribe, no, each member of the body of Christ would carry a responsibility of priestly duties.

I Peter 2:5-10 (lively stones, a spiritual house and a holy priest)

> Ye also, as lively stones, are built up a spiritual house, an holy priesthood, to offer up spiritual sacrifices, acceptable to God by Jesus Christ.
>
> Wherefore also it is contained in the scripture, Behold, I lay in Sion a chief corner stone, elect, precious: and he that believeth on him shall not be confounded.
>
> Unto you therefore which believe he is precious: but unto them which be disobedient, the stone which the builders disallowed, the same is made the head of the corner, and a stone of stumbling, and a rock of offence, even to them which stumble at the word, being disobedient: whereunto also they were appointed.
>
> But ye are a chosen generation, a royal priesthood, an holy nation, a peculiar people; that ye should shew forth the praises of him who hath called you out of darkness into his marvelous light; which in time past were not a people, but are now the people of God: which had not obtained mercy, but now have obtained mercy."
>
> — I Peter 2:5-10

God's glory can now be seen upon our faces because Jesus lives within us. We were to shine as lights in a darken world. (Matthew 5:14-16). God would live in the hearts of every believer; Jesus would be able to touch lives through our hands. Jesus would speak through our mouths. That's exciting! Supernatural light emanates from our human vessels, even though we cannot see into the spirit world. The name of Jesus Christ is upon our forehead, yet we don't notice it. However, the demonic realm sees it and trembles! The very power of God abides inside of us, we, born-again Spirit-filled believers, have a HUGE, TREMENDOUS responsibility to crucify the flesh and its appetites – the world is watching us.

I will say here, that God's power combined with a person who has not subdued himself, is beyond embarrassing, it's humiliating. It's this point – this *"pivotal point"* that makes unbelievers and the world around us say, *I love Jesus Christ, but I don't like His children.* The radio speaker who shared that thought was Ravi Zacharias. With the revelations that have recently taken place in the past three years of the reputation of this known Canadian apologist, (who has since passed away), I find it ironic and terribly tragic. However, we must remember the words of Jesus Christ: *If you want to be my disciple, you must deny your flesh. You must choose to pick up your cross (daily), and follow me in all things.* (Paraphrased from Luke 9:23). Not one person on earth has ever arrived at a place where temptation cannot take them out!

ALL POWER AND DOMINION BELONG TO GOD!

Remember all Satan's brilliant light came from the God of the Universe. The Scriptures tell humanity this spiritual truth: *"Without God, we can do nothing!"* (Paraphrased from John 15:5 – True Vine and Branches). Well, that goes for Satan as well. Think of the scientific differences between the sun and the moon. Both bring light upon the earth. Now, think of the biblical reasons for the sun and the moon. It's found in the very first chapter of our Bible.

The light was good. The light divided day time from night time.

> "And God said, Let there be light: and there was light. And God saw the light, that it was good: and God divided the light from the darkness. And God called the light Day, and the darkness he called Night. And the evening and the morning were the first day."
> — Genesis 1:3-5.

The light was for signs and season; marking days and years.

> "And God said, Let there be lights in the firmament of the
> heaven to divide the day from the night; and let them be
> for signs, and for seasons, and for days, and years: And let
> them be for lights in the firmament of the heaven to give
> light upon the earth: and it was so.

**Two great lights: the Sun and the Moon so that mankind didn't walk
in utter darkness. Even stars in the heaven serve God's purpose.**

> And God made two great lights; the greater light to rule
> the day, and the lesser light to rule the night: he made
> the stars also. And God set them in the firmament of the
> heaven to give light upon the earth, and to rule over the
> day and over the night, and to divide the light from the
> darkness: and God saw that it was good. And the evening
> and the morning were the fourth day."
>
> — Genesis 1:14-19

What makes the moon shine in the darkness?

The reflective light from the sun bouncing off the moon. Satan, in essence
is like the moon. Light really isn't shining from the moon: the light that
comes from the moon is an optical illusion. Moonlight is light coming
from the sun bouncing back. In actuality, the moon only reflects about
12% of the light. God's glory and true light is blinding! It is said in our Old
Testament; no man can look upon God's glory and live. (Exodus 33:20).
The Bible says that the person would be utterly consumed!

As I have said before, Satan's design and luster were meant for a purpose –
a divine purpose. He was to lead in the worship and praise to Yahweh,
Jehovah God Almighty. He would usher in the presence of God. He
would announce the King! Similar to opening acts on a main event. In the
heavens today, the multitudes of God's angels still resound the praises of
King Jesus! The faithful cloud of witnesses who went before us, still sing
along with the heavenly host – glorious hallelujahs! Satan was the first to

lead in concerts and amaze his audience. Think for a moment, what are some of the most spectacular musical event s ever seen?

> "For many bands, the light show is almost as integral to the live act as the music, so much so, in fact, that lighting directors are often heralded as an additional member of the group. These illumination wizards have the most open and creative space to work in, and as a result, they are able to create some of the most complex lighting schemes. Westword; the Independent voice of Denver. From Phish to Floyd, the ten best light shows. (www.westword.com/ music.) See: the bands, Genesis – Abacab and Mama Tours, Pink Floyd – Division Bell tour. Muse, STS9, Saxton Waller, Widespread panic, uses former Grateful Dead lighting director Candace Brightman; Nine Inch Nails, "Lights in the Sky" tour, the Disco Biscuits, Johnny R. Goode III brings cannons as well as lasers, the Ghostland observatory, Phish, and Umphrey's McGee .

My mind automatically thinks of performers who have been obnoxiously overdressed and over-beaded, (to bedazzle, to sparkle and amaze), and I think of Liberace, Elton John or Elvis Presley. It leads us to ask, *where did their genius come from?* Am I saying they are demon possessed? No! Absolutely not, but I am saying they can be inspired by a darker element than they realize, and humanity takes it in. Oh, how we love the lights, the music, the enticing lyrics, the rhythm, and movement of song. The vibrations travel through us; our heart pounds with those vibrations; our eyes open wide to see the show! The impeccable talent of solar guitarists, pianist, or drummer amazes! As we watch their fingers move gracefully, or mightily upon their instruments – and the tune is in our head; we become one with the performer for just that moment; the experience takes our breath away!

Satan is, and has always been in the music industry. Some heavy metal and jazz bands have spoken openly that Satan himself appeared to them, with a contract in hand, promising them great success if they would offer up their soul for payment. *"Sell their soul to the devil and he will give them fame, riches, and fortune."* David Bowe said, *"Rock has always been the Devil's music. I believe rock'n'roll is dangerous."* Jimmy Page said, *"I was living it. That's all there is to it. It was my life – that fusion of magic and music...yes, I knew what I was doing. There is no point in talking about it, because the more you discuss it, the more eccentric you appear to be. But the fact is, as far as I was concerned, it was working, so I used it."* (2007 Guitar World – about Rock and Religion). Satan has the ability to give them what they physically ask for, but it is obvious that the Rock and Roll legends, the Jazz experts, the Singer and Song writers don't understand eternity. This life is brief, it's last only for a moment in time. But eternity is FOREVER.

> "Whereas ye know not what shall be on the morrow. For what is your life? It is even a vapour, that appeareth for a little time, and then vanisheth away. For that ye ought to say, If the Lord will, we shall live, and do this, or that."
>
> — James 4:14-15

Fact – the Sad Truth: *No one remembers their name in hell; as they toss and turn in the billows of flames.*

They will remember every life regret, every missed moment to love their family, they will remember every lost opportunity to do good to someone in need. They will remember every mistake they made for the temporary element of fame and glory for one season in time. No, it's not a fair trade, but when people covet, (lust) money, power, fame, and status, they can't seem to resist the sparkling temptation before their eyes. You have to ask them, is it worth it to have ten years of success, to thousand times ten thousand years of pain, sorrow, grief, and torment? It's interesting the artists, and even Hollywood stars soar high into heavens, with awe and wonder, popularity, and influence; their beauty captures our attention and imagination, but many died shortly after the pact was agreed upon. There have been many unexplained plane crashes, automobile accidents, falls, trips, drowning, and drug and alcohol overdoses, all leaving us with the thought, *"What could have been...and was it all worth it?"*

YOUR ADVERSARY THE DEVIL

> "Be sober, be vigilant; because your adversary the devil, as a roaring lion, walketh about, seeking whom he may devour: Whom resist steadfast in the faith, knowing that the same afflictions are accomplished in your brethren that are in the world."
>
> — I Peter 5:8-9

When I first began this chapter and contemplated, *who is Satan?* A barrage of ideas immediately flooded in. Satan is calculated. He was the first blasphemer against God. The first anarchist. The first rebel. The first manipulator and a deceitful liar. Satan is a boaster and a braggart. First to be consumed with his own beauty and pride! He was the first narcissist ever recorded in human history. He's a creature completely consumed with himself. He's wicked. The Bible tells us that there is no truth in him! He is absolute darkness, and yet can appear as an angel of light. Satan is ruthless, but withstanding him can be accomplished even by a human being.

> "Submit yourselves therefore to God. Resist the devil, and he will flee from you."
>
> — James 4:7

That reference from the book of James gives me hope: *when you are being tempted, submit yourself to God; hang on, eventually Satan will flee from you and God will send forth His heavenly angels to minister to you!*

I Corinthians 10:13 says this: *"There hath no temptation taken you but such as is common to man: **but God is faithful, who will not suffer you to be tempted above that ye are able;** but will with the temptation also make a way to escape, that ye may be able to bear it."*

Notice: God is faithful! He knows your breaking point. He will give you the strength to go through your trial or make a way of escape for you.

SATAN'S DESIRE

Satan is (devilishly) determined to bring others with him to a fiery abode in the very depths of hell. There is no mercy in Satan; so why would anyone seek it from him?

Satan has crushed families, wage wars in nations; divided people, (ethnicity groups), filled them with hatred and racism. He has gone after babies and children; molested them and raped them; he's even lessened the laws to make molestation and sodomy misdemeanors instead of felonies. He has attempted to destroy our marriages; or at least redefine it within our legal system. With the redefinition of marriage Satan has loosed a legal warfare on mankind! Even attempting to remove pronouns from our vocabulary or the official roles of mother and father.

Satan beats down those that are good, pure, honorable and kind. He is the original tempter and the enticer. Remember: In the Bible, God established order and boundaries. Through a course of time, Satan came against that natural order to loose chaos. He has acted upon our human frailty and weaknesses and used it against us. He has intensified our addictions; and savagely tormented his victims to the point of despair, depression, hopelessness, and suicide. He is the world's first bully; first passive aggressive manipulator. He blankets this earth with his negativity and wickedness.

Again, I say, NOTHING GOOD CAN COME FROM HIM! We must resist Satan.

Satan was responsible for the fall in the Garden of Eden and making our lives harder on earth. He presented the temptation, (like bait on a hook), and then waited for the response. Eve rationalized what he said; just like that, Satan talked her out of mankind's dominion. They really were vulnerable little lambs of God. But the simple creatures possessed great qualities; even if they were not aware of it. 1.) God gave to them His Word, (Command), and 2.) God gave them the power of free will and choice. Adam and Eve had a beautiful, clean mind. Eve was persuaded out of her blessings; she was able to reasoned out of obedience to God. Sin was birthed through the exploitation of human beings.

Satan is a murderer. He is the founder of drugs, narcotics, trafficking, gangs, and rape. He's the first pervert who ever existed; he's the first child molester. Satan is a deviant. Anything twisted; disturbing, or rancid, is Satan or thought to be satanic. He is the reason debauchery exists in the world. We know misery and sorrow because of his influence. Satan is the master of illusion, the master betrayer. The origins of sorrow, sadness, and want, (covetousness).

Satan loves secrets! Satan is the whisperer who separates friends. The accuser of the brethren. (Revelation 12:10). It is right here where God's children must be careful not to gossip. It is a sin that brings us to the same level of the Devil. We do not want to become or morph into *the accuser of the brethren.* (Revelation 12:10). Satan is the one who hates all that is good, pure, true, and righteous. He hates God and He hates God's children. The best description is a twisted, deformed, slithering snake entangling its victim and slowly squeezing them to death. The sad part of all, is that those who follow Satan, will be just like him – his disciples. In the words of Jesus Christ, John 8:44-45. Jesus openly rebuked fake religious leaders:

> "Ye are of your father the devil, and the lusts of your father ye will do. He was a murderer from the beginning, and abode not in the truth, because there is no truth in him. When he speaketh a lie, he speaketh of his own: for he is a liar, and the father of it. And because I tell you the truth, ye believe me not."
>
> — John 8:44-45

SATANIC ATTACK ON OUR SEXUALITY AND TRADITIONAL MARRIAGE!

February 26, 2021, Dan Bongino downloaded a congregational debate in the House of Representative W. Gregory Steube, Rep. Florida, he said this, and I quote:

"It's not clothing or a personal style that offends God. But rather the use of one's appearance to act out or take on a sexual identity different than the one biologically assigned by God at birth. In His wisdom God intentionally made them uniquely. He made each individual either male or female. When men or women claim to be able to choose their sexual identity, they are making a statement that God did not know what He was doing when He created them. I want to quote from Dr. Tony Evans commentary bible on this passage of Scripture. (Genesis 1:26). *Men and women equally share in bearing the image of God. But He has designed them to be distinct from and complementary towards each other.* The gender confusion that exists in our American culture today is a clear rejection of God's good design. Whenever a nation's laws no longer reflect the standards of God, that nation is in rebellion against Him, and will inevitably bear the consequences. I think we are seeing the consequences of rejecting God here in our Country today. This bill, (the Equality Act), is going to redefine what a woman is and what a man is."

— Representative W. Gregory Steube,
Republican from Florida,
Washington D.C. State Capitol

Listen to this thought by Pastor John Macarthur:

"Simply stated, there is no such thing as *"transgender."* You are either xx or xy, that's it. God has made man male and female. It is determined genetically, that is physiology, that is science, that is realty. This notion that you are something other than your biology is a *"cultural construct."* It is intended on an assault on God. That's really what it is all about. I was reading an article by R.C. Sproule just yesterday, in which he said, *the greatest revolution in American history were neither the American revolution nor the industrial revolution, but it is the sexual revolution.*

This has become the more far reaching, damning of all revolution that has ever occurred in this country or any other. The problem with buying into this is it is a kind of personal suicide. It is literally the end of your existence in the way that God designed you. A person in the transgender world is 19 times more likely to commit suicide, (to kill herself or himself). It is because you have completely cut yourself off from reality and from normal relationships. This is the end of your identity, this is the end of your ability to have a God designed marriage, it's the end of your ability to have a family. It is the end of your ability to connect, and be part of your society and your culture, to have a future and belong. It is extreme isolation that can be no more extreme. You cannot get more extreme then saying, *I am not who I actually am?!"*

—John Macarthur, (How to deal with transgenderism?)
YouTube Question and Answer series
regarding Transgenderism

We defeat the allurement of sin by the blood of the Lamb! We have the power of choice and free will. We must resist the devil! We must recognize his strategies against mankind and flee youthful lusts.

ONE OF THE GREATEST GIFTS OF GOD – THE GIFT OF REPENTANCE!

"Likewise, I say unto you, there is joy in the presence of the angels of God over one sinner that repenteth."
— Jesus Christ (Luke 15:10).

As we come to Christ, all of those sins must be addressed, confessed, repented of, and given to God to help, fix, restore, or heal. We should not play around with the supernatural. We should not indulge in things we don't fully understand, nor have the full power to control: spells, portions, witchcraft, etc. It's dangerous! You just don't know the price you will pay for the answer you are seeking.

Today, in 2021, as we stream through movies on Netflix, Prime, HBO, or other network programming, we see the abundance of idolatry: witchcraft, incantations, devil worship, vampires, dragons, demons, and werewolves in its script. Our young children take it in and become desensitized to it all. They watch the dark supernatural events; they see the hideous imagery… they are numb to how real that all is. All God has ever asked us in return is to love him; be faithful to Him and serve Him with our whole hearts. He's promised His blessings and good fortune to those who would believe in Him and put their trust in Him. He's promised us his divine protection; a heavenly host of angels to encamp round about us; He has promised us so many good things.

SATAN'S DEMOTION AND JUDGMENT

As we read the story in the book of Isaiah, we still are coming in in the middle of some event. Isaiah 14 describes what will be the end. Satan's ultimate demise.

Isaiah 14:10-18

> "Hell from beneath is moved for thee to meet thee at thy coming: it stirreth up the dead for thee, even all the chief ones of the earth; it hath raised up from their thrones all the kings of the nations.
>
> All they shall speak and say unto thee, Art thou also become weak as we? art thou become like unto us?
>
> Thy pomp is brought down to the grave, and the noise of thy viols: the worm is spread under thee, and the worms cover thee.

How art thou fallen from heaven, O Lucifer, son of the morning! how art thou cut down to the ground, which didst weaken the nations!

For thou hast said in thine heart, I will ascend into heaven, I will exalt my throne above the stars of God: I will sit also upon the mount of the congregation, in the sides of the north: I will ascend above the heights of the clouds; I will be like the most High.

(REMEMBER SATAN'S TEMPTATION OF EVE — Genesis 3:4-7)

Yet thou shalt be brought down to hell, to the sides of the pit. They that see thee shall narrowly look upon thee, and consider thee, saying, Is this the man that made the earth to tremble, that did shake kingdoms; that made the world as a wilderness, and destroyed the cities thereof; that opened not the house of his prisoners?

All the kings of the nations, even all of them, lie in glory, everyone in his own house.

But thou art cast out of thy grave like an abominable branch, and as the raiment of those that are slain, thrust through with a sword, that go down to the stones of the pit; as a carcass trodden under feet.

Thou shalt not be joined with them in burial, because thou hast destroyed thy land, and slain thy people: the seed of evildoers shall never be renowned."

— Isaiah 14:10-18

Here we see the word *"hell"* mentioned in the Holy Bible directly related to the angel Lucifer. It is said to be moved for him, (welcoming him in). *"Your pomp has brought you down to the grave."* Pride. Lucifer is literally the first

narcissistic personality disorder. We've all heard of the word, Narcissist–
today it seems like such a popular phrase.

> Narcissistic personality disorder — one of several types
> of personality disorders — is a mental condition in which
> people have an inflated sense of their own importance, a
> deep need for excessive attention and admiration, troubled
> relationships, and a lack of empathy for others. But behind
> this mask of extreme confidence lies a fragile self-esteem
> that's vulnerable to the slightest criticism."
>
> — Mayo Clinic,
> Narcissistic Personality Disorder.

THE FIVE I'S – I WILL, I WILL, I WILL, I WILL, I WILL....ZAP!

Lucifer, son of the morning wanted to be God in heaven. Here we see a
challenge of authority. *"I WILL ascend into heaven. I WILL exalt my throne
above the stars of God! I WILL sit also upon the mount of the congregation!
I WILL ascend above the heights of the clouds; I WILL be "like" the Most
High God."*

It leads every creature to ask the question Satan: *How'd that work out for you?*

I would say, *not well at all!* Lucifer loses the challenge to be like God – to
replace God. Satan even drew 1/3 of the angels with him. He has been
thousands of years studying us; seeking how to injury, how to hurt, how to
cripple us. One of the best revelations given to me by another elder sister in
Church was this thought: *Dear, Satan may have taken with him one-third of
the angels, but my math tells me that they are two-thirds for us! You don't have
to worry about Satan. Just love God and He will keep you safe from harm!"*

"I SAW HIM FALL AS LIGHTNING!"

Satan's name is changed from morning star to become the diabolical Adversary – the Devil. Immediately Satan is stripped of all his glorious covering; he's greatly disfigured in the altercation. Satan changes; changes in appearance, changes in heavenly anointing and position. Satan's attempt at a heavenly coup are thwarted and Satan is cast out of heaven!

In the Gospel of Luke, Jesus gives his account of what happened that day in heaven. *"I saw Satan fall as lightning…!"* It's always reminded me of the first Thor movie, when the lead character, (Chris Hemsworth), is so full of himself, that his father must strip him of his pride, remove all his power and authority from him, and then banish him from the world of Asgard. *"I therefore cast you out!"*

People may ask, why can't Satan have a second chance; God gave man a second chance?

Because Satan never repented of his evil but relished in it. It is in the makeup of the creature called Satan, and in the world of the supernatural which he came from: Satan was disgustingly evil to the very core. Also, *salvation belongs to humanity, not angels!* (I Peter 1:12). Humanity does not have full access yet to all of God's mysteries, but Satan knew the spiritual realm he existed in. He knew, truly knew, right from wrong and the full weight of consequences to his quest to usurp God's kingdom from Him. Satan was created as an intelligent creature. The children in the garden of Eden, Adam and Eve, had no knowledge of evil or the events that would follow them. They were created and lived in a state of perfection and innocence. They were like children. Satan had all knowledge, he wasn't like the first human beings in the garden of Eden.

SATAN KNEW THE HIDDEN MYSTERIES OF GOD

Again, I will say, Satan knew his boundaries; he knew his penalty for challenging God. Yet, he made the decision to usurp the authority – to proceed; thinking he would gain a kingdom and power, he took the chance, and lost. Satan was blinded, (consumed) by his pride and arrogance – and so he fell. The judgement was sound. The decision was perfect – excellent, in fact! Our God in Heaven, our Eternal Father of Glory not only can see us physically; but we can be internally seen by him: every fiber of our being, every muscle, every nerve, every thought, every ambition. Our heavenly Father discerns motives.

> "For the word of God is quick, and powerful, and sharper than any two-edged sword, piercing even to the dividing asunder of soul and spirit, and of the joints and marrow, and is a discerner of the thoughts and intents of the heart. Neither is there any creature that is not manifest in his sight: but all things are naked and opened unto the eyes of him with whom we have to do."
>
> — Hebrews 4;12-13

We learn why God is called omnipotent, omniscient, and omnipresent. Our God will never share His eternal glory with another. Have you ever heard of the Barringer Crater or the Canyon Diablo Meteorite in Arizona? Look it up!

> "It is a meteorite impact crater approximately 37 miles east of Flagstaff and 18 miles west of Winslow in the northern Arizona desert of the United States. The crater came to the attention of scientists after American settlers encountered it in the 19th century." (Wikipedia, Barringer Crater)

The first time I saw it I thought, *"That looks like where Satan landed!"* and I laughed at that thought. But, can you imagine how hard Satan landed when he was cast out of heaven? The book of Revelation tells the finality of Lucifer, son of the morning – the end of the fallen angle, Satan. But, it also brings more into focus: a Beast, a mark of the Beast, and a false Prophet who can perform miracles. All of them are destroyed.

WHAT IS PRIDE?

"Pride is the disorder of love of one's own excellence to the point of contempt for God."

— St. Thomas Aquino

"Satan's perceived moment of victory becomes the very moment of his defeat. God used Satan's actions against him. Satan played right into God's hands, (in fulfillment of prophecy). The Church is a seed of the kingdom of God. Now Satan focuses his attack on the Church. He attempts to try and impede the growth of it. Satan's desire is to get humanity to REJECT God. He stirs up persecution, heresies and dissension."

— Father Vincent Lampert

"The fear of the Lord is to hate evil: pride, and arrogancy, and the evil way, and the froward mouth, do I hate. Counsel is mine, and sound wisdom: I am understanding; I have strength. By me kings reign, and princes decree justice."

— Proverbs 8-15

CHAPTER SIX

THE EFFECTIVE, SPIRITUAL TOOLS AGAINST SATAN

GOD'S HEAVENLY PROTECTION

The list was given to the Church by the Late Rev. Kenneth Reeves. It was brought back to our knowledge through the Ladies ministry and teaching of Pastor's wife, Sister Claudette Walker of Faith Apostolic Church of Troy, Michigan.

- The sinless blood of the Lamb of God – that covers us!
- The name of our LORD and Savior, Jesus Christ – the name above all names in heaven, on earth, or beneath.
- The word of our personal testimony: our conversion stories and personal examples of God working in our lives; our miracles we have seen and experienced!
- The infilling of the Holy Spirit of God, in speaking in tongues – our seal of adoption, our prayer language, and the Spirit of God praying for us.
- The Holy Bible – The Sword of the Spirit that cuts!

All of these are extremely powerful weapons and when used lawfully are precise, magnificent, and authoritative in the workings of the supernatural Spirit of God! Let me repeat that: *They are extremely powerful!* However, we must be consistent in the disciplines and practices of our Christian faith.

In the above-mentioned bullet points, most of the body of Christ use one, two, or three of these very well (every day), without even realizing what their actions or words are accomplishing in the spiritual realm or the supernatural world around us.

What are they accomplishing?

They are playing their part in pushing back the forces of darkness around them, and where ever they are sending their prayers to. For example, a Christian may have a discipline of every morning reading the Bible or praying. As they read the words out loud it brings those words into their home. Even more importantly, it brings God's words before their eyes and in to their mind. It reminds them of what is right. As they pray, they are talking or communing with the LORD. Just those two simple actions draw you closer to God. Will you allow the Spirit of the living God to break you, change you, and get ahold of you? Will you surrender your life to Christ and allow Him to use your life for His greater purpose?

- Will you get off the internet, social media accounts?
- Will you get off your cell phone?
- Will you stop binging on Netflix, Prime, HBO?
- Will you interact with people who do not know Jesus Christ?
- Will you have the courage to speak to them about Jesus?
- Will you be sensitive to the prompting of the Holy Spirit?

Many churches do not want to touch on the topics of demons and spiritual encounters. Many deny the power of the infilling of the Holy Ghost that Christian believers receive in speaking in tongues. They teach their congregations that those supernatural events were just for the Early church in 33 A.D. Somehow, they feel it's too spooky and better left unsaid then to open the door to the Book of Acts experience.

- I assure you that all of this is very real!
- Our ignorance doesn't wish it all away,

- It makes us susceptible to being tormented by the forces of darkness
- Ignorance makes us easy prey for satanic attacks.
- More importantly, it makes us ill-equipped to defend ourselves!

Your holy life in Jesus Christ is a living example of God working inside of you! Other Christian believers see it and the world around you sees it. The world cannot deny the working of the Spirit of God. They know deep inside, it's all true!

I personally anoint my children's head with oil before I leave my home; and I am doing it in the name of Jesus Christ. I am asking God to cover my daughters spiritually. My husband, Frank, leaves very early in the morning, so I anoint his pillow. I anoint my own head in the name of Jesus Christ. I desire God's anointing. As I drive to work each morning, I say three prayers out loud: The *"Our Father"* prayer in Matthew 6, the *"Lord is my Shepherd,"* prayer from Psalm 23, and I put on the armor of God, found in Ephesians 6:10-20. I pronounce blessings where I go every day! In fact, these are blessings we are entitled to as beloved children of God. I bless my neighbors, I bless my schools, I bless my community. I bless my work. And I keep in mind, everywhere I go, the LORD is with me. I bring Jesus into my Radiology department in my tabernacle – my human body! I remember that God is watching over me; every patient I touch, Jesus has seen and heard him, as I have.

THE RESOURCES THAT ARE AVAILABLE TO US:

- Great Faith – and faith brings hope and experience!
- God's Holy Knowledge – Truth! God's Truth brings freedom and liberty!
- God's Faithful Shepherding – Protection and Care!
- God's overflowing and abundant resources – Provision!
- His heavenly host of angels, (multitudes of angelic hosts - or armies), their role in mankind's life every day to aid and help humanity – to aid and help humanity!

DRAW NEAR TO GOD AND HE
WILL DRAW NEAR TO YOU

Now, when the Christian believer(s) involve dedicated fasting with the above mentioned: Bible reading, prayer, and the use of anointing oil, it's like adding gasoline to that spiritual fire! Then add loving adoration through heartfelt praise and worship, next, learn the gift of thanksgiving. Thank God for who He is and what He has done for you. This is how believers live, move, and have our being inside the body of Christ. (Acts 17:28).

Now, you have just touched the heartstrings of your Creator – by making efforts to draw closer to Him. He will take notice of you; a door to the miraculous has been opened by faith and faith in action. At this point, some may say, *"Hey that's legalistic. We don't have to do all of that for Him to take notice of us!"*

Let me ask you this: *What is the difference between Christian disciplines and Legalism?* It's a matter of the heart. It will always be a heart issue. You don't *"have to DO all of this,"* but you get to. As we do these disciplines, we becoming more like our Great Creator. We are learning about Him – growing in Him. We personally are drawing near to Him because we love Him. We are not in a forced relationship; just like you are not in a forced marriage. If you look at the above disciplines – think of holy matrimony. ***The more time you spend with your mate, the stronger the marriage. It's not legalist, it's the signs of a loving relationship build on mutual respect and admiration.*** I want to know you more, because I love you. In order to know you better, I need to invest my time in you. It's exciting to hope for better – to wait upon the LORD! Ephesians 3:20, (paraphrased) says, *"...God is able to do exceeding abundantly above all that we ask or think, according to the power that works in us."*

Think on just that promise: *The power that works in us?* That's beyond wonderful! Again: *My God IS ABLE to do "exceeding abundantly" above all that we ask or think according to His power that works in us and through us.* Wow!

Keep steadfast because your breakthrough is around the corner and it won't be a small thing. No, it will be grand! Our spiritual and physical identity is found in our relationship with God, through His Son, Jesus Christ.

> "Blessed are the undefiled in the way, who walk in the law of the Lord. Blessed are they that keep his testimonies, and that seek him with the whole heart. They also do no iniquity: they walk in his ways."
> — Psalm 119:1-3

> "Blessed be the God and Father of our Lord Jesus Christ, which according to his abundant mercy hath begotten us again unto a lively hope by the resurrection of Jesus Christ from the dead, to an inheritance incorruptible, and undefiled, and that fadeth not away, reserved in heaven for you, who are kept by the power of God through faith unto salvation ready to be revealed in the last time. Wherein ye greatly rejoice, though now for a season, if need be, ye are in heaviness through manifold temptations"
> — I Peter 1:1-6

God is our loving Father who provides good things for His children. God honestly fulfills His responsibility towards us in our personal healing and developing our education and in understanding Him Psalm 68:19, says, *"Blessed be the Lord, who daily loadeth us with benefits, even the God for our salvation. Selah."* Did you catch that? God is daily loading us with benefits!

- Divine problem-solving abilities,
- Artful skilled negotiations where both parties win,
- Improved communication skills,
- Charity and concern,
- Heavenly wisdom and revelation,
- Abounding hope, even in the worst circumstances,
- Genuine kindness,
- God's goodness and mercy,

- God's abounding peace, and joy, and long-suffering patience,
- As well as dreams, visions, and prophecy,
- Kingdom knowledge and discernment, and
- The operation of the gifts of the Spirit.

— Kari Quijas, *What is Our Christian Purpose,*
Unplugging from the World Wide Web
and Discovering Christ within us."

GOD CANNOT LIE AND HIS WORD IS SETTLED IN THE HEAVENS!

Our heavenly Father has promised each of us to get us to the others side from earth to heaven! We have been extended an invitation into His kingdom through Jesus Christ, the Son of God. We don't have to jump through hoops to earn His love; no, His love is pure and natural. When we make mistakes, as human beings do, He does not disown us nor withdraw His affection from us, even if we shame Him. No, our loving Father gently extends His hand, helps us on our feet, and then confirms He has not left us. We, through relationship, learn nothing can touch us or harm us without His consent.

In knowing our heavenly Father, we lay our lives down and give Him full control. But, it takes time to get to this point of relinquishing our own hold on our lives, but it does come!

THE NATURE OF GOD

What an honor to be chosen by God and fully adopted into the Kingdom! (I Peter 2:9; Ephesians 1:4-5; Ephesians 2:10; John 6:44; Romans 8:28-9). When you have been adopted, you are entitled by law to all the privileges and blessings of that family – in name, in relationship, in abundant resources, and in all protection! This world may not choose you, but the One who loves you, called you out of darkness and into His marvelous light; (I Peter 2:9), the very one who has call you by your name, adores you forever. Know this deep inside your spirit, God desires you and without a doubt, He has chosen you to be His!

If you had dysfunctional lives before your Christian conversion, know that your new life hidden in Christ is promised healthy functionality, soundness, and all of God's goodness. Our Father is faithful, He is trustworthy, and He is a defender of the weak! He is one hundred percent responsible for all His children. Our God NEVER lets us down and He never fails! (I Chronicles 28:20; Joshua 1:8-9; Isaiah 51:6; Lamentations 3:22-23; and I Corinthians 1:9-11). Friends may come and go and jobs may change, this culture may shift, but our heavenly Father diligently and lovingly watches over each child. It is my opinion that every new believer should study the book of Ephesians, especially chapters one through three, to understand what God has done for them and given to them spiritually.

> "...for he that cometh to God must believe that he is, and
> that he is a rewarder of them that diligently seek him." –
> Hebrews 11:6 (b)

Ask God to help you understand your place in Him. Ask God if He would allow you to see yourself through His loving eyes. We need to get our heads out of this world, it's chaos and mess, and into the heavens!

In 1918, Ms. Helen Lemmel wrote the song, *Turn Your Eyes Upon Jesus*. She describes in her classic hymn of our eyes gazing upon the face of God and realizing the things of earth will grow strangely dim. It is so true. What you put before you, will be the world you create for yourself. I choose to be a citizen of heaven. J.R. Baxter wrote the lyrics to "*This World is Not My Home*" in 1936. Above all, let us live well in Jesus Christ. If you are looking for peace, you will find it in Him. Try this exercise: Shut off the news for one month. Turn off your cable channels. In its place, (or time frame), go for a walk outside. Preferably somewhere majestic like a nice walking trail. Get into God's creation, (nature), and out of the world.

HAVE YOU EVER STUDIED THE LIFE OF JOB?

The book of Job gave us a glimmer of the supernatural behind-the-scenes of God's heavenly throne room. In this story, the LORD God mocks Satan, *"Have you considered my servant Job?"*

Why would God taunt Satan like that?

Because He is not afraid of Him. Satan is a defeated foe! (Revelation 12:9). He always has been. Satan is a bully, but God beat this bully and puts him down in his place. Let's quickly look at the story. I want you to place your name where Job's name is.

Job 1:6-10

> "Now there was a day when the sons of God came to present themselves before the Lord, and Satan came also among them.
>
> And the Lord said unto Satan, Whence comest thou? Then Satan answered the Lord, and said, From going to and fro in the earth, and from walking up and down in it.
>
> And the Lord said unto Satan, Hast thou considered my servant Job, that there is none like him in the earth, a perfect and an upright man, one that feareth God, and escheweth evil?
>
> Then Satan answered the Lord, and said, Doth Job fear God for nought?
>
> Hast not thou made an hedge about him, and about his house, and about all that he hath on every side? thou hast blessed the work of his hands, and his substance is increased in the land."
>
> — Job 1:6-10

Isn't that exciting!

Let's look at Job 1 again. First of all, did you really think that God didn't know where Satan had gone, or what he had been doing before Satan's summons? Of course God did! Satan had been prowling around the borders of Job, his family, his house, and his possessions, looking for a way in and God called out for it. God knew what Satan had been up to and relished in the fact that Satan could not penetrate His holy shield of defense! Just because God is silent, doesn't mean He isn't taking notice, or won't address it on a later date. This was that moment for Satan. The Bible records that each person in the world will stand before the LORD and give account. (Proverbs 20:8; Psalm 11:4-7; II Corinthians 5:10; and Revelation 20:13-11).

The Prophet Daniel saw the judgement seat of God. Look at his description of God!

> "I beheld till the thrones were cast down, and the Ancient of days did sit, whose garment was white as snow, and the hair of his head like the pure wool: his throne was like the fiery flame, and his wheels as burning fire. A fiery stream issued and came forth from before him: thousand thousands ministered unto him, and ten thousand times ten thousand stood before him: the judgment was set, and the books were opened."
> — Daniel 7:9-10

You might ask the question, in Job one, why was Satan in heaven before God? God had called them all before Him. *"It was the day when the sons of God came to present themselves before the LORD, and Satan came among them."* Here we see Satan almost as an afterthought. He was no longer first, but last. Still, Satan is accountable to the Divine Creator of the universe. All knew he was the fallen angel. God addresses him and all watch. *"Have you considered my servant Job, that there is none like him (a human being), a perfect and upright man; one that fears God and escheweth evil?'* (Paraphrase from Job 1). Why would God phrase it like that? Because here, (even in man's fallen state), a human being on earth can demonstrate what it means to walk a good life in God with love and reverential fear. Here, Job's example shows the reader how to be upright through the power of choice. God is saying this to Satan, *Satan, this is what you should have done!*

The book of Job was not so much about Job, as it was about Satan and those that will follow his evil ways. Another revelation takes place in the book of Job; for every accusation against God, He made a way through the Son: a Comforter, a Counselor, a Friend. Yes, Job was behaving himself, (righteous and eschewed evil), but the insult was to Satan who was a far more intellectually superior creature.

On earth we operate in the knowledge available to us: that which we are born with, (our personal intelligence or I.Q. intelligence quotient). We all know people are at different levels; we also operate in knowledge that has been established through personal experience – which develops our wisdom. We operate in knowledge developed through our education, (academic learning). But, that's not what the supernatural world operates in. Listen to what I am telling you: There is a heavenly kingdom that exists right now. It's as real as earth is to you today. There is also a demonic underworld called hell, and it is just as real. I'm not sure who said this, but I will quote it: *There are NO unbelievers in hell.* Meaning: When the unbeliever dies, He will meet God face to face; his life will be judged according to the books, and God will give that individual their full reward. There is an unbeliever's reward of eternal damnation. All in known in the heavens; nothing is concealed and they will know that they rightly desire it.

> But when that which is perfect is come, then that which is in part shall be done away. When I was a child, I spake as a child, I understood as a child, I thought as a child: but when I became a man, I put away childish things. For now we see through a glass, darkly; but then face to face: now I know in part; but then shall I know even as also I am known."
> — The Apostle Paul, (I Corinthians 13:10-12)

There is perfect wisdom and judgement in God and He extends it, or gifts it to every creature in heaven, on earth, or below. Satan demonstrated a lack of fear of God Almighty and that disgusting creature did not eschew evil. In the book of Job, a man, (a lesser creature or even a weaker creature), had given to God glory due His name – even without having a full revelation of Him. Oh, there was so much to the above discourse of Job, chapter one. Our human minds cannot understand the weight of the insult or the sting of the personal rebuke: God Almighty judges Satan in front of his peers. But, look here another example that Satan gives us a revelation that we should KNOW! Satan cannot touch us, we are guarded and protected by God!

> *"Hast not thou made an hedge about him, and about his house, and about all that he hath on every side? thou hast blessed the work of his hands, and his substance is increased in the land."*
>
> — Satan

Praise God! This is wonderful news! Beloved, that same protection is around every believer. If you say, *what about the atrocities that have taken place against the Christians of the world around us?* If we are going through trials and tribulation, God has equipped us for the battle. God has confidence in you, in your faith and knowledge of the scriptures. You will be victorious in Christ! The preacher in Ecclesiastes 10:8 says this: *"He that diggeth a pit shall fall into it; and whoso breaketh an hedge, a serpent shall bite him."* Let me say the second part to that scripture again, *"He or she that breaks a hedge, a serpent shall bite him."* Be careful what hedges you tear down. This warning especially goes to our young people who have been raised in church. Some traditions may seem silly, but it just may be the very thing that is keep Satan from being able to touch you!

PART THREE

CHAPTER SEVEN

YOUR PERSONAL WELLBEING

"After He had sent them away, He went up on the mountain by Himself to pray. When evening came, He was there alone."

— Matthew 14:23

If our Savior needed to find that time in the morning to pray and restore His soul, so do we. I would say even more so! Jesus Christ was God Almighty in flesh, and yet He makes the time (often) it's recorded, to find a solitary place, withdraw himself from others, to pray: (I Timothy 3:16 – the mystery of godliness). Jesus Christ's life, ministry, and actions, gives us our examples on how to maintain a holy *"wholeness"* and mental wellbeing. The conclusion is this, we cannot fight, give out, and minister to the needs of others without caring for your own emotional, mental, and physical wellbeing. Every day we must be renewed in our mind and spirit. Think of it like a car. Your car needs oil and water to drive well. Being renewed or replenished in mind and spirit can only come from being in God's holy presence. Look at this very sad statistic.

"A 2013 study from the Schaeffer Institute (1) reports that 1,700 pastors leave the ministry each month, citing depression, burnout, or being overworked as the primary reasons. According to the study, 90% of pastors report working 55 to 70 hours a week, and 50% of them feel unable to meet the demands of the job." (*Burnout in Pastors and Church Leadership*).

—M1 Psychology Loganholme –
Brisbane Psychologist & Counseling Centre

The above reference is one of thousands; and it is not just pastors giving up in ministry, but saints. We all must rest, find that quiet moment with Him to refresh us. We must learn how to safeguard our spiritual wellbeing. Our greatest example will always be Jesus.

WARRING IN THE SPIRIT

Warring in the Spirit will be exhausting - it will draw from you in ways you cannot imagine. But it is worth the battle. We must learn how to pray every morning before we leave the house! I need to engage the LORD to cover my mind and emotions, and you will need the same - to ready you for the day you are about to have. Every day I need God's wisdom imparted unto me, because I do not know what I will face; and so do you!

The only way to refresh our soul is being in the presence of God. If you are looking for a guide on *"how to pray,"* I would recommend Pastor Anthony Mangun's book, *Heaven to Earth.* He is the pastor of the Pentecostals of Alexandria. His father, Gerald Mangun, mother, Vesta Mangun, and his loving wife, Mickey have developed the most amazing praying Church in the city of Alexandria, Louisiana.

My husband, Frank, and I pastor in Morgan Hill, California. But we, and other pastors watch their Sunday on-line services through Facebook or YouTube. Pastors need to be preached to and Pastors need to be refreshed often. As you learn how to pour out yourself to pray for family, friends, coworkers, neighbors, and your community, you must learn how to be filled and renewed again, (to spillover).

If Jesus Christ, (who was God Incarnate into human flesh as the Son of God) needed this refreshing and ministry how much more should His earthly children? I would say a lot more. You will also need a (Pastor)

shepherd to watch over you. Remember the role of the (Pastor) shepherd. He inspects the sheep for fleas and ticks; he anoints their head with oil; he checks their ears. Shepherds examine their animal's feet because they are prone to hoof rot. Shepherds also trim their wool so the beast is not overburdened. I will go into all that in more description in future chapters.

Yes, Jesus Christ is our Good Shepherd, but he also appoints (earthly) under shepherds and the five-fold ministry for the Christian body's maintenance. See the importance of the five-fold ministry in Ephesians 4:11. Let me show the full thought in Paul's letter.

"And he gave some, **apostles**; and some, **prophets**; and some, **evangelists**; and some, **pastors** and **teachers**; for the perfecting of the saints, for the work of the ministry, for the edifying of the body of Christ: till we all come in the unity of the faith, and of the knowledge of the Son of God, unto a perfect man, unto the measure of the stature of the fulness of Christ:

That we henceforth be no more children, tossed to and fro, and carried about with every wind of doctrine, by the sleight of men, and cunning craftiness, whereby they lie in wait to deceive; but speaking the truth in love, may grow up into him in all things, which is the head, even Christ: From whom the whole body fitly joined together and compacted by that which every joint supplieth, according to the effectual working in the measure of every part, maketh increase of the body unto the edifying of itself in love."

— The Apostle Paul's letter to the New Testament Church at Ephesus (Ephesians 4:11-16)

- The perfecting of the saints of God
- For the work of the Ministry
- For the edifying of the Body of Christ
- To bring unity and structure to our faith

- To increase our knowledge in the Son of God
- To be transformed into that *"perfect man"*
- To grow in Love

THE ESSENTIAL CHURCH

Chapter eighteen, *"Everyone Needs a Place to Call Home"* will go into more detail. I feel I need to place these thoughts right here. The organization structure of the Christian Church isn't just a meeting place, like a coffee house. God spoke to Isaiah and declared: *"There shall be a tabernacle for a shadow in the day time from the heat, and for a place of refuge, and for a covert from storm and from rain."* (Isaiah 4:6).

> Church is accomplishing the supernatural purpose of God on earth today. When Jesus Christ told his disciples, *"You are the light of the world."*
>
> "Ye are the light of the world. A city that is set on an hill cannot be hid. Neither do men light a candle, and put it under a bushel, but on a candlestick; and it giveth light unto all that are in the house. Let your light so shine before men, that they may see your good works, and glorify your Father which is in heaven."
> — Jesus Christ, (Matthew 5:14-16)

He really meant that the light of God would shine through us and others would come to that light! The Church is also a place where the lost find refuge. Through faithful attendance a human life is transformed into the very image and character of Jesus Christ.

Sporadic attendance makes the process take longer, and it also decreases your sensitivity to the Spirit of God. The more of the world you let in, the less the flesh wants to come to church. Several things happen when saints are not faithful to their congregations. First, it discourages the members that are coming and attempting to do great things. Think about your job's (secular employment) attendance policies. What happens when people miss work? You are short-staffed and others have to take on more work. After a while, what happens? It hits the morale of the entire group. Fatigue sets in and it weakens the whole. The Church is no different on this point. People missing in action affects the whole in a negative way. The Bible says,

> "Not forsaking the assembling of ourselves together, as the manner of some is; but exhorting one another: and so much the more, as ye see the day approaching."
> — Hebrews 10:25

The word *"exhort"* means to strongly encourage; admonish, beseech, summon, to instruct and strengthen. (Parakaleo). The word is Greek. It's an action verb.

THE REDACTED ANSWER THAT WOULD HELP THE WORLD!

It's a sad fact that we know the disciplines of Jesus Christ work for the good of all people, but we are not allowed to share it. Christianity makes for good citizens on earth today. They work, they pay their bills on time; they are good neighbors; they are helpful and give. But, today's society is trying other methods that are disconnected from God and His righteousness because they want to live in a world without Him. My question for you is this: *How's that working for us all?* I would say emphatically, not well at all.

Again, I reiterate, strong families, make strong communities.

I find it ironic that Bibles are allowed inside of prisons, yet are not allowed in public schools. What are schools afraid of? We hear of *"jail-house conversions,"* perhaps if we, as a society, started learning about morality, and character from the Bible in schools there would be no need for prisons. We will never know because they don't allow it. They don't allow the Ten Commandments, nor prayer, nor reading the Holy Bible, or even discussing some of the principles that Jesus talk in parables. Jesus always dealt with the heart of humanity. Fact, during the revivals of the 1900's in

Welsh, or even in the great awakenings in England and America, noticeable behaviors changed: bars emptied and jail house were not needed. People paid debts owed and men sung hymnals in their work places. Families were brought back together and strengthened.

Jesus Christ inside of our lives, develops us to be better than we realized we could be

1. The first order of business is understanding what we bring to the fight. We are divinely created and equipped to protect ourselves and our family in a *"defensive"* manner; but also to push back hard and take a background in an *"offensive"* manner. Yes, just like American football.

2. The second order of business is to help you stay hidden with Christ. Staying *"hidden"* with Christ is accomplished through inner purity, holy consecration, and our own personal holiness - or commitment to God. Note: We are NEVER to compare ourselves one to another, (Galatians 6:4-6), but are to compare ourselves to Christ. He alone is our perfect example and our Great Shepherd. (II Corinthians 10:12). We use the Holy Bible to judge or weigh our behaviors, attitudes, reactions, and motives.

3. The third order of business is to get you to fully understand the carnal man versus the spiritual man, versus Satan. (What causes us to lose our strength and stamina). It's called developing discernment - *who am I really battling?*

PRAYER

Pastor David Barton, of Wallbuilders.org, wrote this on Why Christians should pray:

Why is it important that we pray for our country and its people?

1. First, because God tells us to (1 Timothy 2:1-4), and it is important that we obey Him (John 14:15, Acts 5:32).

2. Second, because God answers prayer (Matthew 21:22, John 14:13-14).
3. Third, God honors prayer and turns His attention to those who pray. He takes note of people who pray and His ear remains open to them (such as in 2 Chronicles 7:14).
4. Fourth, prayer not only gives God a vehicle by which He can respond and answer prayers but prayer also changes those who pray, for praying helps us to be God-conscious, and when we are God-conscious as individuals, our behavior is different than if we rarely think about God (Romans 1:28).

Read those listed scriptures, they are TRUTHFUL and compelling. I would recommend that as you read number one, look up Pastor David Barton's scripture references. There are only four bullet points; it doesn't take long. I ask you to really examine it. Truth is good for your soul and kingdom knowledge is empowering. Share these aspects of prayer. Memorize it. This is called becoming sound in doctrine. Doctrine is a Greek word, *"didache or "didaskalia"*. (Teaching what is taught; the act of instructing; learning/teaching precepts).

> Merriam-Webster says that the word doctrine means, *"A principle or position or the body of principles in a branch of knowledge or system of beliefs; dogma. A statement of fundamental government policy; a principle of law, (established through past decisions).*

Ask yourself, *"What is my doctrine of faith?"* Only you can answer that.

Then allow me to ask you, *Have you ever sat down and wrote out your family's beliefs?* It's important for your family today, but more for your future posterity. Examine it every New Year. Sit down with the family and declare: *This is what we believe!* And tell your children, *This is who we believe in, and why!* Allow me to share this Bible study lesson on morning prayer:

WHY PRAY IN THE MORNING? BECAUSE JESUS PRAYED IN THE MORNING!

Written by Tonya & Anthony Brannon (posted on Facebook)

> "And in the morning, rising up a great while before day, he went out and departed into a solitary place, and there prayed."
>
> — Mark 1:35

Prayer in the morning is so important because:

- It will be where you meet God before you meet the devil.
- It is where you meet God before you meet your circumstances in life.
- You talk with God before you talk with many people.
- You fellowship first with God before you fellowship with one another.
- You listen first to God's beautiful voice before you hear the voices of the world around you.
- You hear the Good News, His news before you receive the breaking news of the day through the media or newspapers.
- You sit before God before you sit before men.
- You honor God before you honor people.
- You sing before our LORD before you hear any other music of the world.
- You get into His holy Presence before you are in the presence of others.
- You sit and eat at His table before you feed your body.
- You call on Jesus before you call on any other name.
- You wash with the Word of God before you wash with water.
- You see Jesus Christ's face before you see your own reflection in the mirror.
- You have swept out your heart before you sweep your home.

So, let us start our day talking with God first!

"Today's word of Blessings," by Brother Anthony Brannon.
He taught me this long ago. He said, **"We must touch
Jesus before we touch the world."**

— Sister Tonya Brannon
Study notes from her husband's sermon

Isn't that excellent! The first time I read his thoughts, I said, *Yes! I agree
with you!* And daily, when I sit down to pray at my kitchen table in the
morning, I remind myself of that by re-reading Brother Anthony Brannon's
list of why we pray. It somehow grounds me and directs my purpose. I am
so thankful for the men and women of faith who share their knowledge
so that others may perfect and succeed in their own ministry.

WHEN DO I PRAY?

My main prayer time is in the morning when I am refreshed and regenerated
from sleep. I love the stillness of that time; it's when everyone else is
sleeping and it just seems like you can touch God. It is like you have His
undivided attention. I laugh when I write that out. I should really say, it's
more like my sweet Savior has my undivided attention. Understand this
point, that doesn't mean that I do not pray at lunch, or in the evening. But
I feel my most effective prayer is before the sun rises on a new day.

Dear Reader, if you have picked up this book, then you must have an
interest in the subject matter: *EFFECTIVELY Defeating Satan!* My
suggestion to you is to have a pen and paper in hand: *Be Interactive!*

- Write down the ideas and try to incorporate them into your daily
  life. It's easy to forget new techniques if you don't take the time
  to write them down.

Pausing, and taking notes will help you. Share them with your family
and friends. Yes, even share them with your coworkers. You never know
what people are going through; be someone's help. The answers, (which
the LORD reveals to us), will probably come from places you already
know about, but maybe forgotten or lost sight of. Sometimes we get so

familiar with the Church, (God's House), that we forget how holy, sacred, and reverent it is; that His presence is there watching over us; and we are surrounded by a heavenly host of His mighty angels who stand guard around His house.

CHAPTER EIGHT

MOVING FORWARD!

"We are either in the process of resisting God's truth or in the process of being shaped and molded by His truth."
— *Charles Stanley*

As I write this book, I am aware that my target audience will be born-again Christian believers. I am also aware that this book may land in the hands of someone who does not know Jesus. Sometimes families come to God unexpectedly when one of their members has serious issues with Satan: such as demon possession or oppression; satanic activities, even suicide attempts, harmful behaviors, cuttings, alcoholism, or drug use; maybe even a life-threatening accident. I desire that my writing will be clear no matter who you are in God's kingdom: a new believer in Christ, a seasoned Christian in the faith, or someone just beginning the process.

DON'T TURN YOUR EYES FROM THE BATTLE! YOU ARE NEEDED! YOUR SKILLSET, YOUR NATURAL TALENTS, YOUR SPIRITUAL GIFTS! YOU ARE DESPERATELY NEEDED IN THE BATTLE!

BUT WHO STARTED THIS FIGHT?!

The most powerful people on the planet are Spirit-filled Christian believers. I know you don't feel like you are, but it is true nonetheless. When God gave to you the Holy Ghost and fire, it was for a divine purpose! (Matthew 3:11; Luke 10:19). Jesus told his disciples, *"I give you power to tread on serpents and scorpions, and over all the power of the enemy: and nothing shall by any means hurt you!"* (paraphrased from Luke 10:19).

However, I have discovered that the most powerful Spirit-filled Christian believers, (overflowing with natural giftings and talents), steered FAR clear from busting open a hornet's nest of demonic activity in their everyday lives by challenging the devil, or attempting to reclaim territory back from him. Yet the nightly news revealed that the war was raging around them; the scriptures told them who they were really battling, (not people, but spiritual wickedness). Instead of spiritual confidence, they felt scared and overwhelmed and withdrew. Still, the call was in the atmosphere; God was bringing the fight to us all! It was time in the spirit for Christian intercession; it was time to care above heaven and earth; yes, it was time to face the darkness and withstand it. It was time to face the reality that their unsaved loved ones who go to an eternal (Biblical) hell if they didn't take the time to pray and ask God for their souls.

DON'T GET ANGRY IF YOU CONGREGATION GOT CAUGHT UP IN THE WRONG FIGHT! DIRECT ALL THAT ENERGY AND RIGHTEOUS INDIGNATION IN THE RIGHT DIRECTION!

During the 2020 pandemic and Presidential elections many Christians actually woke up - to a sheer panic of the national and world events. They stepped up to the plate, voiced their opinion(s), attempted to persuade even their most staunch Democrat in their sphere of influence: family, friends, co-workers, etc. And their political candidate lost! It was an obvious U.S. Presidential heist of the 21st Century. Elaborate voter fraud became apparent as eyewitnesses in the droves came out to share what they experienced.

In January 2021, in a Christian conference, the speaker got up, (microphone in hand) and disciplined the congregation for being caught up in U.S.

politics. In his rebuke, people took in his thoughts. After, many quietly returned home and just turned their local NETFLIX series on and was lulled back to apathy. Yes, they gave up the fight with the idea, Christians shouldn't get involved in politics. I say here, though we should not be CONSUMED with American politics, we are very much responsible to be part of the process and pray for elected leaders and, yes, know the policies that they are attempted to pass in the House of Representatives and the Senate. You should, as an American citizen, know who your elected officials are and feel confident as a part of your local community to write to them if you are concerned on how they may vote. You have a voice. In fact, I say, Christians have a greater voice because it should come from their Biblical teaching and from their own prayer life with God. However, The devil did a stupendous job of squashing some very powerful voices by shaming them for getting involved in the wrong fight.

So, now they are sitting on the couch waiting for the coming of the LORD and the enemy is just rolling into their lives, into their state, and into their country. I shake my head in utter disbelief. But, I took a different approach. Don't rebuke Christians for getting involved in the game of life. Direct them to the real fight! We should know what's happening around us. We should study and show ourselves approved, like God said! (II Timothy 2:15). We should be able to defend our opinion and Christianity. What you see in the natural, is what is playing out in the supernatural. It's a battle. If the policy is on unborn life, if the policy is on certain groups in elementary schools, if the policy will hurt our American families and jobs, make us more relying on Government, than God, then yes, we must get involved.

> "I exhort therefore, that, first of all, supplications, prayers, intercessions, and giving of thanks, be made for all men; For kings, and for all that are in authority; that we may lead a quiet and peaceable life in all godliness and honesty. For this is good and acceptable in the sight of God our Savior; who will have all men to be saved, and to come unto the knowledge of the truth. For there is one God, and one mediator between God and men, the man Christ Jesus."
> — I Timothy 2:1-5

THE PROBLEM – FEAR AND APATHY

In 2020, the Blood-bought Church had a subtle, (unspoken) mindset, *"If Satan leaves me alone, I'll leave him alone, too."* The most anointed, educated, powerful people on the planet were not getting involved in the debate, in the community life around us, on in the making of American policy.

Know this, it is now 2021 and God has sanctioned the fight!

When I type those words I hear in the recesses of my mind from my very younger days: *Fight! Fight! Fight!* And I am immediately taken to the 7th or 8th-grade class watching some helpless wimp get pulverized by a horrible bully. I can assure you that you are NOT a helpless wimp. Think of David, the lowly shepherd. He was able to destroy a monstrous giant, in his youth! And David did it in the name of the God of Israel! David trusted that if he fought for God's honor, God would have his back!

Think of young Gideon, hiding, threshing wheat because the Philistines kept stealing their food. (Judges 6:12). Yet the angel of the LORD called him a *mighty man of valor*. He did NOT feel like that. God weeded his 10,000-man army down to 300! (Judges 7). Do you think he felt fear? Of course Gideon did. Fear is a natural expression to scary circumstances! Nevertheless, walk forward.

I honestly don't know if we really ever get over feeling afraid; some say, *"I have no fear of anything!"* I'm not sure that is too smart. Fear heightens our senses; fear causes us to be alert. Our mind responds differently when we are afraid; and adrenaline is released. Fear is natural. We are instructed not to fear man, but to have a holy reverential fear of God.

Understand this, God loves underdogs! In order to have an underdog, you have to have an undeniable bad situation with a big, ugly, fierce opponent. God loves insurmountable odds! I find it nail-biting.

The battle is meant to help you grow spiritually; to mature you as a saint, or even reveal to you another level of God you were unaware of. My friend, beautiful, meek Christian brother or sister, your birth was not an accident; you were made for the battle! And these horrible circumstances will allow you (later) to be used by God for intercessory prayers (birthing compassion and empathy inside your heart) and help you aid in the deliverance of others. This trial of your faith will be beneficial to you. However, you must walk forward in your calling and accept the challenge. Yes, your current suffering will become a huge blessing for others. The Apostle Peter wrote of the trial of our faith is more precious than gold: I Peter 1:5-10

> "Who, (Christians), are kept by the power of God through faith unto salvation ready to be revealed in the last time. Wherein ye greatly rejoice, though now for a season, if need be, ye are in heaviness through manifold temptations: That the trial of your faith, being much more precious than of gold that perisheth, though it be tried with fire, might be found unto praise and honour and glory at the appearing of Jesus Christ: Whom having not seen, ye love; in whom, though now ye see him not, yet believing, ye rejoice with joy unspeakable and full of glory: Receiving the end of your faith, even the salvation of your souls. Of which salvation the prophets have enquired and searched diligently, who prophesied of the grace that should come unto you."
>
> — I Peter 1:5-10

WHEN GOD ALLOWS THE BATTLE - HE'S ALREADY EQUIPPED YOU TO WIN IT!

Question: *Do you really believe that God provokes the fight?"*

Yes, I do. There are so many examples from the Old Testament to the New Testament; our God never changes! Some of the best-known Bible stories on this topic are the story of Job; (Book of Job), the story of Samson, (Judges 13-16), the story of Gideon, (which I just mentioned), Joshua and Caleb, (Numbers 13), the story of David! All through the books of Judges, Kings, and Chronicles tells of many battles God pushed Israel into. The Bible says,

"And he changeth the times and the seasons: he removes kings, and setteth up kings: he giveth wisdom unto the wise, and knowledge to them that know understanding."
— Daniel 2:21

People are afraid of change; they resist it!

In the New Testament, the greatest battle was the temptation of Jesus Christ in the wilderness. (Luke 4). The Bible says, *"Jesus was led into the wilderness by the Spirit of God to be tempted by Satan."*

CHRISTIAN PERSECUTION: The Early Church, (1ˢᵗ Century 40 A.D), was forbidden to teach or speak the name of Jesus Christ for fear of imprisonment and death. They record these words, *"It is better to obey God than men!"* (Paraphrased from Acts 5:29). So, in spite of the fear of imprisonment and persecution, the Early Church demonstrated civil disobedience in order to fulfill God's Commands! The entire book of Acts speaks of many accounts of the fighting of the Apostles to further the Gospel of Jesus Christ. Despite the government and officials commanding them to stop, the Disciple followed Christ.

Here are just a few references:

"So the word of God continued to spread. The number of disciples in Jerusalem grew rapidly, and a great number of priests became obedient to the faith."
— Acts 6:7

"But the word of God continued to spread and multiply."
— Acts 12:24

"When the proconsul saw what had happened, he believed, for he was astonished at the teaching about the Lord."
— Acts 13:12 NIV

"So mightily grew the word of God and prevailed."
— Acts 19:20

Only one Apostle made it out alive and he was boiled in oil, beaten, and then banished to the Isle of Patmos. That's our beloved John. (revelation 1:9).

Revelation 1

> *"I John, who also am your brother, and companion in tribulation,* and in the kingdom and patience of Jesus Christ, was in the isle that is called Patmos, for the word of God, and for the testimony of Jesus Christ. I was in the Spirit on the Lord's day, and heard behind me a great voice, as of a trumpet,
>
> Saying, I am Alpha and Omega, the first and the last: and, What thou seest, write in a book, and send it unto the seven churches which are in Asia; unto Ephesus, and unto Smyrna, and unto Pergamos, and unto Thyatira, and unto Sardis, and unto Philadelphia, and unto Laodicea.
>
> And I turned to see the voice that spake with me. And being turned, I saw seven golden candlesticks; And in the midst of the seven candlesticks one like unto the Son of man, clothed with a garment down to the foot, and girt about the paps with a golden girdle.
>
> His head and his hairs were white like wool, as white as snow; and his eyes were as a flame of fire; and his feet like unto fine brass, as if they burned in a furnace; and his voice as the sound of many waters. And he had in his right hand seven stars: and out of his mouth went a sharp twoedged sword: and his countenance was as the sun shineth in his strength. And when I saw him, I fell at his feet as dead. And he laid his right hand upon me, saying unto me, Fear not; I am the first and the last:
>
> I am he that liveth, and was dead; and, behold, I am alive for evermore, Amen; and have the keys of hell and

of death. Write the things which thou hast seen, and the things which are, and the things which shall be hereafter."
— Revelation 1:9-19

So we see, yes, God can pick fights but He is always victorious!

Our Heavenly Father loves for us (His beloved children), to accompany Him into the battle! Right by His side. His desire for us is to partake in the glorious victory! Yes, God will shut the mouth of all His enemies and He will judge the nations in His righteousness according to His Word. (Isaiah 66). Every knee will bow to Jesus Christ as LORD! (Philippians 2:10-11). It is written therefore it will happen.

CHAPTER NINE

PROVOKED TO MINISTRY

The Apostle Peter wrote this letter,

> "Humble yourselves therefore under the mighty hand of
> God, that he may exalt you in due time: Casting all your
> care upon him; for he careth for you. Be sober, be vigilant;
> because your adversary the devil, as a roaring lion, walketh
> about, seeking whom he may devour: Whom resist
> stedfast in the faith, knowing that the same afflictions
> are accomplished in your brethren that are in the world.
>
> But ***the God of all grace, who hath called us unto his
> eternal glory by Christ Jesus, after that ye have suffered a
> while, make you perfect, stablish, strengthen, settle you.***
> To him be glory and dominion for ever and ever. Amen."
> — The Apostle Peter, (I Peter 5:6-11)

Note: After you have suffered a while, God shall make you perfect, establish
you, (soundness), strengthen you, and then settle you.

That's a tremendous promise, but it comes through adversity. In metals,
there is a boiling point that boils away impurities. In clay, there is a
pounding and molding. In olive oil, there is a pressing of the first fruit.
And for humanity, *"iron sharpens iron,"* (Paraphrased from Proverbs 27),
and sparks fly!

ENOUGH! WHEN THE BARREN WOMB CRIES OUT TO GOD!

I want to introduce you to Hannah. Allow me to share her story with you. It comes from the first chapter of Samuel. I Samuel sets up all the characters: Elkanah, (Husband), Hannah, (first wife), and the other, Peninnah, (second wife that bore children). They were orthodox Jewish believers. The story will show their pilgrimage to Jerusalem. I Samuel tells us a very valuable piece of information: The LORD had shut up Hannah's womb. 3000-4000 years ago, in Jewish history, the role of the women was to bear children. It was her responsibility to produce an heir, a son. If she was unable to accomplish it, then the husband would have to take a second wife. In this case, the second wife easily could have children. This set up inner conflict; competition between the women. The second important fact was this: Elkanah cared for Hannah, for he loved her.

I Samuel 1

> "Now there was a certain man of Ramathaim-zophim, of mount Ephraim, and his name was Elkanah, the son of Jeroham, the son of Elihu, the son of Tohu, the son of Zuph, an Ephrathite: and he had two wives; the name of the one was Hannah, and the name of the other Peninnah: and Peninnah had children, but Hannah had no children.

> And this man went up out of his city yearly to worship and to sacrifice unto the Lord of hosts in Shiloh. And the two sons of Eli, Hophni and Phinehas, the priests of the Lord, were there.

> And when the time was that Elkanah offered, he gave to Peninnah his wife, and to all her sons and her daughters, portions: But unto Hannah he gave a worthy portion; for he loved Hannah: but the Lord had shut up her womb.

> And her adversary also provoked her sore, for to make her fret, because the Lord had shut up her womb. And

as he did so year by year, when she went up to the house
of the Lord, so she provoked her; therefore she wept, and
did not eat.

— I Samuel 1:1-7

Note: the Crisis: "Her adversary also provoked her sore - to make her fret because she was barren." Women can be cruel. Peninnah was relentless; her behavior never stopped. It's recorded year by year she tormented the first wife.

"Then said Elkanah her husband to her, Hannah, why weepest thou? and why eatest thou not? and why is thy heart grieved? am not I better to thee than ten sons? So Hannah rose up after they had eaten in Shiloh, and after they had drunk. Now Eli the priest sat upon a seat by a post of the temple of the Lord.

And she was in bitterness of soul, and prayed unto the Lord, and wept sore. And she vowed a vow, and said, O Lord of hosts, if thou wilt indeed look on the affliction of thine handmaid, and remember me, and not forget thine handmaid, but wilt give unto thine handmaid a man child, then I will give him unto the Lord all the days of his life, and there shall no razor come upon his head."

— I Samuel 1:8-11

Note: Amazing how her husband couldn't understand why she was so sad. But, Hannah found her comfort in the LORD and so can we. If you find yourself in a position like this one and it seems like God is silent, know that *"all things work for our good."* (Paraphrased from Romans 8:38.)

"And it came to pass, as she continued praying before the Lord, that Eli marked her mouth. Now Hannah, she spake in her heart; only her lips moved, but her voice was not heard: therefore Eli thought she had been drunken. And Eli said unto her, How long wilt thou be drunken? put away thy wine from thee.

— I Samuel 1:12-14

Note: It's pretty sad when Eli couldn't tell the difference between heart-felt prayer and drunkenness. Understand, when your family doesn't understand you, your spouse cannot seem to relate to how you feel, and even if your pastor seems against you, you (beautiful intercessory) can find grace to help you in your moment of need. Today, we know him by name, Jesus Christ, our Lord.

> And Hannah answered and said, No, my lord, I am a woman of a sorrowful spirit: I have drunk neither wine nor strong drink, but have poured out my soul before the Lord. Count not thine handmaid for a daughter of Belial: for out of the abundance of my complaint and grief have I spoken hitherto.
>
> Then Eli answered and said, Go in peace: and the God of Israel grant thee thy petition that thou hast asked of him. And she said, Let thine handmaid find grace in thy sight. So the woman went her way, and did eat, and her countenance was no more sad.
>
> — I Samuel 1:15-18

Note: Prayer and Worship was part of her life. Hannah was a Jewess.

> "And they rose up in the morning early, and worshipped before the Lord, and returned, and came to their house to Ramah: and Elkanah knew Hannah his wife; and the Lord remembered her.
>
> Wherefore it came to pass, when the time was come about after Hannah had conceived, that she bare a son, and called his name Samuel, saying, Because I have asked him of the Lord. And the man Elkanah, and all his house, went up to offer unto the Lord the yearly sacrifice, and his vow.
>
> But Hannah went not up; for she said unto her husband, I will not go up until the child be weaned, and then I will

bring him, that he may appear before the Lord, and there abide forever.

And Elkanah her husband said unto her, Do what seemeth thee good; tarry until thou have weaned him; only the Lord establish his word. So the woman abode, and gave her son suck until she weaned him.

And when she had weaned him, she took him up with her, with three bullocks, and one ephah of flour, and a bottle of wine, and brought him unto the house of the Lord in Shiloh: and the child was young. And they slew a bullock, and brought the child to Eli.

And she said, Oh my lord, as thy soul liveth, my lord, I am the woman that stood by thee here, praying unto the Lord. For this child I prayed; and the Lord hath given me my petition which I asked of him:

Therefore also I have lent him to the Lord; as long as he liveth he shall be lent to the Lord. And he worshipped the Lord there."

— I Samuel 1:19-28

HANNAH'S CLOSENESS TO GOD, (LITERALLY HER DRIVING FORCE) WAS BIRTHED THROUGH A PERSONAL CRISIS. HER ANSWERED PRAYER CAME THROUGH THE TAUNTING OF A CRUEL ADVERSARY!

Peninnah's name actually is Hebrew for *"jewel."* I am certain that Hannah didn't feel like her adversary was a precious stone, a *"jewel"*, but more like a thorn in her side. A woman who legally shared her husband's bed and was able to produce his sons when Hannah could not! The vicious fires of misfortune opened Hannah's womb to produce a Samuel - in God's timing. It would eventually shut Peninnah's mouth and seal her womb shut! Hannah's child, Samuel, was a prophet of God. He has two books named after him in our Old Testament. He could distinctly hear the voice of God in full conversation; communities feared when he came to the town of what he would say. Would he come for judgment or peace? Samuel anointed kings by the hand of God! His counsel would direct Israel's armies and Peninnah's children are never mentioned in the scriptures again.

My question for you is this: *Have you ever had a bully in your life?* Have you ever gone through psychological abuse by another woman?

In 2003, I read a book called, *Odd Girl Out, The Hidden Culture of Aggression in Girls,* by Rachel Simmons. She stated: *"Aggression in women manifested through nonstop, cruel emotional attacks,"* and it is a very sad part of the American culture.

Even Kaiser Permanente has their employees watch videos through KP Learn regarding bully awareness and preventing hostile work environments. Yet, despite their training, it still very much alive in their corporation; especially amongst female upper management and supervisor leads. **Kaiser cites the following ramifications to bullying:** *Lower productive and poor-quality work because employees are distracted. Increased absenteeism, low staff morale, increased stress levels among staff, and higher employee turnover.* You may ask, *I thought you said it works for our good?* It does. The following examples are when the person has not yet chosen to fight back, but has accepted defeat.

Meredith Brandt, from Career minds blog wrote *"the Queen Bee Syndrome is defined as a situation where high-ranking women in positions of authority treat the women who work below them more critically than their male counterparts."* (Blog.careerminds.com, Queen Bee). Her article was inspired by reading a Wall Street Journal piece, *"Women who achieve success in male-dominated environments."*

THE JEWEL IN HANNAH'S LIFE

If Hannah had not a *Peninnah* in her life, *and if she hadn't gotten to the boiling point of, "ENOUGH!"* Hannah would have remained barren. Meaning, the fires of adversity produce more in individuals than what they could have done on their own. And like Hannah, if we did not have a Peninnah in our lives, we would not produce or reach our true potential. We need the battle because we are driven to our knees in prayer. Many easily recognize thanksgiving and praise when we receive the good in life, such as blessings and favor, but few have learned the depth of thanking God and praising Him for the challenges that cause us to grow up: our own hardships, our disappointments, our heartbreaks, and life's natural down side.

Laura Story, song, Blessings.

> *"What if my greatest disappointments*
> *Or the aching of this life*
> *Is the revealing of a greater thirst this world can't satisfy?*
> *What if trials of this life*
> *The rain, the storms, the hardest nights*
> *Are your mercies in disguise?"*

Thank God for the fires that burn us up - and provoke us to action. Hannah could never have known what the LORD was doing and it seemed so ruthlessly cruel. Hannah would endure (for over 10 years) Peninnah's taunting; needling, teasing. Often Hannah was made a public spectacle within her own home and community. Without a doubt, she felt rejected by God over and over. Yet, Hannah quietly remained in her dignity. She suffered in silence. She held her peace and waited on the LORD...but it seemed like He wouldn't come. In the Old Testament, the Bible says,

> "Thy wife shall be as a fruitful vine by the sides of thine house: thy children like olive plants round about thy table."
> — Psalm 128:3

But, Hannah felt, *I am not that. I am not a fruitful vine?*

Can you imagine what Hannah felt like each time a child's conception and birth were publicly announced? As her adversary's belly grew with a beautiful child forming inside, and Hannah's womb would not conceive. She felt empty or cursed of God.

In case you don't know, a pregnancy takes nine months to come to fruition. That's almost a year. Can you hear the words of an adversary, *"Oh, look, the baby is kicking! Husband, come feel my tummy."* Peninnah warms up to her husband in front of Hannah, *"Do you think it will be another son for you?"* And the praises of Peninnah's friends and community. *"Oh, Peninnah, look how beautiful you look pregnant; look how you shine! You can feel each gift received into Peninnah's hands was given in front of the barren Hannah's view.* You can sense the women then look back at Hannah. *"Is the other one having babies yet? No, hum, maybe next year."* Then you could hear the laughter of women mocking another. Hannah suffered. At night she laid in bed with tears streaming down her cheeks.

But, Hannah was not forsaken as she thought herself to be. God was there; He was right by her side. Hannah was actually the anointed chosen one of God - hand-selected for a miracle, not Peninnah - though for ten years it appeared like she had been. Hannah needed to get to her place of ENOUGH!

If Hannah could just make her way to a holy altar and pour out her heart to God. It took her years to come to wit's end and finally declare it and do something about it. It was an extraordinary miracle in the making forged in the fires of a living in disappointment. And exactly like the book of Job, Job passed his test and Hannah passed hers. That gives me hope that we shall pass ours, too. Yes, God still works like that today and nothing can draw humanity to its knees than some event, person, confrontation, trouble, or hardship that is bigger than them. In Christian circles, we understand reality,

YOU CANNOT HAVE A TESTIMONY WITHOUT THE TEST; AND YOU CANNOT FULLY COMPREHEND THE SWEETNESS OF YOUR VICTORY UNTIL YOU HAVE PHYSICALLY EXPERIENCED THE BITTERNESS OF YOUR SOUL!

Hannah offers to God her praise and rejoices in His mighty works! I Samuel 2 Is Hannah's Song can be read verses 1 through 10. But I would like to share another song. I first heard this song by Rev. Marvin Walker. It is Philip, Craig, and Dean's song, "The Blessing in the Thorn."

> "When does the thorn become a blessing? When does the pain become a friend? When does the weakness make me stronger? When does my faith make me whole? I want to feel His arms around me in the middle of my raging storm so that I can see the blessing in the thorn."
> — Song by Rev. Marvin Walker after his sermon, Reverse the Curse, (4-3-2016), Faith Apostolic Tabernacle. Written by Philip, Craig, and Dean

Please allow me to give you another person whose direction was changed by adversity. It may seem like a long read, but it is worth knowing. I want to encourage you if you are in a place like Hannah. Peninnah's reign will not last. Hold on; humble yourself before God and He shall exalt you in due time.

OTHERS PROVOKED TO THE MINISTRY – MISTER ROGERS?!

From my book, *What is Our Christian Purpose? Unplugging from the World Wide Web and Discovering Christ within Us.*

"Who is Mister Rogers to you? This answer depends on what generation you're from.

I believe today, besides Jesus Christ, the kindest man in the world was Fred Rogers, of KQED's Mister Rogers' Neighborhood. He was a minister who touched thousands of lives in the most positive of ways in his lifetime. Lives were changed because of his goodness. He was tenderly shy and overweight as a young boy and cruelly picked on. They called him "Fat Freddy" and chased and humiliated him. He was picked on so mercilessly that he had to be driven to and from school. One day, he got out of school early and was again the victim of bullying. He found shelter at a neighbor's house. His older neighbor tried to console him in a certain way and help him with life skills: "Just don't let them know it bothers you." But it did bother him. He couldn't understand how grown-ups would say, "Don't be afraid of them." When he was obviously afraid of them. Their prescribed coping mechanisms were not comforting him. For years, the experience bothered him."

WHAT DID MISTER ROGERS SEE, (AS AN ADULT) THAT BOTHERED HIM ENOUGH TO CHANGE HIS CAREER FROM THEOLOGY TO PUBLIC BROADCAST T.V.?

Fred Rogers humbled himself and wholeheartedly asked for the Lord's guidance and sought to right a wrong, or at least change the direction into something better; a positive thing that would help people. Fred Rogers was born in 1928. So, television was new to his generation. On a black-and-white TV set, he saw a comedy skit where pies were being smashed in people's faces. He was so appalled at this behavior, it moved him. He felt, *"If this new invention of T.V. was going to be used like this ...then he would come into the profession and use it for another way - one that will inspire, lift up, and educate."*

The key to his intervention was in his own past.

If you've never experienced that type of singling out or being the center of abuse, then you would not understand how easy the decision was for him to make. But, for those who have endured public humiliation of bullying, it was the right thing to do. Mr. Rogers exemplified Proverbs 25:11: *"A word fitly spoken is like apples of gold in pictures of silver."* He was always so careful to pick his words, for the purpose to edify and lift up so many. His quote: *Look for the helpers in the world!*

> "You don't set out to be rich or famous, what you set out to do is to be helpful. If the other comes along with it, that's okay. But that's not what you set out to be."
>
> — Fred Rogers

> "He was quietly powerful."
>
> —John Donovan, 2001

Author and Pastor's wife, Amy Hollingsworth wrote about Mr. Rogers. He was her mentor and very much like a father to her. Amy had received this letter.

> *"I don't know if this will mean anything to you or not, Amy. But my brother credits Mister Rogers for his being alive. He was always a big boy, and was bullied by his classmates, and abused by his teacher. He developed ulcers before he reached 13. He says if it weren't for Mister Rogers he would have either died from the strain on his body, or by killing himself. He says that it was the love and acceptance that Mister Rogers exuded on the program that made him feel loved and comforted. My brother was a few years older than the target audience, but he still maintains that Mister Rogers saved his life."*

Listen to this thought: Fred Rogers told Amy Hollingsworth,

> "That the space between the television set and the viewer was holy ground."

Fred Rogers was a devout Christian man and he knew the fallen nature of man. If they were going to use the T.V. for bad, he was going to put on T.V. that which was good, healthy, and sound. He said, *"What we put on television, can by the Holy Spirit, be transmitted to what that person needs to see and hear; and without that, it's all dross."*

PREPARING GOD IN YOUR WORK

Fred Rogers had that mindset. He prayed over his scripts, and he prayed for his studio, *"Dear Lord, let some word that is heard be yours."* So when Mister Rogers heard these stories from young people, (and he got thousands of letters from young people), each week. He said that was the Holy Spirit translating what I said, to what that person needed to hear and see."

— Amy Hollingsworth with Wayne
Shepard (WDRV Radio Host).

If we consider the life of Fred Rogers, we should be inspired; also encouraged by his life. We should be moved to be a little more like him. My prayer for all us is this: *LORD, let our lives impact the world around us for good. I pray others would have sweet memories of me...that something I had done, in a random act of kindness, or in a carefully chosen word, would bless others to help them along the way. In Jesus' name I pray.* Let whatever has been provoking you, taunting you, and crushing you be the platform into God on a greater dimension. When you have come to the end of yourself and the circumstances are too big, go to your Heavenly Father. He has a master plan for your life.

SATAN THOUGHT HE CONQUERED CHRIST

When Satan crucified Jesus; (and believe me, when Satan was finally allowed to physical hurt Christ – he relished in the savage abuse). He thought it was the end of the promise of God because their Savior was dead. (Isaiah 53). Jesus Christ would die on the cross, but it was only the beginning! He would even descend into hell, (preach unto the captives), and be raised on the third day!

All Satan's actions did was fulfill the scriptures. God accepted the blood of Christ. That same blood washes over every believer today! Christ's body was beaten by sinful men and his life poured out from Calvary's hill running into nations around the world, yes, even in the 21st Century! I am a living witness and testimony of the Salvation found in Jesus Christ; and Christian believer, so are you! And it all came through His suffering and breaking – beyond what man could do on his own.

"But we speak the wisdom of God in a mystery, even the hidden wisdom, which God ordained before the world unto our glory: **Which none of the princes of this world knew: for had they known it, they would not have crucified the Lord of glory.** But as it is written, Eye hath not seen, nor ear heard, neither have entered into the heart of man, the things which God hath prepared for them that love him."
—The Apostle Paul, (I Corinthians 2:7-9)

"And he that searcheth the hearts knoweth what is the mind of the Spirit, because he maketh intercession for the saints according to the will of God. *And we know that all things work together for good to them that love God,* to them who are the called according to his purpose. For whom he did foreknow, he also did predestinate to be conformed to the image of his Son, that he might be the firstborn among many brethren. Moreover whom he did predestinate, them he also called: and whom he called, them he also justified: and whom he justified, them he also glorified.

What shall we then say to these things? If God be for us, who can be against us?"
— The Apostle Paul, (Romans 8:27-3)

Allow the process; and when you weep, let your tears fall on Jesus' lap.

CHAPTER TEN

WE DO NOT HAVE TO BE AFRAID!

"Nothing in life is to be feared, it is only to be understood. Now is the time to understand more, so that we may fear less."

— Madame Marie Curie

When you learn,

- God cannot lie. (Ever!)
- Satan is the father of lies and there is no truth in him. So stop listening to him, and stop believing everything he tells you. He threatened, but if he could actually do it, he would have done it.
- God is the Great Creator of all things, (visible and invisible).
- Satan is one of those creative beings subject to God. He is NOT ever more powerful. He likes to tell people that his power is equal to God. That's a lie. He is a created being that is under God's thumb! He seriously can do nothing to touch you or your family without permission from the Almighty God.
- The Word of God is my sword of the Spirit; *It is a Lamp to my feet and the light to my pathway.* (Psalm 119:105). I am safeguarded by God's Holy Word!
- God does have angels surrounding us.
- God never sleeps, and He is never tired.
- God is victorious in battle - always!

- The End of Satan has already been written through Old Testament scriptures, but also in the Book of Revelation.
- There is more for you than are with Satan.
- Our life choices will direct our eternity.

Sister Walker revealed in her teaching ministry: The 21ˢᵗ Century Church deals with three demonic entities.

1. Seducing Spirits
2. Doctrines of Devils
3. The Spirit of Antichrist

You have to ask yourself, *"Are you being seduced by this world?"* The Bible records Jesus telling his disciples, I will send you forth amongst wolves, false prophets, false brethren. There will be those who peddle doctrines of devils. How will you recognize them? By their works!

> "Even so every good tree bringeth forth good fruit; but a corrupt tree bringeth forth evil fruit."
> — Jesus Christ (Matthew 7:17) Sermon on the Mount

> "Little children, let no man deceive you: he that doeth righteousness is righteous, even as he is righteous. He that committeth sin is of the devil; for the devil sinneth from the beginning. For this purpose the Son of God was manifested, that he might destroy the works of the devil.

> Whosoever is born of God doth not commit sin; for his seed remaineth in him: and he cannot sin, because he is born of God. In this the children of God are manifest, and the children of the devil: whosoever doeth not righteousness is not of God, neither he that loveth not his brother. For this is the message that ye heard from the beginning, that we should love one another. Not as Cain, who was of that wicked one, and slew his brother. And wherefore slew he him? Because his own works were evil, and his brother's righteous.

Marvel not, my brethren, if the world hate you."

— I John 3:7-13

The next spirit was the spirit of the Antichrist. It would come in the end days. I believe it is already here. We need to look for these. It's time to clean the house. It's time to ready our own vessels for God, (holy sanctification and recommitment), then it's time to sanctify our own Church.

SISTER CLAUDETTE WALKER SHARED THIS REVELATION – WHAT GOD THINKS OF HIS CHILDREN:

She had been in prayer and she felt the LORD ask her, *Claudette as you look through 20 years of journals, how do you see your life in Me?* She internally responded, *"I see ups and downs, Mountain tops and some deep valleys. In the valley is where I feel I let you down, or I could have done better."* She used her hand to show the congregation what she felt it was, like an AC Current. She said then the LORD spoke again, *Let me show how I see your last twenty years.* God took an eraser and erased the lower portions of the deep valleys. God spoke, *When you repent, I no longer see the low points of your life; I have placed them as far away from you, as the east is to the west.* (Psalm 103:12). Now, equipped with this spiritual truth, do your part.

CRUCIFY YOUR FLESH AND CONTROL YOUR EMOTIONS!

Understand this fact: We do not tame the flesh, we crucify it and all its lusts and appetites. Mortify the deeds of the flesh! We don't suppress evil within us, but repent, (recognize it for the evil it is), and ask God to purge it from you; all the sin and shame involved with it. Even if you have to excuse yourself, go into the bathroom, drop on your knees, lift up your hands, and cry to God. Do it! God will run to help you! There have been times I stood in silence in the bathroom and inwardly called out to God, *Please help me!* Then I waited for my help. It always came. Next, research scriptures that will help you. Write them out; keep them on flashcards in your pocket. Instead of scrolling aimless of mind-numbing social media, memorize the word of God. Try something educational: learn new vocabulary words, read a book; do something edifying and constructive. Work with your hands and begin a creative hobby that engages abilities and talents. Stimulate your mind to think. Build something. Volunteer your time. Give of yourself.

FACE YOUR FEARS!

Examine yourself. If you think there are no weak areas in your life that the devil can attack, ask your spouse. Are there any areas that you could be better, nicer, kinder, or more patient? find the scriptures regarding that area. Study the scriptures every day; read the commentary behind the thought or story. Determine within yourself to be victorious in your weak area. You must face your fear. When I was studying for Radiology, my first year in the hospital was terrifying. The lesson they instilled in us,

> "If you discover a procedure that you are struggling with, or afraid of, let the control person, (supervisor in charge) know that any time that procedure comes up you would like to volunteer for it; or at least assist the senior technologist in it."

They forced us to do the exams that had intimidated us the most, in order to master it. Yes, face your fear! It worked. I have some spiritual areas right now that I have been working on for the past year. I will continue them until I am adept at them. Just keep doing the right thing and God's Word will do its part. Learning new skill sets takes being disciplined: new disciplines take practice; dedicated practice blossoms a skilled mastery, (and believe it or not, those types of mastery can come in a short amount of time). When God is in it, it can be quick work! All of this really can be used on any topic; business dynamics, or simple hobbies.

The depths of Christian comprehension and knowledge partnered with the biblical application is very pleasing to God! You will always have the favor and goodness of God if you submit your will to His. If you are honest with

Him and ask for His help, He will come through for you. He will bring happiness to your life. Yes, it is the world of the Holy Ghost who subdues our unruly flesh! Let God work on you. He will reward your faithfulness to him - even in your struggles and tears. (Proverbs 24:16). The Bible says a just man falls seven times, so be kind and patient with yourself. God is for you. He is in your corner and He is on your side. (Genesis 31:42; Psalm 118:6). This is how we cultivate holiness in Christ. (There is great confidence in knowing that He is on your side! (Psalm 124:1).

Praise God! Especially, if you are doing it to bring glory to His Name and to keep yourself wholly for Him. Jesus said,

> "Ye are the light of the world. A city that is set on a hill cannot be hid. Neither do men light a candle, and put it under a bushel, but on a candlestick; and it giveth light unto all that are in the house. Let your light so shine before men, that they may see your good works, and glorify your Father which is in heaven."
> — Jesus Christ, (Matthew 5:14-16).

LUKE-WARM CHRISTIANITY, DEFILED VESSELS OR EMPTY VESSELS!

Those above phrases should cause each Christian believer to pause. No one wants to believe that they are a *"Luke-warm Christian."* Or, that their vessels is marred or defiled. The idea that our LORD would evaluate us and be displeased with us - should make us shudder. I once made this statement:

> "The triumphant crown of glory does not hang on the head of the half-hearted, lukewarm Christian."

And it still holds true today. An empty vessel refers to the Holy Ghost leaving it altogether. (See Luke 11:25). Luke 11 paraphrased: Jesus Christ tells of a story of a wandering, (unclean) spirit who cannot find rest on earth. He makes the declaration, *"I will return to the vessel, (body), which I came from."* He finds the person, and inside their body, the spirit notices how nice it is. He says, *"It was clean and swept, but empty."* The idea of cleaning and sweeping out the human heart and soul refers to the work of the Holy Ghost. The empty vessel demonstrates to the reader, *"The Spirit of God had departed from the person."* At this, the unclean spirit declares, *"I shall go and find seven more spirits to abide with me here."* The Bible says that the end of that fact made the person's life worse than the beginning of when he knew not God.

Luke 11:15-28

'But some of them said, He, (Jesus) casteth out devils through Beelzebub the chief of the devils. And others, tempting him, sought of him a sign from heaven.

But he, (Jesus), knowing their thoughts, said unto them, Every kingdom divided against itself is brought to desolation; and a house divided against a house falleth. If Satan also be divided against himself, how shall his kingdom stand? because ye say that I cast out devils through Beelzebub. And if I by Beelzebub cast out devils, by whom do your sons cast them out? therefore shall they be your judges. But if I with the finger of God cast out devils, no doubt the kingdom of God is come upon you.

When a strong man armed keepeth his palace, his goods are in peace: But when a stronger than he shall come upon him, and overcome him, he taketh from him all his armour wherein he trusted, and divideth his spoils. He that is not with me is against me: and he that gathereth not with me scattereth.

When the unclean spirit is gone out of a man, he walketh through dry places, seeking rest; and finding none, he saith, I will return unto my house whence I

came out. And when he cometh, he findeth it swept and garnished. Then goeth he, and taketh to him seven other spirits more wicked than himself; and they enter in, and dwell there: and the last state of that man is worse than the first. And it came to pass, as he spake these things, a certain woman of the company lifted up her voice, and said unto him, Blessed is the womb that bare thee, and the paps which thou hast sucked.

But he said, Yea rather, blessed are they that hear the word of God, and keep it."

— Jesus Christ, (Luke 11:15-28)

I'm going to point something out here: If you are a Christian believer and once knew the tremendous experience of your conversion, but something has changed...look to this story. If we know that our God changes not, (Malachi 3:6), then something has changed in our hearts. Somewhere we have lost our first love. (Revelation 2:1-7). Here God removes His presence from Israel and allows the Ark of the Covenant to be captured.

PART FOUR

PART FOUR

CHAPTER ELEVEN
ENTRY POINTS OF SATAN

On December 26, 1973, (the day after Christmas), the Exorcist was released in theater. It was called *a supernatural horror film*. The movie was based on a true story of a little girl who had dabbled with a Ouija board and had become possessed by thousands of devils. The Catholic church had to be called in to exorcise the child. It was the most famous, talked about movie for the young actress, Linda Blair. I pulled Wikipedia up and this is there description of the movie: *"The Exorcists was released in 24 theaters in the United States and Canada in late December. Despite mixed critical reviews, audiences flocked to it, waiting in long lines during winter weather and many doing so more than once."* It makes you ask the question, why are we so interested in the supernatural?

In the true story of the Exorcist, the entry point for Satan was the Ouija board. At this point, I want to say here that I am astonished that this board is sold in children toys stores across our nation and that parents buy it for their kids. But it happens.

UNCLE BOB'S TESTIMONY OF THE EXORCIST

My uncle, Bob, shared this with me. He told me, *There were many Catholics who actually saw this film.* He was one of them. He said there was never a movie that disturbed him more his entire life as seeing the devil manifest through the young girl and talk through her in a man's voice; the voice of demons. This was the first movie of its kind. Grown adults slept with the lights on. It bothered them to the core. When he returned home that evening, he used the automatic door opener to his garage. My uncle, Bob, had a huge German Shepherd, Duke. He raised him from a puppy. The dog adored him and would only listen to my uncle. He was trained German Shepherd; ferocious. My uncle would bring the animal with him to the San Jose Probation department where he worked as a Probation officer. That night, when my uncle returned home and Duke heard the garage door, Duke ran out to meet him and stopped in the middle of the garage; he stared at my uncle's car. Then the dog began to growl and cower away. My uncle saw his dog's reaction and got out of the car. As the car door opened, the dog fled back into the house and out the doggie door to the back. He jumped over the fence and took off. Duke had never done that before. The dog returned home two days later. My uncle said, I don't know what came home with me that night from the movie, but my dog sensed it and ran off.

Allow me to introduce another elder, an American Roman Catholic Priest, Vince Lampert. He is the designated exorcist Archdiocese of Indianapolis. According to Father Vince Lampert, there are eight points of spiritual entry doors.

1. Ties to the Occult.
2. The Entertainment Industry
3. Curses- Curses said against you, or curse you speak out.
4. Abuse: Mental, Physical, Sexual
5. A Life of Habitual Sin
6. Inviting a demonic presence into your life.
7. Brokenness/Broken Relationships

Question: Can Spirit-Filled Believers Be Possessed? No.

Spirit-filled believers cannot be demon-possessed, but they can be spiritually oppressed by the demonic realm - especially if they have invited something into their homes. They can, (through their own vices) put shackles back on themselves, (I Thessalonians 5:19), especially if they have invited the evil into their lives.

Question: Can evil influence a Christian's life? Yes. They can through an area of infestations of demons, (demonic area/open doors), through demon vexation, (which is outward tormenting), and through oppression.

DON'T QUENCH THE SPIRIT OF GOD

Christian believers can also *"quench"* the Spirit of God in their lives; lose sight of God and get a (kind of) spiritual amnesia. This is why daily reflection and true repentance is so vital to the longevity of our spirituality. Yes, Believers can *"back-slide"* or turn their back on God and the church. The Bible warns us in II Peter

> "For if after they have escaped the pollutions of the world through the knowledge of the Lord and Savior Jesus Christ, they are again entangled therein, and overcome, the latter end is worse with them than the beginning. For it had been better for them not to have known the way of righteousness, than, after they have known it, to turn from the holy commandment delivered unto them. But it is happened unto them according to the true proverb, The dog is turned to his own vomit again; and the sow that was washed to her wallowing in the mire."
>
> — II Peter 2:20-222

Note the words Peter used: *"Entangled with the pollution of the world again."*

Jesus tells us a story of the supernatural in Matthew 12.

> "When the unclean spirit is gone out of a man, he walketh through dry places, seeking rest, and findeth none. Then he saith, I will return into my house from whence I came out; and when he is come, he findeth it empty, swept, and garnished. Then goeth he, and taketh with himself seven

other spirits more wicked than himself, and they enter in
and dwell there: and the last state of that man is worse
than the first. Even so shall it be also unto this wicked
generation."

— Jesus Christ, (Matthew 12:43-45)

Jesus warns the corrupt religious leaders – continue and this shall be
your fate. It's time to reevaluate our lives if we have let *"unclean things,"*
behaviors, and lifestyle choices back in that God had cast out! Where the
Spirit of the LORD is, there is liberty! (II Corinthians 3:17). And full
freedom and liberty brings great joy!

Allow me to share this interview with Father Vince Lampert.

> Father Lampert was ordained a priest in 1991. (29 years
> ago, now). He received his exorcist training in Rome
> in 2005. (15 years ago). He serves as the pastor of two
> churches in Cincinnati Ohio. He is also an author. His
> book is called Exorcism, which goes into the processes of
> casting out a demon. (*October 20, 2020 - Bone Chilling
> Interview with a Real-Life Exorcist - Fr. Vince Lampert*).
> He was interviewed by a young man named Cameron
> Bertuzzi. The interview is worth listening to.
>
> One of the questions that Cameron Bertuzzi asked Father
> Lambert was, *"How do you know a person is demon-possessed?"*
>
> Father Lampert expounded, "There are four signs of the
> demonic:
>
> 1. The ability to speak and understand languages,
>   (otherwise unknown to the individual),
> 2. Super-human strength, (beyond the normal capacity
>   of the individual),
> 3. Having elevated perception, (knowing about things
>   that that person should not otherwise know),

4. And inversion to anything of a sacred nature, (such as being blessed with Holy water, crucifix, the Bible placed on their head during prayer.

All of these can be indications of demonic presence. The Vatican has put out a question to their exorcists, *what was the entrance point?* Have you ever been involved in the occult? Have you been engaged in satanic practices or rituals? Are you involved in witchcraft or magic? What types of books or literature do you read? After the exorcism, Fr. Lambert said, "Step #5, help the person to resume their normal, healthy spiritual life; or to help them create it for the very first time.

— (October 20, 2020 -
Bone Chilling Interview with a Real-Life Exorcist
- Fr. Vince Lampert).

PERSONAL TESTIMONY: A TIME TO CLEAN HOUSE

In 1998, I was a new graduate from Radiology school, I was also a new convert to the Christian Pentecostal faith. I was so happy that my testimony naturally came out. I wanted to share Jesus with everyone! At times, it did catch people off guard. We've been programed not to discuss Jesus.

A couple of weeks after I received the Holy Ghost, I began to change my own house around. I began to decorate it with my new faith. I began to use yellow post-it notes with scriptures around my house to remind of the promises of God. I eagerly made these changes as I was changing from the inside out! God's glorious light shined through me and others saw it. The transformation was undeniable. My countenance had changed overnight from dark to light. I wasn't who I once was, and my family and coworkers knew it. I experienced being a *New Creature in Christ.* (II Corinthians 5:17).

I remember one weekend feeling the desire to clean the house! Not just straightening up, but a serious spring-cleaning type of cleaning: a purging, so to speak. I went through my drawers, cabinets, closets, etc., and threw out anything that checked me as dark, demonic, unholy, or questionable. I threw out figurines; little things that I had purchased here or there. I threw out jewelry that my old boyfriends had given to me and the sin that was attached to it; I didn't care how much it cost. To me, it represented my old life of fornication and the bond that person had on me – despite how that trinket shined. Those pieces of gold, diamonds, and gems represent relationships that were unhealthy and they represented to me, the person I no longer was anymore. I wanted it out of my house. I threw out books, (which I felt were occultist or New Age). I dusted shelves and pictures. I cleaned, I scrubbed my apartment. I refolded all of my shower and hand towels. I re-organized my dressers.

I had a second chance at life. A better life! One with Jesus Christ in it and I was clean!

Oh, how I could breathe! My physical house was put in order! As I tossed the world out: its music, its symbols, its influence, God was even more pronounced; recognizable! It feels good to get your house in order; to know what's in it; to have full authority of your space!

DO YOU WANT TO KICK SATAN OUT OF YOUR HOUSE? INVITE GOD INTO YOUR PHYSICAL HOME!

My physical house became God's dwelling place! And so is my body. I remember when I asked the LORD to live in my home; it was such a great feeling.

One afternoon, I had just come home from my shift at the hospital. I had not picked my daughter, Brittany, up from school. I walked over and turned the T.V. on to relax; I had to wait a couple of hours before she was out of school. As I sat in my living room, I noticed a haze in my home. I blinked a couple of times - yes, it was there. It was white smoke. I thought to myself, *"Did I leave the oven on?"* I went to the small kitchen and opened it. It was off. The oven is cold. I turned around and stared at the white mist in my home. Then it dissipated - literally vanished before my eyes.

The realization that the LORD God had just welcomed me home. That may seem like a funny statement. But when I was converted, I was a single mother. My daughter Brittany would spend every-other-weekend with her dad. For the first time in my adult life, I was single, and by myself. I wasn't dating anyone - it was just me and God. On Friday evenings, I would prepare my dinner and leave a plate of food at the head of the table. Yes, I would sit and have dinner with the LORD of hosts. During this new time in my life, I had read from the book of Isaiah and I took it to heart. I want you to understand, I was reading these scriptures for the first time in my adult life. I felt they were for me.

Isaiah 54:4-17

"Fear not; for thou shalt not be ashamed: neither be thou confounded; for thou shalt not be put to shame: for thou shalt forget the shame of thy youth, and shalt not remember the reproach of thy widowhood any more.

For thy Maker is thine husband; the Lord of hosts is his name; and thy Redeemer the Holy One of Israel; The God of the whole earth shall he be called.

For the Lord hath called thee as a woman forsaken and grieved in spirit, and a wife of youth, when thou wast refused, saith thy God.

Note: Yes, how I truly felt like this. Look at the description. Think of a single mother: shame, confounded; mistakes made; the memories of my sins. But God was telling me, You will not remember your reproach anymore!

For a small moment have I forsaken thee; but with great mercies will I gather thee. In a little wrath I hid my face from thee for a moment; but with everlasting kindness will I have mercy on thee, saith the Lord thy Redeemer.

For this is as the waters of Noah unto me: for as I have sworn that the waters of Noah should no more go over the earth; so have I sworn that I would not be wroth with thee, nor rebuke thee.

For the mountains shall depart, and the hills be removed; but my kindness shall not depart from thee, neither shall the covenant of my peace be removed, saith the Lord that hath mercy on thee.

> **Note:** God was telling me "With great mercy He gathered me." He promised me an everlasting kindness. The word, Redeemer, I would later learn. He offered to me His sweet peace.

O thou afflicted, tossed with tempest, and not comforted, behold, I will lay thy stones with fair colors, and lay thy foundations with sapphires. And I will make thy windows of agates, and thy gates of carbuncles, and all thy borders of pleasant stones.

And all thy children shall be taught of the Lord; and great shall be the peace of thy children.

> **Note:** My Heavenly Father would become a husband to me. And He promised that all my children would be taught by the LORD; and they would have peace.

In righteousness shalt thou be established: thou shalt be far from oppression; for thou shalt not fear: and from terror; for it shall not come near thee. Behold, they shall surely gather together, but not by me: whosoever shall gather together against thee shall fall for thy sake.

> **Note:** God would establish me in His Righteousness. What did that mean? I didn't know. It sounded wonderful. He promised me that I would not be afraid anymore.

Behold, I have created the smith that bloweth the coals in the fire, and that bringeth forth an instrument for his work; and I have created the waster to destroy.

No weapon that is formed against thee shall prosper; and every tongue that shall rise against thee in judgment thou shalt condemn. This is the heritage of the servants of the Lord, and their righteousness is of me, saith the Lord.

> **Note:** God promised to protect me and my reputation. Oh, how could I not love Him and commit my life to His.
>
> — Isaiah 54:4-17

As a single mom, this chapter meant so much to me. Yes, I would allow the LORD to be the Head of my home. Now ask yourself, *Since your conversion, have you let things sneak back in? Have you removed Christ as the headship of your life and home and replaced him with some worldly idol?* It's time to throw the idol down; break it in pieces and reestablish God's holy Covenant again. It's time to get your house in order!

BLESS YOUR HOME

Invite your pastor and the elders to come and pray for your home. Consecrate the home to Jesus Christ. If you can't find some member of the ministry to bless your home, then bless it yourself. Have Bible studies in your home with other believers. It brings God's Presence and His angelic angels into your home. Prayer and believers gathering together, summons the great Creator, the God of the Universe! The more you pray and use your home for God, the more you will feel His peace in your home.

FOLLOW THE SUCCESSFUL ELDERS WHO CAME BEFORE US

I began my books by quoting the late Rev. Billy Cole. I shared stories about Sister Claudette Walker, (pastor's wife and Ladies Minister), and incorporated the late Rev. Kenneth Reeves revelations on the tools of the Spirit of God. They are from my United Pentecostal organization; they are my elders in the Spirit. I also want to share a book with you that transformed my prayer life: *Heaven to Earth,* by Pastor Anthony Mangun, (Pentecostals of Alexandria). If you want to learn how to pray with order and effectiveness, follow his guide. He has a praying pattern that models the Tabernacle Church in the wilderness. I've included those notes on prayer and my own prayers from his study series: Praying Through the Tabernacle!

Sometimes, (actually a lot of time), we need to ask for help; we need to take the time to study, to observe, to try new things.

I've shared the life of Mister Fred Rogers. His ministry was birthed through a very difficult time as a young boy. Have you ever felt helpless and small? Allow your difficulties and hardships to help you reach your potential. Fred McFeely Rogers' natural love reaches thousands of people! Our world was better because he was in it - making a safe place for children to find a friend if they didn't have one. In my book, I will reference men like the late Rev. Evan Roberts. He was just a simple man. His burden for his nation birthed the great Welsh Revival, (1904-1905). His calling came and no one recognized that Christ was using him. His pastor allowed him to stay after service and preach, (if anyone really was interested in what he would say). Mr. Roberts truly felt God had spoken to him; now if only others listen to the message. Five women made the choice to stay. Five women gave this young man an audience. When Mr. Roberts had finished and they confirmed the message had been sent by God. They grabbed hold of it as manna from heaven and together turned their world upside down right side up! This was the message:

- Remove all doubt from your life.
- Confess all known sin
- Be sensitive to the Spirit of God - obey Him!
- Openly, and boldly share your faith in Jesus Christ and share what He had done for you.

You will find in this book that I have shared the testimony of a Catholic Priest/Exorcist, Father Vincent Lampert. Most people ask him, How is he not fearful when he helps to deliver people from the demonic world? ''

He shares how he is not afraid, *"It comes from understanding how great Jesus Christ is, the work that was done on the cross."*

His confidence wasn't in himself, but in God: he understood that he was protected by God to exorcise the demons out! He understood that God was more powerful and greater than any created being here on earth, or beneath.

Father Lampert relied on the God-given authority and ordination he obtained and his training, but in his trust in the one who gave to him his calling. I will also include some of the words of Reverence Billy Graham; especially excerpts from his book, *Angels, Angels, Angels, God's Secret Agents*. My question for you, dear Reader, who inspires you to be better than you are? Who is your encourager in the faith? Who has challenged you to go deeper than you have ever gone? Find that person. Explore books on faith. Read the testimonies on how God works in our lives, everyday people. Learn to pray and ask God to help you truly become what He meant for you to be. Ask for help; listen to godly counsel; allow a pastor to speak into your life and give you correction when you need it. We all need a pastor. Even a pastor needs a pastor. We really need someone to hold us accountable. I was told a successful Christian believer should have three types of relationships around him.

1. He will have an elder/pastor to give him guidance. He will have someone he submits to and receives correction from.
2. He will have a peer; a friend in the faith to share with and encourage.
3. He will have someone he is helping; someone who looks up to them as a mentor; confident; instructor in the faith.

The person who has these three relationships in their life will be rich indeed with good works. The Christian believer should also be faithful to his church and congregation - *"Moreover it is required in stewards, that a man be found faithful."* (I Corinthians 4:2). They will be individuals others can count on, rely on. It will be obvious that they are fully committed and they care.

CHAPTER TWELVE

DON'T BURY YOUR HEAD IN THE SAND!

IGNORANCE IS NOT BLISS, IT'S DANGEROUS.

Once again, I will repeat myself: Many churches do not want to touch on the topics of demons and spiritual encounters. Many deny the power of the Holy Ghost to completely infill the Christian believers body, where they speak in tongues. They teach their congregations that those supernatural events were for the first century Christian. Somehow, they feel it's too spooky and better left unsaid then to open the door to the Book of Acts experience.

- I assure you that all of this is very real!
- Our ignorance doesn't wish it all away
- It makes us susceptible to being tormented by the forces of darkness
- Ignorance makes us easy prey for satanic attacks
- More importantly, it makes us ill-equipped to defend ourselves!

IGNORANCE IS BLISS. IS IT?
(NO, IT'S DANGEROUS!)

I once heard a man say, *"We just don't know what we just don't know."*

Here is the sad truth: I believe it is a sin issue. We really have become lukewarm. A lukewarm Christian has no anointing, no power to resist demonic attacks, and does not have what is needed to change their atmosphere around them – or push back hard against the demonic. Basically, they are just sitting ducks. The word *luke-warm* is found in the Bible, Revelation 3:16. It is from the Greek adjective called chliaros. Meaning, " *Tepid, lukewarm; of the condition of the soul wretchedly fluctuation between a torpor and a fevour of love."*

For those of you who don't know what it's meaning is, the best description that I can give you is, *"Lukewarm is a little Christianity mixed with worldly habits."*

Think of a water color painting class. One bowl of water is crystal clear. The next bowl has light blue paint. Dip the brush into the light blue paint. Paint your picture; smear the color around; use all the paint off the brush until you think it's all gone. Then, dip the used brush into the clean bowl of crystal-clear water. Even though you visibly cannot see paint on your brush anymore and you feel it was all used on the image, that brush still holds the colors of the light blue paint. As you take your brush and dip it into the crystal-clear water in the clean bowl, a strange thing happens. The paint (that you could no longer see) bleeds into the clean bowl. You watch it effortlessly drift and swirl into the bowl. That's sin.

Their vessels are too polluted with the world, their ears are deaf to the voice of their Savior and their eyes are blind to perceive. The devil doesn't fear them nor does he have to respond to their commands. Here is a story in the New Testament that best shows the effects of playing around with things too high for them. It is found in Acts 19:13-20.

THE STORY BEGINS:

> Then certain of the vagabond Jews, exorcists, took upon them to call over them which had evil spirits the name of the Lord Jesus, saying, We adjure you by Jesus whom Paul preacheth. (13)

Anytime you see the word: *Vagabond,* know it's not meant as a compliment. It was first used to describe Cain, in Genesis 4. No, it is not a good description. It means, *"a person not really in"* or a person that will not submit to the church leadership and correction. They are rogue - operating at their own will and for their own motives: usually self-glorification.

Also note: *"We adjure you by Jesus, whom Paul preaches."*

They were poisers or pretenders! They were attempting to steal Paul's consecrated holy anointing as their own. It was a joke to the supernatural and the devils leaped all over the infraction! They call out the sons of Sceva, *"I don't recognize your authority!"* (That's terrifying!)

"And there were seven sons of one Sceva, a Jew, and chief of the priests, which did so. And the evil spirit answered and said, Jesus I know, and Paul I know; but who are ye? And the man in whom the evil spirit was leaped on them, and overcame them, and prevailed against them, so that they fled out of that house naked and wounded.

And this was known to all the Jews and Greeks also dwelling at Ephesus; and fear fell on them all, and the name of the Lord Jesus was magnified. And many that believed came, and confessed, and shewed their deeds.

Many of them also which used curious arts brought their books together, and burned them before all men: and they counted the price of them, and found it fifty thousand pieces of silver. So mightily grew the word of God and prevailed."

— Acts 19:13-20

The moral of the story is: *Don't play around with the dark spiritual dimensions!*

But, IF YOUR HAVE THE RIGHT, HOLY,CONSECRATED STUFF, *fight back!* COMMAND YOUR GOD-GIVEN ATHORITY AND WATCH THE DEVILS SCATTER LIKE ROACHES!

How do I know if I have the right stuff? If you are doing everything you know to do; if you are faithfully attending church, actually attentively listening to the messages over the pulpit, examining your own life and repenting from all known sin; if you are keeping your vessel pure and your personal relationships are all in order, then you have NOTHING to fear from the devil; and HE IS VERY MUCH AFRAID OF YOU! KNOW THAT!

SATAN BLUFFS

When I was a new convert, I didn't understand this facet of Satan. One year had gone by after my Christian conversion in 1998, I was working at El Camino Hospital, Radiology department. I had learned the story of the sons of Sceva.

A young woman in her twenties came into our department for a chest x-ray. She was from One-South ward of the hospital. Meaning, the Psych ward. But everything seemed fine about her. Then she blurted out to me, *"That department is weird. They say that I am crazy, they are the ones that are crazy!"* It came out of nowhere, so it took me by surprise. This is what I saw in her: *A young troubled girl.*

According to her chart, she had tried to commit suicide. I evaluated everything about her, I found her to be troubled, but not crazy. She answered all the right questions. She maintain eye contact; she wasn't acting bizarre. She could have been my neighbor or a friend; I found her to be reasonable. We got the exam done and I wheeled her back out to the caretaker. I knew that guy; he was odd. In fact, I felt that ward was odd. So, I had compassion for her. I actually felt bad for her having to go back to that ward. So, I offered her, *after my shift would you like me to come visit you?* I was thinking at least she could have someone normal to talk to. I was true to my word and walked over to that part of the hospital. It gave me the creeps. I really didn't like it and sometimes we had to do portables in there. I got to the locked door and the nurses buzzed me in. I walked over to the nurses station and told them who I was there to see. At their desk there had been cameras inside the patients room – a live feed from all the lock down patients. My patient was one of them. The nurses looked at me, then looked at each other. Then both their eyes glanced down to the screen. They shrugged their shoulders. Pointing, one of the nurses said, *She's over there.* I went to the room. I walked in. The lights were dimmed and my normal, healthy patient was lying on the floor on her stomach, her head turned to the side. There were no blankets on her, no pillow. She literally was on the ground. I said her name. She didn't respond. I asked if she was okay; if she needed me to get someone for her. No answer. I had brought with me a Holy Bible. I didn't hide it; the nurses saw me bring it in. I knelt down to her and moved the hair from her face. Her eyes were rolled back and foam was coming out the side of her mouth. I thought, *did they medicate her?* So, I leaned down and said in her ear her name; and introduced myself again, *Hi, it's Kari, remember I told you I would come and visit you after my shift.* No response. Eyes still rolled back; she gurgled a little; drool came out the side. I said, I brought my Bible. I thought maybe we could read some passages. The room was still. I went to lean down to her ear again, but this time I heard in my mind, *"Jesus I know, and Paul I know, but who are you?"* It was the scripture from the story of the sons of Sceva. This was demonic! I shot back up. I was not ready for that. This was my first experience with the demonic; or the demonically possessed. It startled me. It made me question myself, *Was I safe?* I knew the story in Acts 19. It was a threat, or what I would call a low growl. The demons didn't want me there. Satan was threatening me that if I stayed, the demons would jump on me. That thought unnerved me. I was too green in my conversion to know how to handle it. Such as, *Rebuke the devil in Jesus name and command it to get out!* Instead, I got on my feet, backed away from her. Picked up my Bible from her table and left.

The point is this, I missed the opportunity because I was unsure of myself. Satan intimidated me out of the room. At that point, I didn't know how to cast out the devil(s). Still, to this day, I'm not sure what took place with the caretakers and the nursing station. I do not know what they saw. I know they were watching me from their live feed. No one else would come into the room.

IMPORTANT PART OF TRUE CHRISTIANITY IS THE RESPECT OF AUTHORITY – AND KNOWING YOU ARE IN GOOD STANDING WITH GOD AND MAN!

My life is hidden in Christ; which means God protects me as an invisible shield of defense. We do not have to be afraid of Satan! When you know that you are doing your part to submit to the spiritual authority in your life, you do not have to be afraid of demonic attacks. The authority is the covering.

Knowledge of your standings: If you know that your relationships in your life are right; and you are following the rules of conduct across the board – your life is hid with Christ!

Marital: if you know that you and your husband are in unison together – you've got it! If your spouse just will not get on board, but you have surrendered all to Jesus, then you've got it. Partner with your pastor; make sure he knows you are going after your jurisdiction.

Boldly and with great confidence I declare to you, *If you are committed to Jesus Christ, you do not have to shrink from the fight!*

PREPARATIONS

Ask the LORD God to wash your (spiritual) eyes so that you may see clearly; ask Jesus to unstop your deaf ears so that you may distinctively hear Him and respond to His voice. Ask God to make you whole, sound, and healthy. The elders, (pastors, evangelists, teachers, apostles, and preachers), have always referenced over the pulpit, *"A prayer less church is a powerless church."* That still holds true today!

In the 1904 Great Welsh Revival, evangelist Evan Roberts lamented,

> *"Prayer is buried, and lost and Heaven weeps. If all prayed the wicked would flee from our midst or to the refuge."*
> — *Evan Roberts*

ONCE AGAIN, EVAN ROBERTS BULLET POINTS FOR THE WELSH NATION:

1. All sin must be confessed to God and repented of.
2. Remove all doubt from Your life.
3. We must obey the Holy Spirit. Do what the Spirit prompts you to do.
4. There must be public confessions of Christ as Savior.

— The Four Points,
The World Aflame, by Rick Joyner
aotfb.com

EVALUATION: WHAT ARE YOU DOING WITH YOUR TIME?

What you do with your downtime matters in God's kingdom. If you have four to six hours to binge on movies and videos; if you have three or four hours to scroll social media, but no time to pray or read your Bible, you need to reevaluate your personal choices. Most Apple iPhones will tell you how much time you use on your device. Again, I will say, what you do with your time matters to God and in eternity. One way will lead to emptiness and fatigue, and the other will lead to eternal life and a feeling of joy. One is baser, and the other is better. Choose a better way.

STEPPING INTO THE CHRISTIAN PURPOSE

I wrote this in prior chapters. I feel to say it again.

- Will you get off the internet, social media accounts?
- Will you get off your cell phone?
- Will you stop binging on Netflix, Prime, HBO?
- Will you interact with people who do not know Jesus Christ?
- Will you have the courage to speak to them about Jesus?
- Will you be sensitive to the prompting of the Holy Spirit?

ALL NIGHT PRAYER MEETINGS

Have you ever heard of all-night prayer meetings?

We just don't pray like the old-timers used to pray. They would gather their families around the living room and pray as a family. They literally would kneel down in reverence to God and cover their family in prayer - every night!

Pastor Anthony Mangun of the Pentecostals of Alexandria has a method of praying through the Tabernacle. (Referring to the Tabernacle in the wilderness). From his book, *Heaven to Earth, page 176, "List of things I pray as I enter the Holy Place"* Anything that I need counsel and direction over; things that I need God to move in a mighty way; the personal needs that only a Father can meet; and the areas of my life that need peace."

Ask yourself, in this modern era of T.V., videos, social media, and electronic devices, what does the average family do at night together? Do they eat dinner at the table together? or do they grab a plate of food and head for their electronic device? I'm convicted to say the American family grabs for the food and heads into their personal space; that includes the Christian families.

CHANGE YOUR ATMOSPHERE!

My goal is to give you examples of lost Christian principles that affect the atmosphere in powerful ways! Want to make one easy change in your life, let the last thing you look at be a Bible scripture. Ponder what is said, and thank God for it. If the elders came back through some bizarre time-warp and landed in 2020, they would be appalled at the blatant sin and worldliness of our generation.

That embarrasses me to type that out, because I have three daughters and three grandchildren, and I know that I am not innocent on the above rebuke. I do not write this because *"I have arrived!"* No, on the contrary. I feel the convictions of my holy God upon me. I have discovered fault within myself; I have fallen short of giving God my very best, my completely undistracted time...and I have been guilty of just penciling God of Glory into my schedule, here or there.

Our LORD has weighed my time and I have been found wanting and so have you. But, our Father doesn't leave us there; He does expect us to make the necessary changes to our life once He has revealed how He feels about it. His loving arms are open wide; His voice calls to us - *come to Me.*

Brothers and sisters, I rejoice in the opportunity presented to me and to you here: An opportunity to change our behavior; repent from our mistakes, and be reconciled to our Beloved Savior! "And when you are converted, strengthen your brethren!"

> "And the Lord said, Simon, Simon, behold, Satan hath desired to have you, that he may sift you as wheat: But I have prayed for thee, that thy faith fail not: and when thou art converted, strengthen thy brethren."
> — Jesus Christ, (Luke 22:31-32)

The Apostle Paul said this to the church at Rome,

> "...now it is high time to awake out of sleep: for now is our salvation nearer than when we believed. The night is far spent, the day is at hand: let us therefore cast off the works of darkness, and let us put on the armour of light. Let us walk honestly, as in the day; not in rioting and drunkenness, not in chambering and wantonness, not in strife and envying.

But put ye on the Lord Jesus Christ, and make not provision
for the flesh, to fulfil the lusts thereof."
                    — Apostle Paul, (Romans 13:11-14).

THE CARNAL MAN VERSES THE SPIRITUAL MAN

Some may declare, *"Oh, okay, Mr. Legality!* As if what I am saying is too
much to ask of them. They may continue, *"we all know everything in
moderation."* God forbid, not sin!

Even Paul asked the church in Rome, *"Shall we continue in sin because grace
abounds?"* (Paraphrased from Romans 6:1). Then he answered it, *"God
forbid!"* Nothing makes me more upset than to hear internet preachers tell
the listeners they really don't need all that *"STUFF"* like Faithful Church
Attendance, Daily Scripture Reading, etc. I think, Wow, "STUFF?!" I
cannot believe you would say that! People need to be encouraged to do
more with God, not less. The natural man will always fall short and it is
because we are naturally selfish.

If they took the statistical data of the 21 Century church prayer life it would
be but a drop in the bucket compared to what it should be – *overflowing
rivers of living waters.* Prayer is our communion with our heavenly Father
and when we are in His presence we are changed. Then we have the ability
to help others recover from the snares of Satan.

You have to start somewhere. Begin with self-evaluation and confession of
sin. Repent! Turn from the direction you have been going and head towards
Christ instead. Ask God to give you the power over your temptations.
Your help is in your asking. Even a muttered sigh, *"Oh, God help me, I'm
wretched. Look at the mess I've made of my life."*

THE LOST CHRISTIAN DISCIPLINES OF BECOMING LOWLY AND MEEK

There are many lost Christian disciplines - things that draw us to a place of lowly humility that the Church no longer performs anymore. These are ceremonial rituals not being done for sake of time. They just don't make the cut in the set hour of worship. I will make this statement, it's hurting the body of Christ. Make the time to perform the holy ordinances. Examples that I can give you are holy communion, foot washing, corporate fasting, and all-night prayer meetings. All of these venues help to naturally walk a believer into personal reflection; reflection that leads to repentance; (or a changed heart). I hope we find it now.

Ask yourself what was the purpose of Holy Communion?

Answer: When you eat of the Bread, you are to do in thanksgiving, remembering Jesus Christ's body that was broken for you. The Cup was the New Testament in His blood! Do often in remembrance of Christ! (I Corinthians 11:23-26).

Question: What was the purpose of foot washing?

Jesus laid aside his garments, took a towel, and girded himself, (for what he was about to do); our LORD poured water into a basin, and washed his disciple's feet, and he wiped them with a towel. (John 13:1-5)

Answer: Foot washing in a Christian-based tradition - a consecrated ritual/ceremony! It is an act of humility; to love your brethren, cover them in prayer as you wash their feet in a basin of water. There is so much that goes on in the supernatural realm than you can understand and it is one of the greatest symbols of love and self-mortification. It is absolutely counter-culture. Do you understand its significance? You choose to show your love for your brethren; you choose to humble yourself and follow the actions of Christ.

Everything in our competitive nature is to promote self - to become the best! We are guilty of overinflated resumes; we are the hero of our own stories; we share exploits of grandeur - everything done to make one great in the eyes of others. When really, we are just regular human beings. The disciples of Christ as Him, *"Who is the greatest in the kingdom of heaven?"* (Matthew 18:1). His answer surprised them.

> "Jesus called a little child unto him, and set him in the midst of them, And said, Verily I say unto you, Except ye be converted, and become as little children, ye shall not enter into the kingdom of heaven. Whosoever therefore shall humble himself as this little child, the same is greatest in the kingdom of heaven. And whoso shall receive one such little child in my name receiveth me. But whoso shall offend one of these little ones which believe in me, it were better for him that a millstone were hanged about his neck, and that he were drowned in the depth of the sea. Woe unto the world because of offences! for it must needs be that offences come; but woe to that man by whom the offence cometh!"
> — Jesus Christ, Matthew 18:2-7

Jesus said, *"Be converted and become as a child."* How is that even possible? The world we live in emanates pride and exaltation, but Christ's Kingdom does not. The flesh and spirit are not friends - they are opposing enemies which war against each other. The carnal reputation hangs on ego, vanity, pride, self-righteousness, competition, etc., but your spiritual accomplishments, worthy of honor, will not. Foot washing compels the body, stoop down, bend, think of others before your own needs. The Biblical Foot Washing is a holy Christian ceremony with these thoughts: *I cover my brother, just as the LORD covered me.* What happens when we conquer the flesh and make ourselves small? We discover the hidden man within us holds more weight on the scales of success in God's eyes.

Christ is exalted and draws humanity to His side. (John 12:32). Jesus said, (speaking of his crucifixion), *"And I, if I be lifted up from the earth, will draw all men unto me."* How much more, if His disciples will follow His lead, deny themselves and die out to their flesh? Answer, they will draw others to Christ?

> "And of some have compassion, making a difference: And others save with fear, pulling them out of the fire; hating even the garment spotted by the flesh."
> — Jude 1:22-23

Question: What is the purpose of fasting?

Answer: We choose to push the plate aside; we abstain from food for a time period. We read our Bible in its place and pray to our Heavenly Father.

During the course of learning spiritual fasting, I was astonished at how long the body can go without food. I was equally surprised at how much water the body truly needs to function well, replenish, and support vital organs.

I am going to say this: Do NOT go without water!

Unless you have personally heard from God, or have an accountability partner, do NOT go without water during your fasting. Dehydration can shut down your kidneys. You don't want to end up on dialysis because you wanted to become more spiritual. I will also share another concern: When you get off the fast - do so slowly. Use Jell-O and broth. Do not jump into a pizza, hamburger, greasy French fries, or a big plate of pasta. Another serious medical condition is bowel obstruction. Please use wisdom and exercise discretion. Speak with your pastor. Have an accountability partner. Christian disciplines will require that you abstain from food for a season - time of purification. Fasting truly accomplished great exploits in the Spirit. I will share stories with you to prove that point: One is from the book of Daniel. He prayed and prayed. Then he waited. Finally, his prayer was answered. The angel Gabriel came with the message. Before he could come, the spiritual prince of Persia withstood the message and stopped

Gabriel from getting through. But God sent the archangel Michael to push back the forces of darkness and Gabriel was able to give to Daniel his answer from God!

The second story will be about Jesus Christ and His three disciples: John, Peter, and James. (Matthew 17:1). They had just come down from the Mount of transfiguration. They beheld the glory of God and saw in the spirit, Moses, and Elijah. Interestingly these men represent water and fire. As they got down from the mountain, (Matthew 17:15) things began to happen. But the disciplines found that they were powerless to cast out the devil. They had to go to Jesus. Jesus performed the miracle. Later, away from the crowds, his disciples asked the LORD, why couldn't we accomplish this great feat? Jesus told them the answer: Because of your unbelief. These kind (of demons) come out by prayer and fasting! (Matthew 17:20.)

DANIEL 10 THE ANSWER GETS THROUGH!

"In the third year of Cyrus king of Persia a thing was revealed unto Daniel, whose name was called Belteshazzar; and the thing was true, but the time appointed was long: and he understood the thing, and understood the vision.

In those days I Daniel was mourning three full weeks. I ate no pleasant bread, neither came flesh nor wine in my mouth, neither did I anoint myself at all, till three whole weeks were fulfilled.

And in the four and twentieth day of the first month, as I was by the side of the great river, which is Hiddekel; then I lifted up mine eyes, and looked, and behold a certain man clothed in linen, whose loins were girded with fine gold of Uphaz: His body also was like the beryl, and his face as the appearance of lightning, and his eyes as lamps of fire, and his arms and his feet like in colour to polished brass, and the voice of his words like the voice of a multitude.

And I Daniel alone saw the vision: for the men that were with me saw not the vision; but a great quaking fell upon them, so that they fled to hide themselves.

Therefore I was left alone, and saw this great vision, and there remained no strength in me: for my comeliness was turned in me into corruption, and I retained no strength. Yet heard I the voice of his words: and when I heard the voice of his words, then was I in a deep sleep on my face, and my face toward the ground. And, behold, an hand touched me, which set me upon my knees and upon the palms of my hands.

And he said unto me, O Daniel, a man greatly beloved, understand the words that I speak unto thee, and stand upright: for unto thee am I now sent. And when he had spoken this word unto me, I stood trembling. Then said he unto me, Fear not, Daniel: for from the first day that thou didst set thine heart to understand, and to chasten thyself before thy God, thy words were heard, and I am come for thy words.

But the prince of the kingdom of Persia withstood me one and twenty days: but, lo, Michael, one of the chief princes, came to help me; and I remained there with the kings of Persia. Now I am come to make thee understand what shall befall thy people in the latter days: for yet the vision is for many days.

And when he had spoken such words unto me, I set my face toward the ground, and I became dumb. And, behold, one like the similitude of the sons of men touched my lips: then I opened my mouth, and spake, and said unto him that stood before me, O my lord, by the vision my sorrows are turned upon me, and I have retained no strength.

For how can the servant of this my lord talk with this my lord? for as for me, straightway there remained no strength in me, neither is there breath left in me. Then there came again and touched me one like the appearance of a man, and he strengthened me,

And said, O man greatly beloved, fear not: peace be unto thee, be strong, yea, be strong. And when he had spoken unto me, I was strengthened, and said, Let my lord speak; for thou hast strengthened me. Then said he, Knowest thou wherefore I come unto thee? and now will I return to fight with the prince of Persia: and when I am gone forth, lo, the prince of Grecia shall come. But I will shew thee that which is noted in the scripture of truth: and there is none that holdeth with me in these things, but Michael your prince."

— Daniel 10:1-21

MATTHEW 17:14-21 THESE KINDS OF DEMON COME OUT ONLY BY PRAYER AND FASTING!

"And when they were come to the multitude, there came to him a certain man, kneeling down to him, and saying,

Lord, have mercy on my son: for he is lunatic, and sore vexed: for ofttimes he falleth into the fire, and oft into the water. And I brought him to thy disciples, and they could not cure him.

Then Jesus answered and said, O faithless and perverse generation, how long shall I be with you? how long shall I suffer you? bring him hither to me. And Jesus rebuked the devil; and he departed out of him: and the child was cured from that very hour.

Then came the disciples to Jesus apart, and said, Why could not we cast him out?

And Jesus said unto them, Because of your unbelief: for verily I say unto you, If ye have faith as a grain of mustard seed, ye shall say unto this mountain, Remove hence to yonder place; and it shall remove; and nothing shall be impossible unto you.

Howbeit this kind goeth not out but by prayer and fasting."

— Jesus Christ, (Matthew 17:14-21)

My Own Testimony on Fasting, (from my book, *What Is Our Christian Purpose?*)

In the beginning of my book I shared a dream with you. This is how my victory came through prayer and fasting:

In 2005, our church did a twenty-one-day fast. It's called *First Fruits*. At this time, I want to declare, I had nothing pending; everything was going well in my life and the lives of my children (no serious concerns, no fires to put out). I had a happy marriage, and our kids were all doing well in school. Our pastor called for prayer, so when the doors were open for prayer, we went. I thanked God; I prayed for my family. I sang and worshiped him, not really expecting anything. I just participated because my pastor asked all the families too. In fact, I had nothing really to pray for myself about. I felt happy and content. So, in the morning, I would wash and anoint my face with oil. I still had to go to work every day. And no one knew I was fasting. After the fast, I had a dream; in my dream."

"And it shall come to pass in that day, that his burden shall be taken away from off thy shoulder, and his yoke from

off thy neck, and the yoke shall be destroyed because of
the anointing."

— Isaiah 10:27

We make our flesh weaker so that our spiritual man may live.

Fasting heightens our five senses and draws us closer to our Heavenly
Father and we gain the knowledge of sonship. Another sense begins to
emerge: a 6th Sense into the supernatural; where you can audibly hear the
LORD's voice speak to you, where you personally can see angels appear...
where you can also see what's behind ugly behavior as you personally see
demons whisper in people's ear; where you see the demonic creatures which
stir up gossip and fighting; but also they begin to see you - to recognize
that they are not hidden, but exposed! They will shrink back from you -
when the anointing rests upon you. My question: are you ready for the
fight?

CHAPTER THIRTEEN

MUSIC AND ENTERTAINMENT THE DEVIL'S PLAYGROUND

MUSIC AND YOUNG CHILDREN

As I have mentioned in earlier chapters, music has always been the devil's playground. Yes, that slithering snake is quite the lyricist; with his subtle hidden meanings. Oh, the evil was written so poetically in song and musically arranged to the point where his melody gets inside your head! Next thing you know, he controls your actions; and you never saw where it was coming from because he's gotten under your skin! Where do the thoughts of murder and suicide come from? The American system of the music market has set up the perfect platform for the devil through subliminal messages. What they may not even realize is who is really behind their jingles, commercials, and script. Ask yourself, as a Christian believer, what is American T.V. program programming inside our children? How much murder, violence, fighting, and wars can they consume? Evening series have become soft porn and the indoctrination of perversity as the "norm." When you open your homes to murder and suicide spirits, then you cannot be surprised at the outcome of depravity.

"Children are like sponges. They soak up everything. Once I was visiting a home. A little six-year-old girl was coloring and singing to herself. I listened carefully to the melody and then finally heard the words to her song. She sang, "Me so horney, oh, me so horney." I was shocked, here was a little six old child not understanding what she was so easily singing. The child's older brother played that type of music in the house and his younger sibling picked it up. If they soak up enough filth ultimately it will be what comes out."

— Father Vincent Lampert (interview, What is evil?)

The serious question is: How do we unplug from it all? How do we turn it off? Sin is never satisfied, and movie binging has proven that fact.

WHEN THE HOLY GHOST LEADS YOU TO CLEAN THE HOUSE!

When one of my daughters was going through her teenage years she would sometimes bring in music that I didn't want her listening to. She thought I was old fashion, and I thought she wasn't mature enough to listen and discern that type of music. Her choice of music: Gangster Rap. Of all things! I had a standard for my home, *"Don't bring it into my house!"*

One afternoon I had a day off. My eldest daughter was at her school. The house was quiet and I sat down on my bed to read my Bible. I looked up; I can't tell you why. I felt like going to check my daughter's room. I cannot tell you why I felt to look in her bathroom. I caught a glimpse of myself in the mirror and then looked down. My daughter's bathroom had all the appearance that a *"teenager"* lives here; curling irons, special brushes, towels on the floor, etc. For some reason, I opened the bottom cupboard and there was a CD. It wasn't the main label, it just looked like a blank CD. I went over to my CD player and put the CD in. The music that sounded and it's lyrics were vile! I was so upset that she would defy my request to not bring that into my house. I was upset that she snuck it in and that she was listening to such garbage. It was so mentally disturbing; the f- word, the b-word; it was violent; and graphic with details of sex and drugs. I still wonder, why would anyone want to listen to that? I turned it off and then waited for my daughter to come home. School ended and I watched the clock. She entered the house in a happy mood and headed for her room. I had placed the CD player on my kitchen bar. I hit play as she walked past me. As soon as it dawned on her what she was listening to she spun around. I took the CD out and went to break it. She begged me not to destroy the CD; claiming it was her friends and she had to give it back to them. I snapped the CD in half and said again, *"Don't ever bring this stuff into my home!"*

We've gotten so used to stuff around us, and may not realize we shouldn't have it in our house: books, (humanistic, secularism, occultists), worldly music, even idols. Here, I would like to say, Ask the LORD God to show you things in your house that are evil and give you the strength to remove it out of your house! The book is about effectively defeating Satan. Don't give him a foothold into your home; no open channels to the demonic world; no windows or doors open to Him. The entertainment in TV, Videos, and music that come from this world, or even from Satan himself all help to pollute your vessel, deaden your sensitivity to God, and turn off your sixth sense into the supernatural.

> "Whatever weakens your reason; impairs the tenderness of your conscience, obscures your sense of God, takes off your relish for spiritual things, whatever increases the authority of the body over the mind, that thing is sin, however innocent it may seem in itself."
> — Susanna Wesley
> Mother to John and Charles Wesley
> Known as the Mother of Methodism

My question for you is this: when you finally get home from a long day at work, what do you rest in? Jesus extends an invitation; do things differently than what you have been doing and you will see a change. Come to me!

> "Come unto me, all ye that labour and are heavy laden, and I will give you rest. Take my yoke upon you, and learn

of me; for I am meek and lowly in heart: and ye shall find rest unto your souls."
— Jesus Christ, Mathews 11:28-30

IN PLACE OF T.V. TRY READING OR LISTENING TO A BOOK (AUDIBLE READ)

Read books. Turn off the TV and its loud, violent imagery and sit quietly and read; ponder the author's thoughts. Even read out loud and think about what you are reading. Enjoy your own presence with God.

Reading is really the only way to get to the heart of deep thought and reflection. The benefits of personal reflection: He knew that silence leads to reflection, that reflection leads to appreciation, and that appreciation looks about for someone to thank.
—Amy Hollingsworth, 2005, speaking of Fred Rogers

TESTIMONY OF FAITH – GOD GAVE ME A DREAM ABOUT TELEVISION.

I was in a garden. The garden was lush and beautiful, and I thought within me, *"This looks like the LORD's garden."* It was so peaceful. I saw a tree with all manners of fruit; the leaves were full and green. The tree was beside a flowing stream. It wasn't just flowing, but the waters were alive. I stared at the stream and the water rushing. Then I saw a golden oil skim across the top of the living waters, then more golden oil came flowing when I stood and watched. I studied it. The oil formed a face and the mouth was moving right before me. I was trying to hear what the mouth was saying, but I couldn't hear. The face became a three-dimensional head that came up and out of the water, and it was speaking to me. God's mouth was moving, but I could not hear a sound from Him. His head was grand

and large. As much as I tried, I couldn't. So, I tried harder to listen, but there was a noise in the background. It made me upset and I looked around to turn it off. I never saw the T.V., but I knew what it was. What I couldn't understand was that we were outside in the garden, and yet, I heard a loud television blaring – it was noise: (A distracting noise). The sound from the television dulled my ears. It made it impossible to hear what God was saying. I woke up, and I knew what it meant. It is not by accident that the TV blares loud on its own. Christians truly do not realize what they forfeit when they lounge in front of the television. T.V., movies, and DVD's dull your spiritual ears, and makes it almost impossible to hear the voice of the Good Shepherd. Turn the TV off! To hear the voice of God clearly, we must turn the world off! Turn the cell phone off; turn the computer and social media off! Listen for the still, soft voice of our LORD. (I Kings 19:12). God doesn't scream, or yell. He speaks softly, lovingly. His desire is to commune with you...will you try? Elijah the prophet heard the voice of God in I Kings 19, "A Still Small Voice"

CHRISTA'S DREAM - MY YOUNGEST DAUGHTER

My daughter Christa shared a dream she had that woke her up to a fright. She said, In my dream, I was at our current house. I woke up, (yet I was still dreaming), and got up to check the front door. I had heard a noise, someone walking in our house. When I got to the doorway, next to the T.V. an image of a man stood there by our television. His shape was of a tall man, but the body was filled with static as you see on a channel. I went to walk away from him and he leaped forward and put his static hand on my head. Then I woke up. It was so real. I will say this, there is more to T.V. than many of us understand. More and more we see it's a doorway to the other side, a dark side. I know some families who actually unplug their T.V. at night. What would be the purpose, to break the connection into their homes.

PART FIVE

PART FIVE

CHAPTER FOURTEEN

THE PRAYERS OF THE SAINTS

MORE THAN, NOW I LAY ME DOWN TO SLEEP...

There is a spiritual truth that when we draw closer to God in prayer, in fellowship with like believers, and in Bible devotional time, we become stronger, wiser, kinder and more loving - in essence, we become like our Heavenly Father. God rewards our intimacy by revealing Himself to us and making us sensitive to His Holy Spirit -until finally it happens, we hear God and see Him more clearly.

God is the truth.
The Spirit of God will always change us
if we seek Him entirely, faithfully, and
With our whole heart.

Satan has successfully placed obstacles in humanity's journey of self-discovery, spiritual development, morality, intellect, and emotional well-being. Now, it's solely up to parents and grandparents to instill these Christian elements or lose their children to the world around them. Once again, let allow me to list these out.

In the same way, mankind misses it with their heavenly
Father and loses out on the spiritual gains, such as

- Divine problem-solving abilities,
- Artful skilled negotiations where both parties win,
- Improved communication skills,
- Charity and concern,
- Heavenly wisdom and revelation,
- Abounding hope, even in the worst circumstances,
- Genuine kindness,
- God's goodness and mercy,
- God's abounding peace, and joy, and long-suffering patience,
- As well as dreams, visions, and prophecy,
- Kingdom knowledge and discernment, and
- The operation of the gifts of the Spirit.

I looked through the *Strong's Concordance* for the true
definition of the word benefits, but it was not given. I
pulled up *Merriam Webster's Dictionary's* definition:
Something that produces good or helpful results or effects
or that promotes well-being: advantage, useful aid. I
used the analogy of an employee benefit to get others to
understand: God is so much higher, bigger, and greater
than that tiny element of this physical world. I strive to lift
the eyes of God's children to fully engage His greatness."
— Kari Quijas, *What is Our Christian
Purpose, Unplugging from the World Wide
Web and Discovering Christ within us."*

THE STORY OF FATHER PADRE PIO - WHEN MAN ENTERS THE BATTLE THROUGH CHRIST!

Please allow me to give you an example: His name, Padre Pio. During
WWII a simple, (obscure) monk stopped allied forces from bombing his
little Italian town. How? He prayed. The fighter pilots saw the appearance

of a large monk in the sky telling them to go the other way. The pilots were terrified at the ghostly apparition and did as the Monk bid them. On other occasions, several other pilots gave testimony that their control panel went berserk; and the pilot(s) would have to return to their base. When they returned the gauges and equipment were fine. There are hundreds of stories of this monk still available on YouTube. Many who experienced some of the miracles, said it was as though the Priest could see right through you – like nothing was hidden. He was gifted with kingdom knowledge. Father Pio was also fearless; he held back no punches. If you came to him to confess sin, he would make you search your soul for all of it. It was uncomfortable, embarrassing, and raw. He revealed everything. I spent many days researching it on line. I found it fascinating, but also this one point struck me, "Why would you confess your sins to a man, when you can take your burden to the LORD? Songs have been written about that fact, called, Leave It There!

The song was written by Charles A. Tindley, (1916).

1. If the world from you withhold of its silver and its gold,
   And you have to get along with meager fare,
Just remember, in His Word, how He feeds the little bird—
Take your burden to the Lord and leave it there.

o Refrain:

Leave it there, leave it there,
Take your burden to the Lord and leave it there;
If you trust and never doubt, He will surely bring you out—
Take your burden to the Lord and leave it there.

2. If your body suffers pain and your health you can't regain,
   And your soul is almost sinking in despair,
Jesus knows the pain you feel, He can save and He can heal—
Take your burden to the Lord and leave it there.

3. When your enemies assail and your heart begins to fail,
   Don't forget that God in Heaven answers prayer;

He will make a way for you and will lead you safely through—
Take your burden to the Lord and leave it there.

4. When your youthful days are gone and old age is stealing on,
And your body bends beneath the weight of care;
He will never leave you then, He'll go with you to the end—
Take your burden to the Lord and leave it there.

THREE PRAYERS I SAY ON MY WAY TO WORK:

1. The Lord's Prayer (Matthew 6:10-15)
2. The LORD is my Shepherd (Psalm 23)
3. The Armor of God (Ephesians 6:10-20)

Start here each morning until you develop your own prayer routine. Each morning, before I leave for work, I anoint my daughters, Micah and Christa Bella, with anointing oil in the name of Jesus Christ. I anoint my husband's pillow and pray over him a simple prayer, *"Help my husband today throughout his day. Keep him safe from harm, and bring him back home to us. In Jesus' name."* I have a daughter, Brittany, who doesn't live at home anymore. I plead the blood of Jesus Christ over her, and my three grandchildren, Isaiah, Elijah Michael, and Harley Rose. I ask God to dispatch angels to watch over my family every day. Every person's prayer is heard and responded to even if you don't notice. Here is where our faith and the ability to trust in God comes in. I know Him as a loving Father that never fails us. I know He hears my prayers and that my prayers, and your prayers, matter very much to him. The historical role as help meet, still carries with it its own authority and power, that is why I pray for my husband and children every day. I sometimes even declare, In the role of help meet, I ask in Jesus' name, protect us against all evil; keep us hidden under the shadow of your wings; let us see you each day…in a kind word, in a smile, in a landscape or sunrise. Then I thank our Father for His loving care.

BUT I'VE PRAYED BEFORE?!

Just keep doing it, until you see things begin to move. You may say, *"I've prayed, and nothing, certainly nothing like that ever happened!"* If I do this well, my book will help you to see things happen.

The Church is entering the season of miracles, signs, and wonders. How can I make that declaration? I know that the LORD's coming is near (Revelation 3:11), or what the Christian body calls the *"Rapture"* of the Church. (I Thessalonians 4:17). Today, many Muslims in the middle east have given testimony over the internet (through YOUTUBE), of having very specific dreams of Jesus coming to them; revealing Himself to them as their Messiah! That's exciting! Revival is breaking out in other parts of the world. In 2020, there is a Christian revival happening in Africa, Ethiopia, and Nigeria. We have revivals happening in the Philippines. We have underground churches in China, North Korea, Hong Kong! God will always have a church! There will always be a remnant of faithful believers. My question for the North American Christian believer is this, *What are you doing with your religious freedom?*

BEGINNING PRAYER

LORD God Almighty, I want to see you face to face. I love You. Please help to bring me into Your presence. I desire to be closer to You. I ask this day, please receive my prayers; fulfill all my petitions. I believe them to be in accordance with Your Holy Will, and in Your Holy Word. I believe my efforts will bring glory to the Name of Jesus Christ, my LORD, my Savior, and King. I thank you for the honor and privilege of intercessory prayer. Let my prayers reach my Nation, and the Nations of the world, in Jesus' name. Amen

PSALM 100 BY KING DAVID - HOW KING DAVID ENTERED INTO GOD'S PRESENCE

"Make a joyful noise unto the Lord, all ye lands.

2 Serve the Lord with gladness: come before his presence with singing.

3 Know ye that the Lord he is God: it is he that hath made us, and not we ourselves; we are his people, and the sheep of his pasture.

4 Enter into his gates with thanksgiving, and into his courts with praise: be thankful unto him, and bless his name.

5 For the Lord is good; his mercy is everlasting, and his truth endureth to all generations."

— Psalm 100

COME BEFORE GOD'S HOLY PRESENCE WITH SINGING

- Find songs about the blood of Jesus
- Find songs that glorify the Name of Jesus Christ
- Find songs that remember His gift of Salvation

Find a song that glorifies Christ; sing to God every morning! This is how we bring the Church into our homes; this is how we invite the Presence of our King into the life of our family - it is through song and adoration. Begin here. Open your hearts to what God will do for you that day. Come to Him in joy, with great expectation. God loves His children; He loves when we reach for Him. He loves our songs that we sing to Him. God desires our fellowship. Begin in worship.

Declaration of faith: My heavenly Father loves me completely. God delights in me; He made me and adores me. I desire to draw closer to him in song and praise. My LORD and Savior Jesus Christ loves me forever!

SING UNTO THE LORD!

I want you to understand, when you sit quietly at your table in your home and begin to serenade the LORD God of the universe. He will come to you. Get passed the oddity of singing by yourself; wait for the promise.

> "But he giveth more grace. Wherefore he saith, God resisteth the proud, but giveth grace unto the humble. Submit yourselves therefore to God. Resist the devil, and he will flee from you. Draw nigh to God, and he will draw nigh to you. Cleanse your hands, ye sinners; and purify your hearts, ye double minded."
>
> — James 4:6-8

THESE ARE A LIST OF MY SONGS:

The Name of Jesus, by Chris Tomlin
Power of Your Love
This Blood
Nothing but the Blood of Jesus
Take Away, by Yolanda Adams
This Blood, by Prestonwood Choir
Blessed Assurance
The Goodness of God
LORD, Prepare me to be a Sanctuary
House of Prayer, by Eddie James
Fill my Cup, by Richard Blanchard
Jesus Again, by Tamala Mann
Trust in You, by Lauren Daigle
Be Thou My Vision
Worth (You thought I was worth saving)
Salt and Light, by Lauren Daigle
Great Is Thy Faithfulness
It is Well

KNOW WHO YOU ARE IN CHRIST (FROM PSALM 100)

"Know ye that the LORD, He is God." He is sovereign and in control of everything. *"It is God that has made us and not we ourselves. We are His people and the sheep of His pasture."* Yes, in this world we may feel very vulnerable, but God ALWAYS protects His children. Not a sparrow can fall to the ground without His knowledge. Jesus Christ is 100% responsible for His children! He calms all their fears; He leads them through the darkness of this world safely into His kingdom.

ADD THANKSGIVING TO YOUR PRAYERS!

- But thanks be to God, which giveth us the victory through our Lord Jesus Christ. I Corinthians 15:57
- Now thanks be unto God, which always causeth us to triumph in Christ, and maketh manifest the savour of his knowledge by us in every place. II Corinthians 2:14
- Thanks be unto God for his unspeakable gift. II Corinthians 9:16
- Giving thanks unto the Father, which hath made us meet to be partakers of the inheritance of the saints in light: Colossians 1:12
- Saying, We give thee thanks, O Lord God Almighty, which art, and wast, and art to come; because thou hast taken to thee thy great power, and hast reigned. Revelation 11:17

PSALM 91 THE PROMISE OF GOD

Because he has known My Name

"Because thou hast made the Lord, which is my refuge, even the Most High, thy habitation; there shall no evil befall thee, neither shall any plague come nigh thy dwelling.

For he shall give his angels charge over thee, to keep thee in all thy ways. They shall bear thee up in their hands, lest thou dash thy foot against a stone.

Thou shalt tread upon the lion and adder: the young lion and the dragon shalt thou trample under feet.

Because he hath set his love upon me, therefore will I deliver him: I will set him on high, because he hath known my name. He shall call upon me, and I will answer him: I will be with him in trouble; I will deliver him, and honor him. With a long life will I satisfy him, and shew him my salvation."

— Psalm 91:9-16

A TIME OF PERSONAL REFLECTION AND REPENTANCE

Humble yourself before God.

"Dear LORD, Search me, O' God. I may not understand what ALL my sins are, but I ask you to examine my life, my heart, and my mind, my attitude. Search me, and try me, and see if there be any wicked way in me. I give you permission in my heart, to make the necessary changes that I need to be holy – and transformed into your image.

Forgive me for ALL my unkind words, the imagination of my mind - thoughts. Forgive me when I should have been more patient or kind. Forgive me when I engaged in gossip. I acknowledge my sin and bring it to the confession table.

Please teach me to have pure speech. Forgive me when I was angry without reason. Help me to understand my feelings better; healthier. Teach me how to express myself in a way that is very pleasing to You, and inviting to others.

O God, I pray in Jesus' name, please break the strongholds that are in my life, and the life of my loved ones, and family, friends, co-workers, neighbors – and those who will come to know you.

Forgive my sins yesterday that I may not have repented from or even noticed; Forgive me of my sins this day. (At this moment, let me reflect on last week, yesterday, and today.) Forgive my family and loved ones.

Job was a man who prayed for his children and family; and asked God to forgive them of their sins. I make the same request for my family. Forgive them of their sins. I do not know if they secretly cursed God in their hearts; merciful Father, send the Holy Ghost to draw my children into your loving fold.

And I thank you for the forgiveness of sin. I receive your forgiveness and am made new. I bless you, Lord. Thank you."

Your Word says,

"If we confess our sins, he is faithful and just to forgive us our sins, and to cleanse us from all unrighteousness."
— I John 1:9

Thank you, JESUS. Teach me to love and worship you in spirit and in truth; and sincerity. In Jesus' name, I pray.

CHAPTER FIFTEEN

A CUP OF ANOINTING OIL

INGREDIENTS OF THE OLD TESTAMENT ANOINTING OIL

Olive oil
Calamus oil
Cinnamon oil
Cassia oil
Myrrh

In Matthew 6:17, Jesus gave the disciples instructions that when they fasted they were to anoint their head with oil. But where could they find this anointing oil to use? The answer was found in their Torah, (the first five books of Moses). It was the very recipe that God Almighty gave to Moses when building the Tabernacle (Church) in the wilderness after leaving Egypt. (Exodus 30). God's special oil served a great purpose.

EXODUS 30:22-31 HOLY ANOINTING OIL

"Moreover the Lord spake unto Moses, saying,

Take thou also unto thee principal spices, of pure myrrh five hundred shekels, and of sweet cinnamon half so much, even two hundred and fifty shekels, and of sweet calamus two hundred and fifty shekels, and of cassia five hundred shekels, after the shekel of the sanctuary, and of oil olive an hin:

And thou shalt make it an oil of holy ointment, an ointment compound after the art of the apothecary: it shall be an holy anointing oil.

And thou shalt anoint the tabernacle of the congregation therewith, and the ark of the testimony, and the table and all his vessels, and the candlestick and his vessels, and the altar of incense, and the altar of burnt offering with all his vessels, and the laver and his foot. And thou shalt sanctify them, that they may be most holy: whatsoever toucheth them shall be holy.

And thou shalt anoint Aaron and his sons, and consecrate them, that they may minister unto me in the priest's office. And thou shalt speak unto the children of Israel, saying, This shall be an holy anointing oil unto me throughout your generations."

— Exodus 30:22-31

In the time of Moses, only one tribe could offer their services to God in the Temple. That was the Tribe of Levi; or what we call the Levitical priesthood. According to Exodus, if any other person entered the Tabernacle, touched any of the holy items found inside, that person would die. (Exodus 30:20). In the book of Leviticus Aaron's son's, Nadab and Abihu, trespassed against God's law and the fire from God devoured them. (Leviticus 10:1-2). Remember the 1981 movie, *Raiders of the Lost Ark*, with Harrison Ford? The Nazi's in World War II were after the Ark of the Covenant. They felt if they had this ark, (which would be placed in front of their troops during a battle), their armies would be unstoppable! They took from the stories in the Holy Bible, how God defended Israel. In the movie, the Nazi's did capture the Ark of the Covenant, open it and the Spirit of God unleashes a holy hell upon them and burnt them up like candles – their faces and bodies melted before God! The exciting part today, is that New Testament believers were now similar to the Levitical tribe.

> "But ye are a chosen generation, a royal priesthood, an holy nation, a peculiar people; that ye should shew forth the praises of him who hath called you out of darkness into his marvelous light;
>
> Which in time past were not a people, but are now the people of God: which had not obtained mercy, but now have obtained mercy.
>
> Dearly beloved, I beseech you as strangers and pilgrims, abstain from fleshly lusts, which war against the soul;
>
> Having your conversation honest among the Gentiles: that, whereas they speak against you as evildoers, they may by your good works, which they shall behold, glorify God in the day of visitation."
>
> — I Peter 2:9-12

Christians are invited and welcomed into the very present of God to offer up praises to God because we have been called out of darkness and brought in to His marvelous, glorious light! How exciting. We are the people who, *"have obtained mercy"* from God. Peter goes on to tell the New Testament believers, *"as strangers and pilgrims on earth, abstain from fleshy lusts which war against your soul!"* In other words, you have a high calling. You are not like you used to be, or like the culture around you. You have been singled out for God's purpose. And even better yet, we are to offer the invitation of salvation in Jesus Christ, to others, that they may obtain the promise of God.

> "How God anointed Jesus of Nazareth with the Holy Ghost and with power: who went about doing good, and healing all that were oppressed of the devil; for God was with him."
>
> — Acts 10:38

PROTECTING THE ANOINTING

First, understand what an *"anointing"* is. The anointing is a Hebrew word, *mishchah*. It is a consecratory gift from God. The word *"anointing"* is found in 28 Bible verses from the Old Testament to the New Testament.

In the New Testament, we find the Greek word, chrisma, meaning the power and unction from God. It is the anointing that was used in an inaugural ceremony for priests. It's beyond special, and extremely powerful. Does the word look familiar to you? This is where we get the English word, *Charisma.*

> Charisma means, *"a strong compelling attractiveness; or that can charm or inspire devotion in others."* Or in other words, *"The divinely conferred power of God to compel and persuade mankind."*

Our anointing (*gift*) is meant for a very specific purpose - to touch those around us, to share the Gospel in our own personality and experience. Our anointing gives to human beings the ability to persuade. God gives to His children hope in a hopeless world, but He also addresses the arena of sin. Our desire is to convince men and women that the word of God is truth; that sin separates us from God, but God made a way back to Him, through the Son. That message tells us the bad news – without God, man is lost in sin, but then follows up with the good news, Jesus Christ became your atoning sacrifice.

Our anointing directly and spectacularly impacts the sinner's future posterity – their lineage! As dad gets saves, he becomes a better father, a stronger one. He becomes a more loving dad who is sensitive to God. The same is true when mom gets saved. God gives to each parent the wisdom to become great parents. When both parents allow God to speak into their lives, they become better people; ethical, moral, and mentally sound. All of that, in turn affects their children. It gives them a better childhood; meaning they will have a better chance at life. I believe our generation is just starting to understand the negative impact that happens when there is an absent father in the family equation. Remember, strong families make for strong, sound, healthy communities.

"In adolescence, the implications of fatherless homes are incredible, as these children are more likely to experience the effects of poverty. Former president George W. Bush even addressed the issue while in office, stating, *"Over the past four decades, fatherlessness has emerged as one of our greatest social problems. We know that children who grow up with absent-fathers can suffer lasting damage. They are more likely to end up in poverty or drop out of school, become addicted to drugs, have a child out of wedlock, or end up in prison. Fatherlessness is not the only cause of these things, but our nation must recognize it is an important factor."*
— A Father's Impact on Child Development,
(Children's Bureau) All4kids.org

God gives to His children a sound mind; the ability to create goodness. The Bible declares boldly,

"The law of the Lord is perfect, converting the soul: the testimony of the Lord is sure, making wise the simple. The statutes of the Lord are right, rejoicing the heart: the commandment of the Lord is pure, enlightening the eyes. The fear of the Lord is clean, enduring forever: the judgments of the Lord are true and righteous altogether. More to be desired are they then gold, yea, than much fine gold: sweeter also than honey and the honeycomb. Moreover by them is thy servant warned: and in keeping of them there is great reward."
— Psalm 19:7-11

That's a lot of positive changes! Let me ask you this, *how do you create goodness?* How about mentoring; how about creating quality schools; how about developing new policies that impact the community?

Understand, there is no greater anointing oil than our Holy Ghost inside of us. See also: Ephesians 5:17-21; I John 2:20, 27; I John 4:13), our faith in Jesus, (as our Healer,) or our trust in God's power.

> "But the anointing which ye have received of him abideth in you, and ye need not that any man teach you: but as the same anointing teacheth you of all things, and is truth, and is no lie, and even as it hath taught you, ye shall abide in him.
> — I John 2:27

> Hereby know we that we dwell in him, and he in us, because he hath given us of his Spirit."
> — I John 4:13

The way we flow in our anointing is through faithful prayer and our holy consecration to God. I do my best to touch God every morning. His anointing helps me to speak with clarity; it gives me the authority to convince and persuade the lost. His anointing flows over me to help me face the fires of adversity. I need my LORD's fresh anointing. Through the obedience to the Holy Scriptures we anoint the sick, calling on His name: JESUS. We believe by faith in the Word, and in the power of God, the sick shall be healed. Have I ever seen a miracle of healing, yes, I have!

There is a fascinating story of anointing oil found in Zephaniah, chapter four, and I wish that I had the ability to draw this passage of scripture:

> "And the angel that talked with me came again, and waked me, as a man that is wakened out of his sleep. And said unto me, What seest thou? And I said, I have looked, and behold a candlestick all of gold, with a bowl upon the top of it, and his seven lamps thereon, and seven pipes to the seven lamps, which are upon the top thereof: And two olive trees by it, one upon the right side of the bowl, and the other upon the left side thereof.

So I answered and spake to the angel that talked with me, saying, What are these, my lord? Then the angel that talked with me answered and said unto me, Knowest thou not what these be? And I said, No, my lord.

Then he answered and spake unto me, saying, This is the word of the Lord unto Zerubbabel, saying, Not by might, nor by power, but by my spirit, saith the Lord of hosts. Who art thou, O great mountain? before Zerubbabel thou shalt become a plain: and he shall bring forth the headstone thereof with shoutings, crying, Grace, grace unto it.

Moreover the word of the Lord came unto me, saying, The hands of Zerubbabel have laid the foundation of this house; his hands shall also finish it; and thou shalt know that the Lord of hosts hath sent me unto you. For who hath despised the day of small things? for they shall rejoice, and shall see the plummet in the hand of Zerubbabel with those seven; they are the eyes of the Lord, which run to and fro through the whole earth.

Then answered I, and said unto him, What are these two olive trees upon the right side of the candlestick and upon the left side thereof? And I answered again, and said unto him, What be these two olive branches which through the two golden pipes empty the golden oil out of themselves? And he answered me and said, Knowest thou not what these be? And I said, No, my lord. Then said he, These are the two anointed ones, that stand by the Lord of the whole earth."

— Zechariah 4

In this story the event has already past. But, there comes a prophecy of story coming, just like this one. It's found in Revelation, chapter 11. Note: This event will come to pass, just like the birth of the Messiah, the story of

Mary and Joseph, just like the Israel rejecting him as their king, just like the crucifixion, burial, resurrection, and ascension! This event is coming to us!

REVELATION 11 TWO CANDLESTICKS STAND BEFORE GOD

And I will give power unto my two witnesses, and they shall prophesy a thousand two hundred and threescore days, clothed in sackcloth.

These are the two olive trees, and the two candlesticks standing before the God of the earth. And if any man will hurt them, fire proceedeth out of their mouth, and devoureth their enemies: and if any man will hurt them, he must in this manner be killed.

These have power to shut heaven, that it rain not in the days of their prophecy: and have power over waters to turn them to blood, and to smite the earth with all plagues, as often as they will.

And when they shall have finished their testimony, the beast that ascendeth out of the bottomless pit shall make war against them, and shall overcome them, and kill them.

And their dead bodies shall lie in the street of the great city, which spiritually is called Sodom and Egypt, where also our Lord was crucified.

And they of the people and kindreds and tongues and nations shall see their dead bodies three days and an half, and shall not suffer their dead bodies to be put in graves.

And they that dwell upon the earth shall rejoice over them, and make merry, and shall send gifts one to another;

because these two prophets tormented them that dwelt on the earth.

And after three days and an half the spirit of life from God entered into them, and they stood upon their feet; and great fear fell upon them which saw them.

And they heard a great voice from heaven saying unto them, Come up hither. And they ascended up to heaven in a cloud; and their enemies beheld them.

And the same hour was there a great earthquake, and the tenth part of the city fell, and in the earthquake were slain of men seven thousand: and the remnant were affrighted, and gave glory to the God of heaven. The second woe is past; and, behold, the third woe cometh quickly.

And the seventh angel sounded; and there were great voices in heaven, saying, The kingdoms of this world are become the kingdoms of our Lord, and of his Christ; and he shall reign for ever and ever.

And the four and twenty elders, which sat before God on their seats, fell upon their faces, and worshipped God, saying, We give thee thanks, O Lord God Almighty, which art, and wast, and art to come; because thou hast taken to thee thy great power, and hast reigned.

And the nations were angry, and thy wrath is come, and the time of the dead, that they should be judged, and that thou shouldest give reward unto thy servants the prophets, and to the saints, and them that fear thy name, small and great; and shouldest destroy them which destroy the earth.

And the temple of God was opened in heaven, and there was seen in his temple the ark of his testament: and there were lightnings, and voices, and thunderings, and an earthquake, and great hail.

—Revelation 11:3-19

THE HIGH PRIEST OF YOUR HOME

You have been placed in a honored position to have your offering accepted by God. As high priests of your home, use the oil to cover your home and family in the name of Jesus.

I buy these ingredients online; and the little bottles that I will put them in. I pray the name of Jesus Christ over each little vial of anointing oil. As a pastor's wife, when I see a person needs it, I hand them out. I will explain what I tell them. These are the very ingredients that were in the Temple of God. Now, as the high priest of your home, anoint yourself and your home with this oil. I anoint the doorposts, I anoint the window seals. I anoint my daughter's room and items. I anoint my husband's pillow and pray for our marriage. I anoint my daughters in the morning before I leave for work. Yes, I place a drop on my finger of this precious oil, and by faith ask Jesus to anoint us for the day.

Scriptures: Exodus 29:7, Leviticus 8:12, Deuteronomy 33:24, I Samuel 10:1, I Samuel 15:1, I Samuel 16:3, James 5:14-16, Matthew 6:17, Mark 6:13, mark 16:1, Luke 7:38-46, John 11:2, John 12:3, Acts 19:11-12, Psalm 23:1-6, Psalm 45:7, Psalm 133:1-3, Genesis 28:18.

CHAPTER SIXTEEN

DEFILE THE TEMPLE, DESTROY THE ANOINTING OF GOD

"What? know ye not that your body is the temple of the Holy Ghost which is in you, which ye have of God, and ye are not your own? For ye are bought with a price: therefore glorify God in your body, and in your spirit, which are God's."
— *I Corinthians 6:19-20*

The world is corrupted by sin; Satan's desire is for your vessel to be polluted by his allurements and pleasures that he offers to humanity: unbridled lusts, covetousness, a mind wretched with filthy thoughts. We have the power and authority to kick Satan out of our lives! When we begin to understand how valuable we are to our heavenly Father, that He sent His only Son, Jesus Christ, to die for our sins and free us from its penalty – which was death, there must come with that knowledge an understanding or responsibility to keep ourselves free from being ensnared again – or free from the pollutants of the world around us: it's images, it's language and expression, it's politics, it's culture, it's humor, it's callousness, it's cruelty, it's selfishness. As New Testament believers we are the *"Living Temple of God"* on earth, just as the Ark of God of the Testament was in the wilderness. (Exodus 25-30; 35-40). So, what you do with your body, mind, soul, and spirit matters today and in eternity.

178 Kari Quijas

In II Chronicles 29 the LORD Jehovah had raised up a young king, his name was Hezekiah. He was only twenty-five years old when he began to reign. King Hezekiah had a burning desire in him to change his nation. You will see early in the story he makes the declaration to open the doors to the house of the LORD and repair them. That meant the doors had been closed down for some time and they needed repairs. Next, King Hezekiah brought back the Levites and the Priest (spiritual leaders) for the service to the Temple. He commanded them to *sanctify themselves*, (make themselves right and ready for God). Then, *Sanctify the house of the LORD*. His public, royal decree: *Remove or carry out all the filthiness of the holy place.* That means things had gotten in that needed to be removed. He told them, *"You have forsaken the LORD God, you have turned your back on Him and shut down the service of God."* I believe here we should consider our church in the 21st Century. The question we should ask ourselves is this, *"Have we allowed the filth of the world into the House of God and into our lives?"*

We should all: *"Make yourself right before God, repent!"* (II Chronicles 29:1-11)

> "Hezekiah began to reign when he was five and twenty years old, and he reigned nine and twenty years in Jerusalem. And his mother's name was Abijah, the daughter of Zechariah.
>
> And he did that which was right in the sight of the Lord, according to all that David his father had done. He in the first year of his reign, in the first month, opened the doors of the house of the Lord, and repaired them.
>
> And he brought in the priests and the Levites, and gathered them together into the east street, and said unto them, Hear me, ye Levites, sanctify now yourselves, and sanctify the house of the Lord God of your fathers, and carry forth the filthiness out of the holy place. For our fathers have trespassed, and done that which was evil in the eyes of the Lord our God, and have forsaken him, and

have turned away their faces from the habitation of the Lord, and turned their backs.

Also they have shut up the doors of the porch, and put out the lamps, and have not burned incense nor offered burnt offerings in the holy place unto the God of Israel. Wherefore the wrath of the Lord was upon Judah and Jerusalem, and he hath delivered them to trouble, to astonishment, and to hissing, as ye see with your eyes.

For, lo, our fathers have fallen by the sword, and our sons and our daughters and our wives are in captivity for this. Now it is in mine heart to make a covenant with the Lord God of Israel, that his fierce wrath may turn away from us. My sons, be not now negligent: for the Lord hath chosen you to stand before him, to serve him, and that ye should minister unto him, and burn incense."

— II Chronicles 29:1-11

So how does this story affect us today?

THROUGH THE VOICE OF OUR ELDERS

Sister Claudette Walker's lists:

1. Seducing Spirits
2. Doctrines of Devils
3. The Spirit of Antichrist

We must ask ourselves, What seduces me, what moves me away from God? What has my attention? Next, ask yourself do I still believe all the Word of God? Or have I been compromised and laid aside the teachings of Christ for worldly doctrines that are easier to follow, or more convenient? (The mind set: If I just go with the flow of the world around, no one gets angry.). We will discover many stories in the Holy Bible where mankind's conscious warnings were slowly eroded away and silenced. So, God rose up people of faith to speak the Hard Truth of the Reality of God and His ways! Each prophet of God, evangelist, or pastor would declare, *"Your ways are in error with your Holy God, turn from your wicked ways: Repent and God shall receive you."* We need to look for these. It's time to clean the house and evaluate ourselves. It's time to ready our own vessels for God, (holy sanctification and recommitment), then it's time to sanctify our own Church.

WHEN CHRISTIANS ACT AND SPEAK LIKE THE WORLD AROUND THEM !

There is a term in our New Testament, called *"grieving the Spirit of God."* To grieve Him means to offend a Holy God. Make no mistake, we serve a Holy God and His expectation for the Church is that we will behave ourselves and strive towards sanctification.

> **Sanctification:** purification and personal consecration. The sanctification of heart and life. (Blue Letter Bible: Sanctification).

CHRISTIAN CONDUCT AND THE 21ST CENTURY CHURCH

To be honest, I'm surprised to see alcohol and the cussing spirit grab hold of our congregants. Know this first off, cussing is the devil's language. (It is unsanctioned, and considered by God as unholy speech). The Bible tells us very emphatically, *"Out of the abundance of the heart, the mouth speaks."* (Paraphrased from the words of Jesus in Luke 6:45). It's a heart issue. If you are swearing or *"cussing like a sailor,"* even if you are thinking about them in your mind, then the enemy has a foothold in your life. Just like I pointed out, the loss of joy, anxiety, depression, and fear serve as warnings that you have lost serious ground back to the enemy forces. Will you allow the Holy Ghost, through this simple work, to redirect your life?

SPIRITUAL TRUTH - YOUR SPEECH GIVES YOU AWAY!

If you say, *"Well, I'm angry, and it just comes out."* Then you need to go back to your great Creator, ask Him to forgive you for using filthy language; ask God to increase your vocabulary in order to better express how you feel. You cannot yield the weapons of God's power and righteousness when you are spewing Satan's foul, four-letter obscenities out of your mouth! The English language is vast; believe me, a well-spoken rebuke with sound words goes further than the f-word, and you will keep yourself respect. Remember, if you used a cuss word, you've already lost the argument.

What this means, is that you will have to begin new exercises; do some homework just like when you were in school or college. Research the dictionary for strong words that would work in the place of cuss words. Used index cards. Understand the words meaning (definition) and how to pronounce it. Believe me, people will take notice if you do not swear when you are angry – and they might just ask you how you do it. Then you can share with others how they can overcome their temper and the temptation to use vulgarity. What helps me is to remember, *"Obscenity, vulgarity and cursing is the Devil's language! I belong to a Holy God and He doesn't speak like that."*

Can you not see the obvious contradiction – a Christian believer says to represent a heavenly kingdom above. So, if you are a new creation in Christ, why are you speaking like an unregenerated sinner on earth? Even, our beloved Peter's speech gave him away. His speech manifested the testimony that he had been with the LORD. (Matthew 26:73). Our language should also demonstrate to others that we too have been with Jesus; that we are His holy disciples. We should be knowledgeable in scripture; studied, approved of God, but even more, our Christian conduct should speak volumes to those around us. As Paul said, *"Christ's love constrains me."* (Paraphrased: II Corinthians 5:14). Let's look quickly what the Apostle Paul said to young Timothy,

"Of these things put them in remembrance, charging them before the Lord that they strive not about words to no profit, but to the subverting of the hearers. Study to shew thyself approved unto God, a workman that needed not to be ashamed, rightly dividing the word of truth. But shun profane and vain babblings: for they will increase unto more ungodliness."

— II Timothy 2:14-16

"Nevertheless the foundation of God standeth sure, having this seal, The Lord knoweth them that are his. And, let everyone that nameth the name of Christ depart from iniquity. But in a great house there are not only vessels of gold and of silver, but also of wood and of earth; and some to honour, and some to dishonour.

If a man therefore purge himself from these, he shall be a vessel unto honour, sanctified, and meet for the master's use, and prepared unto every good work. Flee also youthful lusts: but follow righteousness, faith, charity, peace, with them that call on the Lord out of a pure heart."

— II Timothy 2:19-22

"And the servant of the Lord must not strive; but be gentle unto all men, apt to teach, patient, in meekness instructing those that oppose themselves; if God peradventure will give them repentance to the acknowledging of the truth; And that they may recover themselves out of the snare of the devil, who are taken captive by him at his will."

— II Timothy 2:24-26

BECOMING AMBASSADORS FOR CHRIST

I want you to consider a real U.S. Ambassador. President Donald J. Trump has appointed ambassadors to 61 countries since assuming office. One you may have heard of is Nikki Haley. She served as a U.S. Ambassador to the United Nations under Donald Trump from January 2107 through December 2018. She was governor of South Carolina from 2011 to 2017. She was the first female and Indian American to serve in office.

Another U.S. Ambassador you may have heard of was J. Christopher Stevens. He was an American career diplomat and lawyer who served as the U. S. Ambassador to Libya from May 22, 2012, to September 11, 2012. He was killed when the U.S. Special Mission in Benghazi Libya was attacked by memoirs of Ansar al-Sharia.

The office of the Ambassador is distinguished. From the United States Embassy webpage, *"The Role of Ambassador"*

- Speaking with one voice to others on U.S. policy–and ensuring mission staff do likewise–while providing to the President and Secretary of State expert guidance and frank counsel. **The one voice is God's. The Policy, is His gospel. The mission: death, burial, and resurrection – new birth!**
- Directing and coordinating all executive branch offices and personnel (except for those under the command of a U.S. area military commander, under another chief of mission, or on the staff of an international organization). **Establishing and directing prayer groups and outreach ministry teams.**
- Cooperating with the U.S. legislative and judicial branches so that U.S. foreign policy goals are advanced; security is maintained; and executive, legislative, and judicial responsibilities are carried out. **Agreeing with leadership, pastors and elders. Safeguarding the church, the Word of God, and establishing Christian disciplines within the body. Communion, Foot washing, Corporate prayer and fasting.**
- Reviewing communications to or from mission elements. **Confirming the strength of all ministry in the local assembly and the district. Asking for help when needed, and aiding those struggling.**
- Taking direct responsibility for the security of the mission — including security from terrorism — and protecting all U.S.

Government personnel on official duty (other than that personnel under the command of a U.S. area military commander) and their dependents. **This is the responsibility of the pastors, elders, and prayer ministry teams together.**

- Carefully using mission resources through regular reviews of programs, personnel, and funding levels. **Regular check and reviews of the above listed.**

- Reshaping the mission to serve American interests and values and to ensure that all executive branch agencies attached to the mission do likewise. **Making the necessary changes: in policy, in personnel, in building, in shutting down programs not successful, and refocusing personnel to new areas.**

- Serving Americans with professional excellence, the highest standards of ethical conduct, and diplomatic discretion. **Note: Professionalism. Excellence. High Standards and Ethical conduct. Asking yourself, in our ministry, are we checking attitudes, behaviors, conduct of our personnel, leadership, and staff.**

Now, think about these responsibilities in the Spiritual realm, being ambassadors for Jesus Christ; which each of us are as born-again Christian believers: *How should our speech be? Eloquent, well spoken with compassion and genuine concern.* That person should be strong, mentally clear on their mission, yet meek in spirit – respectful. Taking great care for those he represents. That person's mindset should be on winning them, persuading them in reason and God's truth, not being brass or offensive. We should never mirror back the world, but the world should see Jesus Christ, His Word, and His self-control.

Colossians 4:2-6

"Continue in prayer, and watch in the same with thanksgiving; withal praying also for us, that God would open unto us a door of utterance, to speak the mystery of Christ, for which I am also in bonds:

That I may make it manifest, as I ought to speak. Walk in wisdom toward them that are without, redeeming the time. Let your speech be always with grace, seasoned with salt, that ye may know how ye ought to answer every man."

— Colossians 4:2-6

Believer, you will lose credibility if you can't control your tongue. James takes it further saying,

"If any man among you seem to be religious, and bridleth not his tongue, but deceiveth his own heart, this man's religion is vain."

— James 1:26

Note the words: *"This man's religion is vain,"* which means that it is empty and amounts to nothing. I am going to be honest with you: if you want to be greatly used in God's Kingdom, it will be on our LORD's terms and in His holy Word. You must be pure in the words you speak, the thoughts you think (every moment), in your attitudes, actions, and responses you give! You are responsible for casting out every evil thought, every silly imagination you think, and yes, you are responsible for what comes out of your mouth - but also too, what you post on social media. Your intellectual property, whether it was expressed outwardly, or in written form, will be held to God's standard of excellence, not man's; not our neighbor's, or friend's, but our LORD's. Be careful!

"The fear of the Lord is to hate evil: pride, and arrogance, and the evil way, and the froward mouth, do I hate."

— Proverbs 8:13

"When pride cometh, then cometh shame: but with the lowly is wisdom."

— Proverbs 11:2

From my book, *What is Our Christian Purpose, Chapter 19, Contending with Sarcasm:*

"There are other hindrances to the moving of the Spirit of God: Besides doubt and unbelief, I believe another limiting factor to the power of God is found in our American expression that equates it with sarcasm, pride/ego, and arrogance.

Sarcasm
is the fluent speech of doubt,
with a purpose or intent to put down and belittle.

God hates the speech of sarcasm in American culture!

Pride and arrogance actually make the top ten list of what God hates. Most Americans would recognize it because it is seen every day on TV, especially sports commentators and political rhetoric. These men and women are so full of themselves. When I come across a station, I just think, How does it all fit, all the commenters, back seat quarterbacks, and their egos? All of that nonsense repels God. He disdains it and turns aside those who engage in this behavior. He will not hear their prayers.

When God says that "He resists the proud", (James 4:6), God really will turn away from those engulfed in it. Pride and arrogance: many have fallen because of it." — What Is Our Christian Purpose? Unplugging from the World Wide Web and Discovering Christ within us.

So, what do we do if we have fallen short?

Acknowledge it and repent! Ask the LORD to give you a new speech, a new way of expressing yourself that brings honor to Him every time; and then receive His forgiveness and thank Him.

CHAPTER SEVENTEEN

SPIRITUAL DISCERNMENT - DEVELOPING SENSITIVITY TO GOD

I will begin with this thought: God's voice will never contradict His Holy Word. Ever! I want to speak on exercising discernment and developing spiritual ears to hear the still, small voice of God! The word discernment means *the ability to judge well*, and that is what is lacking today. The Bible says we need to exercise discernment. (Hebrews 5:14).

> "But strong meat belongeth to them that are of full age, even those who by reason of use have their senses exercised to discern both good and evil."
> — Hebrews 5:14

FROM SISTER CLAUDETTE WALKER - PREACHED FROM HER CHURCH IN JANUARY 2019, BABY DEDICATION

"Let's look at Samuel 2. We shall look at five verses: 11, 18, 26, 35, and I Samuel 3:1.

> And Elkanah went to Ramah to his house. And the child did minister unto the Lord before Eli the priest. (11)

But Samuel ministered before the Lord, being a child,
girded with a linen ephod. (18)

And the child Samuel grew on, and was in favour both
with the Lord, and also with men. (26)

And I will raise me up a faithful priest, that shall do
according to that which is in mine heart and in my mind:
and I will build him a sure house; and he shall walk before
mine anointed forever. (35)

and the child Samuel ministered unto the Lord before Eli.
And the word of the Lord was precious in those days; there
was no open vision. (1) I Samuel 3

If you take just those 5 verses and we easily recognize we have a special
child here. He's living in the House of God. He ministers to the LORD.
He ministered to Eli the priest. He doesn't even have a home life. He has
a small bed near Eli. The young child Samuel lives in the Houses of God.
The child is surrounded by the Presence of the LORD; He helped to trim
the wick for the Golden Candlestick. He was around the holy of the holies.
Yet, we see that when God first calls to Samuel, His voice wakes the child
out of sleep, but Samuel had not learned to recognize the voice of God. It
sounded like his pastor's voice, it sounded like Eli the priest. (End)

I Samuel 3:7

Now Samuel did not yet know the Lord, neither was the
word of the Lord yet revealed unto him. (7)

It says, *"he did not (yet) know the LORD, neither was the Word yet revealed
to him."* There is a process of maturation. The child was raised in the
presence of God and around the holy things his entire life, but the Bible
says young Samuel did not know the voice of God and the Word was not
yet revealed to him.

The LORD God wants to encourage parents: If you have brought your children up in a wonderful home, if you have trained the children in the way they should go in the LORD, If you never missed church; if you have done your part, God will make himself known to your child. You see we can foster an environment for our children, but it is God who calls. We serve a very jealous God over the salvation of each person. He wants longingly for it to be a very personal experience!"

— Sister Claudette Walker

Other scripture references on learning to discern the voice of our Father (Jeremiah 33:3; 1 Samuel 3:10; Psalm 32:8–9; Proverbs 2:1–5; John 10:27–30; Hebrews 5:14).

I Samuel 3:3-8

And there the lamp of God went out in the temple of the Lord, where the ark of God was, and Samuel was laid down to sleep; That the Lord called Samuel: and he answered, here am I. And he ran unto Eli, and said, Here am I; for thou calledst me. And he said, I called not; lie down again. And he went and lay down. And the Lord called yet again, Samuel. And Samuel arose and went to Eli, and said, Here am I; for thou didst call me. And he answered, I called not, my son; lie down again. Now Samuel did not yet know the Lord, neither was the word of the Lord yet revealed unto him. And the Lord called Samuel again the third time. And he arose and went to Eli, and said, Here am I; for thou didst call me. And Eli perceived that the Lord had called the child.

—1 Samuel 3:3–8

"We as parents foster an environment of God for our children; we can place them around God, but when it comes time, God will speak to your child and they will hear Him because we have taught/trained up our child(ren)."

— Sister Claudette Walker,
January 2019, Baby Dedication

EXERCISING OUR FAITH AS AN ADULT

You must exercise your giftings and confirm everything by the Word of God, an elder, or a pastor. Ask God to give you a fresh anointing. If you believe God has personally spoken to you, then you should be able to find a story in the Word of God, and your pastor should confirm the voice of God, as Eli did to young Samuel. In 1998, I was surprised when I heard the LORD call my name. I was sound asleep, but God woke me. It was the voice of my mother, *"Kari Ann!"* I woke up quick! My mother had been the voice of authority in my life. God was calling me to prayer; He wanted to spend time with me.

SERMON: "THE VOICE OF GOD" YOUTUBE VIDEO. (1980'S) BY THE LATE REV. BILLY COLE

He began, "How the LORD will speak to you. To me, it is a very gentle impression on my mind. To my wife, it is very dramatic. And the LORD still speaks to her in that fashion. You may not be with either one of those extremes; you may be somewhere in the middle. You can find how the LORD's speaks to you. We always call it the Voice of God, but that means so many different things. You're going to learn how the LORD speaks to you through trial and error. You have to EXERCISE faith, amen! And you have to exercise faith in what you have learned. But, this can be a problem if you lack the courage to do God's will once He has spoken. When you learn how God speaks to you, then you have to exercise faith in what He said.

You have to develop with the LORD a child-Father relationship, not a servant-Father relationship. It is true that we serve the LORD, but we are not His servants, but children of God.

Henceforth I call you not servants; for the servant knoweth not what his lord doeth: but I have called you friends; for all things that I have heard of my Father I have made known unto you."

— Jesus Christ, (John 15:15)

"And because ye are sons, God hath sent forth the Spirit of his Son into your hearts, crying, Abba, Father. Wherefore thou art no more a servant, but a son; and if a son, then an heir of God through Christ."

— the Apostle Paul, Galatians 4:6-7

"Behold, what manner of love the Father hath bestowed upon us, that we should be called the sons of God: therefore the world knoweth us not, because it knew him not. Beloved, now are we the sons of God, and it doth not yet appear what we shall be: but we know that, when he shall appear, we shall be like him; for we shall see him as he is."

— John the Beloved, (I John 3:1-2)

Billy Cole said this, "Get up off your knees, lift up your head to your Father. Exercise some faith in Him, and who you are in Him. Have faith in the voice of God in your life. When the LORD God speaks to you, be obedient to Him. Get a clear-cut direction from God. This happens in prayer and Bible reading. This is why fasting is so important to us as the body of Christ. Greatness lies in the vision. This is why we need a Pastor in our lives; and the fellowship of the body of Christ. Your faith inspires you to trust in God."

— Rev. Billy Cole,
YouTube (the Voice of God).

All of this is learned. Do you have a teachable spirit? Can you be corrected? Do you know how to follow your Pastor, and how to follow God?

BECOMING SENSITIVE TO GOD AND THE ANGELS AROUND US

If a donkey can speak out and have the ability to see angels, then surely human beings can become more sensitive to God! See Numbers 22:21-35.

> "And Balaam, (the prophet), rose up in the morning, and saddled his ass, and went with the princes of Moab.
>
> And God's anger was kindled because he went: and the angel of the Lord stood in the way for an adversary against him. Now he was riding upon his ass, and his two servants were with him.
>
> And the ass saw the angel of the Lord standing in the way, and his sword drawn in his hand: and the ass turned aside out of the way, and went into the field: and Balaam smote the ass, to turn her into the way.
>
> But the angel of the Lord stood in a path of the vineyards, a wall being on this side, and a wall on that side.
>
> And when the ass saw the angel of the Lord, she thrust herself unto the wall, and crushed Balaam's foot against the wall: and he smote her again.
>
> And the angel of the Lord went further, and stood in a narrow place, where was no way to turn either to the right hand or to the left.
>
> And when the ass saw the angel of the Lord, she fell down under Balaam: and Balaam's anger was kindled, and he smote the ass with a staff.
>
> And the Lord opened the mouth of the ass, and she said unto Balaam, What have I done unto thee, that thou hast smitten me these three times?

And Balaam said unto the ass, Because thou hast mocked me: I would there were a sword in mine hand, for now would I kill thee.

And the ass said unto Balaam, Am not I thine ass, upon which thou hast ridden ever since I was thine unto this day? was I ever wont to do so unto thee? and he said, Nay.

Then the Lord opened the eyes of Balaam, and he saw the angel of the Lord standing in the way, and his sword drawn in his hand: and he bowed down his head, and fell flat on his face.

And the angel of the Lord said unto him, Wherefore hast thou smitten thine ass these three times? behold, I went out to withstand thee, because thy way is perverse before me:

And the ass saw me, and turned from me these three times: unless she had turned from me, surely now also I had slain thee, and saved her alive.

And Balaam said unto the angel of the Lord, I have sinned; for I knew not that thou stoodest in the way against me: now therefore, if it displease thee, I will get me back again.

And the angel of the Lord said unto Balaam, Go with the men: but only the word that I shall speak unto thee, that thou shalt speak. So Balaam went with the princes of Balak.

If a donkey can perceive angels and be sensitive to God, so can we.

We are His beloved sons and daughters. We have a soul. Jesus Christ died for our sins! We have been led by the Spirit of God, and know Jesus as our LORD, God, Savior and heavenly Father – God is our King! You could only have that kingdom knowledge unless God Himself personally gave it to you. So, rejoice!

Accept the challenge of the book! Defeat Satan. Take back your God-given territory: Your marriage, your children, your career, your neighbors, your community and your state. Yes, even your nation. There is ownership. You are where God placed you in life. Take back your true jurisdiction in the spiritual realm; your anointing, and save your family, save your community, save your nations, and make a spiritual difference in the world around you. Our prayers can travel where we cannot. Our prayers can touch places God sends them to! He just needs you to be available to Him, and be consistent!

PART SIX

CHAPTER EIGHTEEN

EVERYONE NEEDS A PLACE TO CALL HOME

"How then shall they call on him in whom they have not believed? and how shall they believe in him of whom they have not heard? and how shall they hear without a preacher?"

— The Apostle Paul,
To the church at Rome 10:14

In the New Testament God has placed offices of authority to speak to the Church. We call it a 5-fold ministry. It's found in the book of Ephesians, chapter 4.

"And he gave some, apostles; and some, prophets; and some, evangelists; and some, pastors and teachers; for the perfecting of the saints, for the work of the ministry, for the edifying of the body of Christ: Till we all come in the unity of the faith, and of the knowledge of the Son of God, unto a perfect man, unto the measure of the stature of the fulness of Christ: That we henceforth be no more children, tossed to and fro, and carried about with every wind of doctrine, by the sleight of men, and cunning craftiness, whereby they lie in wait to deceive;

but speaking the truth in love, may grow up into him in
all things, which is the head, even Christ."

— Ephesians 4:11-15

This is how God speaks to the body of believers in word, through the
men and women of God in these above offices. Notice, it does not show
the office of Priest. That's an important point. God choose for the New
Testament the office of Apostles, Prophets, Evangelists, Pastors, and
Teachers to perfect the saints and for the very work of the ministry – this
accomplishes God's will, *"Edifying the bod of Christ"* The idea, *"Until we
all come in the unity of the faith and of the knowledge of the Son of God –
becoming perfect in Him!"* If God has founded these five offices today, and
did not include the role of Priest, as it was in the Old Testament, then we
must accept the guidelines established in the New Testament.

Why not the role of Priest?

Question: Are we still in the Old Testament Covenant, and are you from
the Tribe of Levi?

The role of the Old Testament priest was to offer up blood sacrifices for
the himself, and the nation of Israel. Only one tribe was allowed the office
or role of priesthood, that was the Levites. (Leviticus). Today, the Church
no longer offers up to God animal sacrifices, (pigeons, bulls, and sheep),
because Jesus was the sinless Lamb of God. (I Peter 1:19). We know that
there is One High Priest in heaven who offers up prayers for us, and that
is Jesus Christ, our mediator. (I John 2:1). There is one High Priest who
alone is authorized to hear the confession of sins, that man is Jesus Christ,
our Advocate with the Father. (I Timothy 2:5-6). Hebrews, chapter eight
goes into more detail:

> "But now hath he, (Jesus Christ), obtained a more excellent
> ministry, by how much also he is the mediator of a better
> covenant, which was established upon better promises.
> For if that first covenant had been faultless, then should
> no place have been sought for the second.

For finding fault with them, he saith, Behold, the days come, saith the Lord, when I will make a new covenant with the house of Israel and with the house of Judah: not according to the covenant that I made with their fathers in the day when I took them by the hand to lead them out of the land of Egypt; because they continued not in my covenant, and I regarded them not, saith the Lord.

For this is the covenant that I will make with the house of Israel after those days, saith the Lord; I will put my laws into their mind, and write them in their hearts: and I will be to them a God, and they shall be to me a people."
— Hebrews 8:6-10

Jesus' death abolished the Covenant that had fault.

The New Testament church was founded in Jerusalem by the Jewish disciples of Jesus Christ on the day of Pentecost. (Acts 1 & 2). Acts one and two are the origins of our New Testament church – or the Early Church in Jerusalem. Christians would need to be transformed into the image of their Savior, through the work of the Holy Spirit. We are directed on Christian conduct, and shown how to live a new life, through the five-fold ministry in the Epistles of the Church and each believer is to read the Bible for themselves.

"Seeing then that we have a great high priest, that is passed into the heavens, Jesus the Son of God, let us hold fast our profession. For we have not an high priest which cannot be touched with the feeling of our infirmities; but was in all points tempted like as we are, yet without sin. Let us therefore come boldly unto the throne of grace, that we may obtain mercy, and find grace to help in time of need."
— Hebrews 4:14-16

AARON'S ROD BUDDED

In the Old Testament, Israel challenged the authority of the leadership of Moses and Aaron. God took care of that insurrection through a public ceremony. Aaron's Rod Budded – and God proved the Spiritual leadership in the Book of Numbers, chapter 16.

Numbers 16

And the Lord spake unto Moses, saying,

Speak unto the children of Israel, and take of every one of them a rod according to the house of their fathers, of all their princes according to the house of their fathers twelve rods: write thou every man's name upon his rod.

And thou shalt write Aaron's name upon the rod of Levi: for one rod shall be for the head of the house of their fathers. And thou shalt lay them up in the tabernacle of the congregation before the testimony, where I will meet with you.

And it shall come to pass, that the man's rod, whom I shall choose, shall blossom: and I will make to cease from me the murmurings of the children of Israel, whereby they murmur against you.

And Moses spake unto the children of Israel, and every one of their princes gave him a rod apiece, for each prince one, according to their fathers' houses, even twelve rods: and the rod of Aaron was among their rods.

And Moses laid up the rods before the Lord in the tabernacle of witness. And it came to pass, that on the morrow Moses went into the tabernacle of witness; and, behold, the rod of Aaron for the house of Levi was budded, and brought forth buds, and bloomed blossoms, and yielded almonds. And Moses brought out all the rods from before the Lord unto all the children of Israel: and they looked, and took every man his rod.

And the Lord said unto Moses, Bring Aaron's rod again before the testimony, to be kept for a token against the rebels; and thou shalt quite take away their murmurings from me, that they die not.

And Moses did so: as the Lord commanded him, so did he.

And the children of Israel spake unto Moses, saying, Behold, we die, we perish, we all perish. Whosoever cometh anything near unto the tabernacle of the Lord shall die: shall we be consumed with dying?

— Numbers 16:1-13

We see in the Old Testament Tabernacle, (Church) that God ordained spiritual leaders over congregations – He called them a priest. He used the tribe of Levi to perform those duties. (See Numbers 18 for the duties of the Priests and Levites).

"And I, behold, I have taken your brethren the Levites from among the children of Israel: to you they are given as a gift for the Lord, to do the service of the tabernacle of the congregation.

Therefore thou and thy sons with thee shall keep your priest's office for everything of the altar, and within the vail; and ye shall serve: I have given your priest's office unto you as a service of gift: and the stranger that cometh nigh shall be put to death.

And the Lord spake unto Aaron, Behold, I also have given thee the charge of mine heave offerings of all the hallowed things of the children of Israel; unto thee have I given them by reason of the anointing, and to thy sons, by an ordinance forever.

This shall be thine of the most holy things, reserved from the fire: every oblation of theirs's, every meat offering of theirs's, and every sin offering of theirs's, and every trespass offering of theirs's which they shall render unto me, shall be most holy for thee and for thy sons. In the most holy place shalt thou eat it; every male shall eat it: it shall be holy unto thee."

— Numbers 18:6-10

If you want to call yourself a *"priest"* then you must be able to perform these duties that are specified in the Old Testament. Jesus Christ became our High Priest in the heaven. We don't need a man operating in the role of priest, here on earth. When Jesus was sacrificed on the Cross of Calvary as the sinless Lamb of God, He alone drank from the cup of the wrath of God. Because of His sacrifice, He, (alone), is the only ordained and qualified mediator of the New Testament Covenant. On the Cross, Jesus said the words, *It is finished!* Meaning Jesus fulfilled it all. No more animal sacrifices; no more Jewish priests; no more false traditions of men.

We were instructed in the New Testament to establish order and to form a five-fold ministry: *And he gave some, apostles; and some, prophets; and some, evangelists; and some, pastors and teachers. (Ephesians 4:11a).* And each of those offices, ordained by God and confirmed by the Holy Spirit of God, serve a purpose on earth. *"...for the perfecting of the saints, for the work of the ministry, for the edifying of the body of Christ."* (Ephesians 4:11 b). The entire body of born-again-Christian believers now operates as a spiritual priesthood to offer up spiritual sacrifices, acceptable to God by Jesus Christ and to show forth His praises, who has called us all out of darkness into His marvelous light! (I Peter 2:5, 9 – Royal Priesthood of God).

I have just proved through scripture that the very life, ministry, death, burial, resurrection, and ascension of Jesus Christ, God changed the order of His ministry and ushered in a better Covenant! Today, the Jew and Gentile Christian believer are the only legitimate ordained, anointed spiritual lineage. It is His order! God said in the New Testament scriptures that He found fault with the first Covenant. (Hebrews 8:6-10).

A BETTER COVENANT – A NEW WAY

II Peter 2:5-11 Commissioning and Anointing – the Saints are the Holy Priesthood.

> "Ye also, as lively stones, are built up a spiritual house, an holy priesthood, to offer up spiritual sacrifices, acceptable to God by Jesus Christ. Wherefore also it is contained in the scripture, Behold, I lay in Sion a chief corner stone, elect, precious: and he that believeth on him shall not be confounded.

> Unto you therefore which believe he is precious: but unto them which be disobedient, the stone which the builders disallowed, the same is made the head of the corner, and a stone of stumbling, and a rock of offence, even to them which stumble at the word, being disobedient: whereunto also they were appointed.

> But ye are a chosen generation, a royal priesthood, an holy nation, a peculiar people; that ye should shew forth the praises of him who hath called you out of darkness into his marvelous light; which in time past were not a people, but are now the people of God: which had not obtained mercy, but now have obtained mercy.

> Dearly beloved, I beseech you as strangers and pilgrims, abstain from fleshly lusts, which war against the soul."
> — II Peter 2:5-11

MORE THAN A BUSINESS! DON'T MISS CHURCH.

The Church is more than a job to perform: products created or services provided. It is not a corporation or business. No, the church is the very body of Christ – it's spiritual and affects the supernatural and physical world around us. We are said to be Jesus Christ's hands and feet here.

Secondly, missing church creates a bad pattern or example for others to do the same thing - miss church. The third point is even more crucial. What happens when the lost make their way into your church service and they see just a small remnant or an inconsistent one? The Church should be responsible and dependable as Christ was. Visitors will feel like they have made a mistake in picking your church to visit.

If the house of God is not important to dad and mom, then it will not be important to their children. Remember, strong families, make strong communities.

The fact is this, the Spirit of God draws each individual into a loving fold. Missing church is selfish, and it is sinful. Deuteronomy 5:7, *Thou shalt have no other gods before me!* Missing church is the physical act of putting something else over God, or in front of God. Missing church weakens all: body, mind, and spirit. In the Ten Commandments, God gave to man a day of rest. *Six days to labor and one to rest in.* Deuteronomy 5:13. He asked Israel, *"keep the sabbath day; sanctify it."* Deuteronomy 5:12. Israel holy day was Saturday. Our day of fellowship, is Sunday. Isaiah 58 said this,

> "If thou turn away thy foot from the sabbath, from doing thy pleasure on my holy day; and call the sabbath a delight, the holy of the Lord, honorable; and shalt honor him, not doing thine own ways, nor finding thine own pleasure, nor speaking thine own words:
>
> **Then shalt thou delight thyself in the Lord; and I will cause thee to ride upon the high places of the earth,**

and feed thee with the heritage of Jacob thy father: for
the mouth of the Lord hath spoken it."
— Isaiah 58:13-14

It is rude to be invited to your Father's house and just dismiss it. Your Father in heaven has provided for you to be fed and to fellowship with other believers. But, more than that, He has desired your presence. The summons has gone out, *Come and sit with me a while. Let your soul be refreshed!* Sadly, many saints do not respond.

Before the pandemic, there were some churches, or radio pastors declaring, *"Don't let someone make you feel guilty about missing church – as if you have to attend to be right with God."* They even called it the Galatian heresy. I disagree with this thought strongly. First, because it is unbiblical. (Hebrews 10:25). Second, because of the damage it will cause to believers. Missing church weakens their faith. When any person misses church, they are missing out on the best God has for them.

Fact, when they choose to miss, it is usually to do something fleshy or carnal.

I'm not referring to having to work on a church day; I am referring to a day of laundry, washing your car, or going to a baby shower. Feeding the flesh, yields no eternal benefits but weakens the body especially since these particular individuals are the ones not doing the very basics of their faith. They are not reading their Bible. They are not stopping to pray. They are still listening to worldly music; they are still binging on violent and sexual movies. These types of saints don't need less church, but more. These individuals need to be encouraged not to miss, because they are the ones that will. When it comes to human beings, we need more of God, not less.

Fact, I am a better person in the presence of my King and so is every Christian believer. I am a more loving wife, a better parent, a better employee and neighbor. God's Spirit heals, corrects, rebukes, and challenges. (II Timothy 4:2). God's presence also cleanses us. God's presence subdues my passions and strong emotions! The word of God spoken over the pulpit washes our soul. (Ephesians 5:26). It also grounds our morality.

Fact, the world has six days to indoctrinate us. Since most churches only have one service, on Sundays, that gives the pastor one day to preach; and usually for an hour message.

I would also like to say at this point, the very pastors preaching *"It's okay to miss,"* are the ones who aren't missing church?" They don't miss services, they don't miss their Bible reading; they don't miss they communication with God. So, why would you encourage your weaker congregants to miss? To me, that doesn't make sense and it is dangerous to their salvation because I don't believe in *"once saved, always saved."* Everything in life is a choice. The Apostle Paul said this to the church in Philippi, *"Work out your own salvation with fear, (Godly reverence) and trembling!"* Here is the full thought:

> "Wherefore God also hath highly exalted him, and given him a name which is above every name: That at the name of Jesus every knee should bow, of things in heaven, and things in earth, and things under the earth; And that every tongue should confess that Jesus Christ is Lord, to the glory of God the Father.
>
> Wherefore, my beloved, as ye have always obeyed, not as in my presence only, but now much more in my absence, work out your own salvation with fear and trembling. For it is God which worketh in you both to will and to do of his good pleasure."
> — The Apostle Paul, (Philippians 2:9-13).

Jesus warned his disciples: *He that shall endure unto the end shall be saved.* (Paraphrased from Matthew 24:13). The full thought is this. Watch the warning that our LORD gave to us all.

> "And then shall many be offended, and shall betray one another, and shall hate one another. And many false prophets shall rise, and shall deceive many. And because iniquity shall abound, the love of many shall wax cold.

But he that shall endure unto the end, the same shall be saved. And this gospel of the kingdom shall be preached in all the world for a witness unto all nations; and then shall the end come."

— Jesus Christ, (Matthew 24:10-14).

Don't miss church!

It really will help you and your family. More importantly, our presence together is powerful. There is a popular saying, *"One can put a thousand angels to flight, and two can put ten thousand angels to flight!"* (Paraphrased from Deuteronomy 32:30-43).

There is a reason why Satan tempts you to miss it. In some areas, he wins. Think of the random conversations that we have with one another is service. Think of those you have laughed with; those you have encouraged, those you have helped just by being there. Don't miss church.

The fourth reason you shouldn't miss church, it hurts your pastor. Pastors spend their time seeking God for the congregation; preparing a message to share. Their minds are on their fold – at least it is for a good pastor. They pray for you, for you family; they pray for your life and what you may be struggling with. They come to give you manna for your soul, but then you are not there to receive it. There is a disconnect.

When saints miss services, it discourages good pastors. It also lets God down, because there might have been something that God was trying to say to them, but you missed it.

"BUT, I DON'T NEED A PASTOR!" IS A LIE FROM THE PIT OF HELL!

I want to mention accountability here. I noticed in the last ten years a new trend in the Christian circles, the thought, *"I don't need a pastor in my life, and I don't need a church."* I strongly disagree and feel that mindset came from Satan. God gives to his men and women in ministry an anointing and discernment regarding evil. That means God imparts to them kingdom knowledge and His wisdom. In Ezekiel 33, God calls these people, *"Watchmen on the Wall!"* It carries with it a great responsibility of blessings or a curse! A blessing to the individual who cries out the warning of what is coming; a curse for those who do not warn them of their wicked ways! Warn them, blow the trumpet!

I have listed what the tools are in the above paragraph, but I will say this before any soldier is sent to the front lines, they first go through enlistment and Bootcamp training.

FROM SISTER VESTA MANGUN!

"The Church should be a training ground, with one active Pastor. Some churches have several assistant Pastors. The Pastor and other leaders are to be the faculty preparing the members for their own ministry. Ministry is everyone's business! It is everyone's responsibility! Every local Church =, in effect, should be a mini-seminary. Sunday school teachers, leaders, greeters, ushers, encourages, ministers of music, ministers of education and youth, intercessors, custodians, secretaries, ministers to hospitals, jails, nursing homes, and shut-ins. No matter the ministry, every calling is great if you will greatly pursue it.

— Sister Vesta Mangun, (page 73)
Pastor's Wife, Ladies' Speaker Pentecostals of Alexandria
From her Book, Vesta Mangun Continues

I would gently make this suggestion to you: Prayerfully find one of those in your area - A Spiritually filled, Bible-believing Apostolic ministry with sound doctrine!

Introduce yourself to the pastor; build a relationship with him and his wife; allow them to speak into your life; faithfully, sit through church services, ask questions and develop your knowledge on the basics of Christianity. Here, doctrine most certainly matters! The foundation you build with, will be the foundation that you will stand upon when the rains come! (Matthew 7:24-29 Jesus' description of sound building). The Bible says in I John 4:1-5 paraphrased, *"Try the spirits, to see if they be of God!"*

Once the LORD's Holy Spirit leads you to a pastor and congregation, grow where you are planted. Be found faithful to your leaders and congregation. Respect your pastor for the office that he holds; some day he will give an account for your soul.

> "Obey them that have the rule over you, and submit yourselves: for they watch for your souls, as they that must give account, that they may do it with joy, and not with grief: for that *is* unprofitable for you."
>
> — Hebrews 13:17

Allow the Pastor and pastor's wife to teach you a Bible study and spend time with you - allow them to help you mature and spiritually grow. Be productive where God places you; get to know the congregation. This is God's perfect, holy will for every soul to belong to a church and to have an over shepherd!

The Bible tells us in Proverbs 1,

> "...To know wisdom and instruction; to perceive the words of understanding; to receive the instruction of wisdom, justice, and judgment, and equity; to give subtilty to the simple, to the young man knowledge and discretion.
>
> A wise man will hear, and will increase learning; and a man of understanding shall attain unto wise counsels: To understand a proverb, and the interpretation; the words of the wise, and their dark sayings.
>
> The fear of the Lord is the beginning of knowledge: but fools despise wisdom and instruction. My son, hear the instruction of thy father, and forsake not the law of thy

mother: For they shall be an ornament of grace unto thy head, and chains about thy neck."
— King Solomon (Proverbs 1:1-9)

FROM THE VOICE OF AN ENGLISH PROFESSOR – ROSARIA BUTTERFIELD

In the book, *The Secret Thoughts of an Unlikely Convert, An English Professor's Journey Into Christian Faith,* written by Rosaria Champagne Butterfield, Rosaria said she was put off by the idea of church membership, until she read the pledge with the Holy Ghost. Our LORD gently led her through each number - and she knew, *Yes, I do agree with these vows.* Christ was asking for all of her. Her denomination: Reformed Presbyterian. I also included her first response next to some of the questions, so that you can see what she considered. Now, I consider myself a Born-Again, Spirit-filled, Apostolic, Pentecostal believer, and I had never considered all the numbered points that her organization had laid out for their congregations, until I read them in her book. And I confess to you, that had I not my own strong personal relationship with our LORD, and the moving of His Holy Spirit, I could not have laid my own life down.

As a pastor's wife I would be weary to hand this list to a new believer. In fact, it took over three years, before Rosaria's pastor asked her to fully commit. The written declaration of faith of each of those bullet points solidified her congregation - each received it gladly and each the new expectations of each member. There was a transparent standard of excellence signed by their pastor and the new member. He promised to be their over shepherd, and they promised to do their part as a church member.

This is covenant agreement with their people:

1. Do you believe the Scriptures of the Old and New Testament to be the word of God, the only infallible rule of faith and life? At this first question, Rosaria said, *"My rule of faith and life had been my own intellect."* Question: would she change her life to match the Word?

2. Do you believe the one living and true God - the Father, Son, and Holy Spirit, as revealed in the Scriptures?

3. Do you repent of your sins, confess your guilt and helplessness as sinner against God; profess Jesus Christ, Son of God, as your Savior and LORD; and deviate yourself to His service: Do you promise that you will endeavor to forsake all sin, and to conform your life to His teachings and examples? Rosaria said this: *"Repent? Sin? Guilt? Helplessness? These were once anathema to my character and life."*

4. Do you promise to submit in the LORD to the teaching and government of this church as being based upon the Scriptures and described in substance in the Constitution of the Reformed Presbyterian Church of North America? Do you recognize your responsibility to work with others in the church and do you promise to support and encourage them in their service to the LORD? *In case you should need correction in doctrine or life, do you promise to respect the authority, and disciplines of the church?*

5. To the end that you may grow in Christian life, do you promise that you will diligently read the Bible, engage in private prayer, keep the LORD's day. Regularly attend worship services, observe the appointed sacraments, and give to the LORD's work as He shall prosper you?

6. Do you purpose to seek first the Kingdom of God and HIs righteousness in all the relationships of life, faithfully to perform your whole duty as a true servant of Jesus and seek to win others to Him?

7. Do you make this profession of faith and purpose in the presence of God, in humble reliance upon His grace, as you desire to give your account with joy at the Last Great Day?

Allow me to ask you this question: *What do you believe in and what will you submit to in your life?* Yes, such as submitting to the authority in our lives with the true fear of God, or learning how to inquire of the LORD and wait patiently for the response, (promise).

Supernaturally you must be clothed with our LORD, Jesus Christ and then you must have a physical (human) relationship covering, called a Pastor. You must first be found FAITHFUL to your local assembly and in good standing.

THE AREA OF TITHING AND SUPPORT

Tithing is biblical. The word tithe means, "tenth." We first see it demonstrated in the Old Testament, during the time of the wilderness Tabernacle. It was developed by God, placed inside the Law of Moses. Israel was to give of their *"first fruits."* Since it was the LORD who caused the increased and blessed the land, He asked something of His people. Financially care for your leaders. God specified one-tenth. In the New Testament, the early Church gave all, even selling properties to further the gospel, care for the needs of the elderly (widows) among them; and feed the body. Now, fast forward to our century. We have seen so much financial mishandlings and abuse over finances, that the Church body does not trust the leadership with their hard-earned money. However, once you have released your tithe into the hands of a pastor, you commitment is recorded in heaven. If the man of God blows the money on African safari trips, European vacations, BMW's for their children, you have to ask yourself, "Is this where God has me; is this leadership where I am supposed to serve?" If you cannot trust your pastor or church with your money, (tithe/offering), then how are you trusting them with your soul, and that of your family? Somewhere you have made a lapse in judgment and you have stopped hearing the voice of God. Look at the full thought of Malachi 3:6-18.

> For I am the Lord, I change not; therefore ye sons of Jacob are not consumed. Even from the days of your fathers ye are gone away from mine ordinances, and have not kept them.

> Return unto me, and I will return unto you, saith the Lord of hosts. But ye said, Wherein shall we return? Will a

man rob God? Yet ye have robbed me. But ye say, Wherein have we robbed thee? In tithes and offerings.

Ye are cursed with a curse: for ye have robbed me, even this whole nation.

Bring ye all the tithes into the storehouse, that there may be meat in mine house, and prove me now herewith, saith the Lord of hosts, if I will not open you the windows of heaven, and pour you out a blessing, that there shall not be room enough to receive it. And I will rebuke the devourer for your sakes, and he shall not destroy the fruits of your ground; neither shall your vine cast her fruit before the time in the field, saith the Lord of hosts. And all nations shall call you blessed: for ye shall be a delightsome land, saith the Lord of hosts.

Your words have been stout against me, saith the Lord. Yet ye say, What have we spoken so much against thee? Ye have said, It is vain to serve God: and what profit is it that we have kept his ordinance, and that we have walked mournfully before the Lord of hosts? And now we call the proud happy; yea, they that work wickedness are set up; yea, they that tempt God are even delivered.

Then they that feared the Lord spake often one to another: and the Lord hearkened, and heard it, and a book of remembrance was written before him for them that feared the Lord, and that thought upon his name.

And they shall be mine, saith the Lord of hosts, in that day when I make up my jewels; and I will spare them, as a man spareth his own son that serveth him. Then shall ye return, and discern between the righteous and the wicked, between him that serveth God and him that serveth him not."

— Malachi 3:6-18

You may say at this point, *"That's the Old Testament. The Cross abolished the Law?"* No, it did not. It fulfilled it! When you feel that something is no longer in practice, then you are obligated to research the New Testament and see if the practice continued in the Early Church. (Acts 2:42-45). Now, I've already said that they gave all. Not one-tenth, but all. Do I feel that God desires your entire paycheck? No. I do not. I still believe one-tenth plus offerings is in practice. It is a safe amount that helps our community.

Old Testament Tithe:

Genesis 14:19-20 Abram's tithe
Genesis 28:20-22 Jacob's tithe
Exodus 35-36 An offering to the LORD
Leviticus 27:26-34 The Law of Moses
Numbers 28:18 Help for the Levites (1/10 of Israel's Inheritance)
Deuteronomy 8:18 Remember your LORD who gives you your wealth.
Deuteronomy 12:5-6 Israel's responsibility towards God
Deuteronomy 14:22 Israel's Festivals
Deuteronomy 14:28-29 Help for Orphans and Widows
Deuteronomy 16:10 Remember your tribute and offering to God.
Deuteronomy 16:16-17 Do not come empty-handed unto the LORD.
I Chronicles 29 The people supplied all the valuable items for the building and rejoiced!
II Chronicles 31:4-5 Abundance of the First Fruits
II Chronicles 31:12 Israel faithfully dedicated gifts to God.
Nehemiah 10:35-37 Nehemiah (the Builder) re-establishes the tithe.
Nehemiah 12:43-44 They rejoiced for their storehouses were full!
Psalm 50:10 It all belongs to God!
Proverbs 3:9-10 Solomon. Honor the LORD with your wealth
Proverbs 11:24-25 those who withhold come to poverty.
Proverbs 28:22 A stingy man will come to poverty.
Proverbs 28:27 Those who care for the poor, will always be cared for by God.
Amos 4 Bring more than required (Israel was getting stingy).
Haggai 1:1-11 Israel neglected their duty and left the House of God in ruin.
Malachi 3 Israel was accused of robbing God of His substance.
Malachi 3:10-12 God tests His people with the Tithe money.

New Testament Tithe:

Matthew 6:1-4 Jesus said tithe without making an open show.
Matthew 6:23-36 Those who are consumed with building their own storehouse will come to nothing.
Matthew 23:23 Tithing does not mean we stop caring for others.
Mark 12:41-44 The faithful giver – the little old widow gave all she had.
Luke 6:38 That which you give willingly shall be blessed, pouring over!
Luke 11:42 Tithing does not guarantee salvation – your heart does.
Luke 18:9-14 Warning by Jesus. Don't get lifted up in your pride over tithing.
Romans 12:13 Contribute to the needs of the saints.
I Corinthians 16:2 Put something in, and bring something with you!
II Corinthians 9:16 Sow bountifully!
I Timothy 6 God richly provides for us!
Hebrews 6:10 God will not forget what you did for Him!
Hebrews 7:1-2 History lesson of Abraham and Melchizedek. Point: Abraham tithed.
Hebrews 13:6 Do not neglect to do good! (Sacrifices are pleasing to God).
I John 3:17 The distribution of this world's goods.

"Therefore I thought it necessary to exhort the brethren, that they would go before unto you, and make up beforehand your bounty, whereof ye had notice before, that the same might be ready, as a matter of bounty, and not as of covetousness.

But this I say, He which soweth sparingly shall reap also sparingly; and he which soweth bountifully shall reap also bountifully. Every man according as he purposeth in his heart, so let him give; not grudgingly, or of necessity: for God loveth a cheerful giver.

And God is able to make all grace abound toward you; that ye, always having all sufficiency in all things, may abound to every good work: (As it is written, He hath dispersed abroad; he hath given to the poor: his righteousness remaineth forever.

Now he that ministereth seed to the sower both minister bread for your food, and multiply your seed sown, and increase the fruits of your righteousness;) Being enriched in everything to all bountifulness, which causeth through us thanksgiving to God.

For the administration of this service not only supplieth the want of the saints, but is abundant also by many thanksgivings unto God;

Whiles by the experiment of this ministration they glorify God for your professed subjection unto the gospel of Christ, and for your liberal distribution unto them, and unto all men; and by their prayer for you, which long after you for the exceeding grace of God in you.

Thanks be unto God for his unspeakable gift."
— II Corinthians 9:5-19

Understand this basic material point: *Your tithes help to pay your pastor (a living/wage), and offset the expenses of running a fully operational church; such as church insurance, the water bill, PG&E, (air conditioning and heating), the janitorial services, and paying the gardener).* Your pastor shouldn't be working for free and having to carry the financial load of the ministry by himself. It's always easier when everyone pays their tithes. As the tithe money comes in, it is also meant to be sent out into the mission fields! Yes, it all matters to God. Not only the *"salary or wages"* perspective. God did say that *a laborer was worthy of their hire.* (Paraphrased from I Timothy 5:18). Meaning, *pay the man of God a fair wage*; and actually an abundant wage because your hearts are full and have been richly blessed by God. But, also money, in tithes and offerings should be going out to missions, to projects, to the community around us. It helps with advertising, marketing, post cards, business cards, banners, musical instruments, speakers, sound systems, microphones. It pays the gardener that keeps your grounds; it pays the janitor that cleans the sanctuary. It pays the daycare provider that watches your children during services. In California, there is a great need to help the homeless; they are encamped all around us. there is a need for clothing, shelter expenses, food.

If the finances are locked up – the work does not go forth as easily as it was meant to.

The book of James says this,

> "Even so faith, if it hath not works, is dead, being alone. Yea, a man may say, Thou hast faith, and I have works: shew me thy faith without thy works, and I will shew thee my faith by my works. Thou believest that there is one God; thou doest well: the devils also believe, and tremble. But wilt thou know, O vain man, that faith without works is dead?
>
> Was not Abraham our father justified by works, when he had offered Isaac his son upon the altar? Seest thou how faith wrought with his works, and by works was faith made perfect? And the scripture was fulfilled which saith, Abraham believed God, and it was imputed unto him for righteousness: and he was called the Friend of God.
>
> Ye see then how that by works a man is justified, and not by faith only. Likewise also was not Rahab the harlot justified by works, when she had received the messengers, and had sent them out another way? For as the body without the spirit is dead, so faith without works is dead also."
> — James 2:17-26

THE WORKS WITH NATURALLY COME TO YOU – AND THEY ARE EASY!

Believe me, if the Spirit of God is in you and you are reading the Word of God, faithfully doing your Christian principles and attending Church, then you will naturally be doing *"works"* or service to God, and it's neither legalistic nor grievous. They come hand and hand with being yoked with Christ. It's called producing fruit.

Question: What naturally brings forth fruit in fruit trees? The warm of the sun, planted in good ground, well-watered…it will produce fruit. It cannot help but, (under these circumstances) to produce fruit. It will do what it was created to do – naturally under the right circumstances.

We must learn to trust God, take Him at His word, and obey the prompting of the Holy Spirit believing the promises and rewards for yourself first.

Yes, you exercise wisdom.

Yes, you must have checks and balances.

Yes, there must be financial transparency in the record keeping; not just the Pastor and pastor's wife, but also those involved such as the financier, and the secretary. At this point I want to bring a letter from Paul, the Apostle, to young Timothy. Look at his bullet points. Review his direction - what mattered to Paul? What message was he getting out? Remember, the end of Paul's life was drawing near and these are his finally recorded words.

Timothy,

> "I charge thee therefore before God, and the Lord Jesus Christ, who shall judge the quick and the dead at his appearing and his kingdom; preach the word; be instant in season, out of season; reprove, rebuke, exhort with all longsuffering and doctrine.
>
> For the time will come when they will not endure sound doctrine; but after their own lusts shall they heap to themselves teachers, having itching ears; and they shall turn away their ears from the truth, and shall be turned unto fables.

But watch thou in all things, endure afflictions, do the work of an evangelist, make full proof of thy ministry. For I am now ready to be offered, and the time of my departure is at hand.

I have fought a good fight, I have finished my course, I have kept the faith: henceforth there is laid up for me a crown of righteousness, which the Lord, the righteous judge, shall give me at that day: and not to me only, but unto all them also that love his appearing.

Do thy diligence to come shortly unto me: For Demas hath forsaken me, having loved this present world, and is departed unto Thessalonica; Crescens to Galatia, Titus to Dalmatia.

Only Luke is with me. Take Mark, and bring him with thee: for he is profitable to me for the ministry. And Tychicus have I sent to Ephesus. The cloak that I left at Troas with Carpus, when thou comest, bring with thee, and the books, but especially the parchments.

Alexander the coppersmith did me much evil: the Lord rewarded him according to his works: Of whom be thou ware also; for he hath greatly withstood our words.

At my first answer no man stood with me, but all men forsook me: I pray God that it may not be laid to their charge. Notwithstanding the Lord stood with me, and strengthened me; that by me the preaching might be fully known, and that all the Gentiles might hear: and I was delivered out of the mouth of the lion.

And the Lord shall deliver me from every evil work, and will preserve me unto his heavenly kingdom: to whom be glory for ever and ever. Amen.

Salute Prisca and Aquila, and the household of
Onesiphorus. Erastus abode at Corinth: but Trophimus
have I left at Miletum sick. Do thy diligence to come
before winter. Eubulus greeteth thee, and Pudens, and
Linus, and Claudia, and all the brethren.

The Lord Jesus Christ be with thy spirit. Grace be with
you. Amen."
    —Apostle Paul, (II Timothy 2 -complete chapter)

It's all spelled out: This is what matters to Paul: Keep your eyes on Christ,
forsake the world, and do the work of an evangelist, (even in your secular
career). Paul passed the Christian baton to his protege, young, fearful
Timothy. You can see the urgency in his writing! If Paul were standing
next to him, his hands would be upon his shoulders looking him directly
in the eyes looking for confirmation!

THE BENEFITS OF OBEDIENCE TO GOD!

I believe that there are true Christian hidden mysteries on spiritual warfare
that Believers are missing in the 21st Christian church. I believe we are
distracted with the world around us: it's pleasures, it's imagery, and its
practices.

The work that our LORD God is calling us to is greater than our normal
lives and *the sin that has truly so easily beset us.* (Hebrews 12:1). If we stood
for Jesus, accepted our place on this battlefield alongside our Savior; if
we really performed our duty towards His kingdom, I believe we would
impact the world around us that could only compare to the American
Great Awakening. This would destroy child pornography and human
trafficking. Destroying Satan worship and occultism. God's Holy Spirit
could overcome destructive governments, shut down FAKE news, and heal
the race wars we are seeing today. How? Jesus said, *"It's all is summed up
in love."* God's power is greater than anything the Devil does against us,
but America must bring God back into our lives. Through Jesus Christ,
we could come against the opiate war, mental disease and sickness, the

confusion we are seeing regarding our human sexuality and the corruption in our land. I believe Jesus Christ is the answer that this world needs. I know His disciplines positively affect the atmosphere around us because it brings God into the equation. We must have all the variables missing, and our Great Creator is missing out of our lives because we asked Him to leave; we are suffering because of it. Satan is having a field day on our ignorance and he's hurting our children.

CHAPTER NINETEEN

TRIALS AND TRIBULATIONS IN THE CHRISTIAN'S LIFE

"And having spoiled principalities and powers, he made a shew of them openly, triumphing over them in it."
— Colossians 2:15

In life we will all have crosses to bear. There is a big spiritual difference between a cross and a battle! One God has placed on you to refine you, prove you, and develop you; the other came by Satan. Vicious Satanic attacks can be fought and won!

Do you know Merriam-Webster calls *"a cross to bear,"* as a problem that causes trouble or worry for someone over a long period of time? Jesus had a cross to bear in order to reconcile man to God. He asked his disciples this poignant question: *"Can you drink form the same cup that I am going to drink from?"* That's is paraphrased from Matthew 20:22. Christ describes our cross to bear in scripture: *If any man will come after me, let him deny himself, and take up his cross daily, and follow me. 1.) Deny ourselves in wants and desires. 2.) Take up His Cross daily* – it's interesting that he phrased it *"daily."* He did because every day is a choice: *Am I going to do it the LORD's way, or my own way? Am I going to apply the scripture despite the fact that my flesh is crying out to do the opposite?*

Allow me to give you an example. You are at work, someone has been unkind or rude to you. Everything in your being screams, "say something unkind back to them." Then an invisible friend (an angel from God), appears at your right side and you suddenly remember: *A soft answer turneth away wrath: but grievous words stir up anger.* (Proverbs 15:1). And then a little more scripture, verse two comes to mind: *The tongue of the wise useth knowledge aright: but the mouth of fools poureth out foolishness.* You silently exhale out your anger and chose to refrain. Verse three: *The eyes of the Lord are in every place, beholding the evil and the good.* Now you have a battle, because tonight you are going to remember that you let it pass; that it embarrassed you and you feel weak for not responding. It may even make you mad. The question again, will you deny yourself, take up your cross, (daily), and follow Jesus Christ?

Other examples of crosses to bear: *The responsibility of caring for others. Especially over long periods of time; suffering hardships for the greater good.* It is when the load falls on your shoulders because you are the most capable and reliable person for the job. I have lived long enough to recognize when God Himself has handed an elder family member to one person in particular. That is a placement of honor, not grief. It meant that the LORD evaluated every person and found you to be the best person to love them and care for them until they die. Your attitude on the matter will help you or hinder you. Again the choice is yours, *Will you do it Christ's way?*

SPIRITUAL DISCERNMENT

Once again: The word discernment means *the ability to judge well*, and that is what is lacking today. The Bible says we need to exercise discernment. (Hebrews 5:14).

> "But strong meat belongeth to them that are of full age, even those who by reason of use have their senses exercised to discern both good and evil."
> — Hebrews 5:14

This is why we must have a very close relationship with Jesus. The more we are in His holy presence, the more we become like Him.

Question, *what is a spiritual, or Satanic attack?*

A spiritual or satanic attack are the temptations that lead to evil, (sin). An ongoing harassment, taunting, teasing and crushing not sanctioned by God. It is something that robs you or areas of God's peace. They can include strongholds of the past, or drugs and alcoholism. It can be sexual addictions, pornography, or seemingly endless dysfunctional and unhealthy relationships: one after another, after another. It is anything that weakens your strength and severs your trust and love of God.

I know they seem similar, *Cross to bear or Satanic Attack.* Especially *"the responsibility of caring for others that no one is capable of caring for."* But the determining factor is: ***Can the blood of Jesus Christ and His atoning sacrifice break the curse? If it can be broken, destroyed, or defeated, it's not a Cross to bear!*** I feel to clarify something here; something I know very well: there is a difference between caring for an aging parent with dementia, and caring for an ungrateful, unruly, ungoverned, dysfunctional child addicted to drugs and alcohol that's putting you through a living hell. It's the sin issue – either your sin or the sin of another. Sin issues are not a cross to bear! More importantly, other people's sin issues are not your cross they certain personality types tell you it's all your fault. (Narcists, Selfish, Spoiled brats). If you are in the web of sin, or someone else is in the web of sin, you have to see it for what it is: This is sin! Sin is not a person, it's an action, behavior, or lifestyle. Then you must acknowledge the behavior is hurting you, what the church calls, *"confession of sin."* Catholics use confessional boxes. Here is where the Christian family talk with elders in our church, or our Pastor. We ask for help. Next, it's time to kill it. Sin must be mortified or crucified! Strong's Concordance's definition of mortify and origin is this: *To put to death! To make die. To destroy or render extinct. It's an action verb! To be liberated by the bond of anything!* How do you kill a sin? Starve it! Stop feeding into it and turn your back on it.

Example: Now, in turning away someone from your home due to their ongoing sins, is the right thing to do. However, you may end up caring for your innocent grandchildren, hurt during the parent child's sins. Here is where we see a transfer take place. It goes from a satanic attack to a cross to bear. A cross in which Jesus Christ will give you the strength to accomplish. Because the two are so close, spiritual discernment is vital! Identifying the fight you are in, is imperative! Strong boundaries must be established – consistent and faithful! It is advisable to obtain counsel from pastors and Christian counsels. They can help you determine what is meant for you to carry, or what's meant for you to cast out! Since the fallen nature of man comes with addictive personalities, we have to be careful not to enable sin in family – and that's difficult. Learn to pray. Learn to humble yourself and ask God for help.

REMEMBER YOUR VICTORIES!

Rejoice Believer, if He allows you to suffer, then it means that God alone has equipped you to defeat Satan! And it will be in such a way: a wonderful, powerful, spectacular way to bring Glory to God. Think: Shadrach, Meshach, and Abednego. (Daniel 3). Remember the stories in your Bible. Think of Joseph, who they cast into prison with FALSE accusations of rape and misconduct against his master. Remember, Hannah's taunting by the cruel Peninnah. Hannah was crushed by her adversary who provoked her sore daily to make her fret. (I Samuel 1). The adversary finally drove Hannah into such a state; broken, on her knees in prayer; pouring out her heart before the LORD in the Temple. Her suffering and agony birthed a prophet of God. Samuel was one of the mightiest prophets, next to Elijah and Elisha. But he was conceived and blessed in the victory of broken prayer.

> "Rejoice not against me, O mine enemy: when I fall, I shall arise; when I sit in darkness, the Lord shall be a light unto me."
>
> — Micah 7:8

Do not fear you are not alone and you have everything you need; rejoice for your name is written in heaven. All Power Has Been Given to Us!

STAY THE COURSE – BE FAITHFUL TO GOD, STEADFAST, AND UNMOVABLE!

We have a mission. We are the Light of the World! (John 8:12). We have the Spirit of the Living God dwelling inside of us. (I John 4).

> Ye are of God, little children, and have overcome them: because greater is he that is in you, than he that is in the world.
>
> They are of the world: therefore speak they of the world, and the world heareth them. We are of God: he that knoweth God heareth us; he that is not of God heareth not us. Hereby know we the spirit of truth, and the spirit of error.
>
> Beloved, let us love one another: for love is of God; and every one that loveth is born of God, and knoweth God."
> — I John 4:4-7

MY PRAYER:

> "LORD, Jesus Christ, Please allow me, and all the Christian believers to drink from this cup which was shed for us, I ask, in Jesus' precious name. Amen."

GREAT REWARDS FOR FAITHFULNESS

Saint of God, it's all going to be worth it!

Even if you feel you are coming in towards the end - even from this point in your life, if you just pluck one other soul or family out of hell, do it! God sees it, and He is a diligent recordkeeper. If you failed God, wasted your time, missed opportunities in the spirit, were not faithful in everything, just confess it. Repent! Turn from all wicked ways, and He shall receive you! Applying the Word of God and the principles of God's statutes will arm you, (fully equip you) to be strong in the Spirit. If we are Christian in all aspects of our lives; follow all the disciplines we have been taught, then a heavenly anointing follows! We can make things happen supernaturally and we can change the atmosphere. Our new kingdom knowledge is meant to break strongholds and set the captive free! Know this, God has given you your own guardian angel for protection. Besides God's watchful eye on your life, he has a heavenly host of angels which encamps round about you. (Proverbs 15:13 and Psalm 34:7). Know this spiritual truth: Where you are right now, is where God placed you. The people in your life are who you are responsible to pray for; make supplications for, intercede for; be thankful for. Look at Jude 1:20-25.

"But ye, beloved, building up yourselves on your most holy faith, praying in the Holy Ghost, keep yourselves in the love of God, looking for the mercy of our Lord Jesus Christ unto eternal life. And of some have compassion, making a difference: and others save with fear, pulling them out of the fire; hating even the garment spotted by the flesh. Now unto him that is able to keep you from falling, and to present you faultless before the presence of his glory with exceeding joy, To the only wise God our Savior, be glory and majesty, dominion and power, both now and ever. Amen."
— Jude 1:20-25

I'm not exaggerating in my expectation for all saints to have the power to have *"compassion and make a difference"* - I'm telling you the truth. "Pull them out of the fire!" When we do things God's way, through the Son of Jesus Christ's ministry and life, we are more than overcomers! (Romans 8:31-39). We are strong, sufficient, competent, potent, victorious, efficacious, anointed and useful in the Master's hand! (F-Fe-Ka-Cious!) Efficacious: Successful in producing a desired result!

CHAPTER TWENTY

WORD THERAPY!

Sister Claudette Walker shared this: She had suffered a stroke. People were calling her to check on her. They asked her over and over, *"How are you feeling?"* What is our natural response; of course, to answer the question honestly, and reflect upon how we are feeling. The LORD gave to her the revelation of *"Word Therapy."* We walk this road by faith, not by sight. God told Sister Claudette Walker, *"try Word Therapy."* When they ask you how you are feeling, find a scripture to quote. This is what she found during her recovery:

How do you feel?

I feel confident! (Philippians 1:6)

> "Being confident of this very thing, that he which hath begun a good work in you will perform it until the day of Jesus Christ."
>
> — Philippians 1:6

How do you feel?

I feel persuaded. (Romans 8:37-39)

> "Nay, in all these things we are more than conquerors through him that loved us.

For I am persuaded, that neither death, nor life, nor angels, nor principalities, nor powers, nor things present, nor things to come,

Nor height, nor depth, nor any other creature, shall be able to separate us from the love of God, which is in Christ Jesus our Lord.

— Romans 8:37-39

WALK BY OUR PRECIOUS FAITH, NOT BY OUR SIGHT

"Therefore we are always confident, knowing that, whilst we are at home in the body, we are absent from the Lord: (For we walk by faith, not by sight:) We are confident, I say, and willing rather to be absent from the body, and to be present with the Lord. Wherefore we labor, that, whether present or absent, we may be accepted of him. For we must all appear before the judgment seat of Christ; that every one may receive the things done in his body, according to that he hath done, whether it be good or bad. Knowing therefore the terror of the Lord, we persuade men; but we are made manifest unto God; and I trust also are made manifest in your consciences."

— II Corinthians 5:6-11

Christian Believers, it's the 21st Century, and we have served God long enough to know that we do not go by what we feel. If we went by how we felt, we wouldn't go into work. We must know the Word of God, read the Word of God for ourselves, Trust in what it says to us, obey it's instructions and guidance, and then we must declare the Word of God out loud. We must quote the Word of God in battle! We, the Church, go by what He says, not by what we think, feel, or see with our own eyes. We can be deceived by a very seductive enemy. Satan preys on our feeling lonely, sad, depressed, or even sick. He prays on our vulnerability. So, God gave to the

Church the mighty Words of LIFE! It says, the *Word of God is FOREVER settled in the heavens.* It was the very Word of God that Jesus quoted in his battle with Satan in the wilderness, always beginning with, *"It is written!"*

REMEMBER: BE THANKFUL FOR WHAT GOD HAS GIVEN YOU

Claudette said,

> "Do you understand that you didn't just stumble into this precious TRUTH? And you have a responsibility to love what He has given to you, with all that is in you. You love GOD'S HOLY TRUTH with all your heart, mind, soul, and strength! God has given to you, through His Spirit, the revelation in the Mighty God in Christ, the power of the Holy Ghost to intercede for you, pray through you, Jesus' name baptism for the remission of your sins! These are TREASURES from heaven and we've got to love it and be so thankful for them! Guard it. It is worth fighting for, young people!"

You are soldiers for Jesus Christ; you are in His army! You belong to Him and to His kingdom! Praise God! So, be alert. Be sober - wake up to your calling, in Jesus' name. You've been called to these *"last-days"* battles. And God knew that when He laid His hand upon you, that if you would just avail yourself of what He has given to you, that you could be a VICTORIOUS overcoming soldier, not just saving yourself, but reaching out in the throngs of darkness and literally pulling souls from the depths of hell. You have power inside of you! Do you know what you have? Do you know what has been given to you? Do you know what you can yield?"

CHAPTER TWENTY-ONE

A GLIMPSE INTO THE SUPERNATURAL - THE ANGELS OF GOD

"Be not forgetful to entertain strangers: for thereby some have entertained angels unawares."

— Hebrews 13:2

We are so used to the physical realm, we forget the spiritual realm that is all around us. Remember in God's holy creation, there is the supernatural workings of angels. They are all around us – watches us.

"Are they not all ministering spirits, sent forth to minister for them who shall be heirs of salvation?"

— Hebrews 1:14

JACOB'S LADDER

Genesis 28:1-22

"And Jacob went out from Beersheba, and went toward Haran.

And he lighted upon a certain place, and tarried there all night, because the sun was set; and he took of the stones of that place, and put them for his pillows, and lay down in that place to sleep.

And he dreamed, and behold a ladder set up on the earth, and the top of it reached to heaven: and behold the angels of God ascending and descending on it. And, behold, the Lord stood above it, and said, I am the Lord God of Abraham thy father, and the God of Isaac: the land whereon thou liest, to thee will I give it, and to thy seed; And thy seed shall be as the dust of the earth, and thou shalt spread abroad to the west, and to the east, and to the north, and to the south: and in thee and in thy seed shall all the families of the earth be blessed.

And, behold, I am with thee, and will keep thee in all places whither thou goest, and will bring thee again into this land; for I will not leave thee, until I have done that which I have spoken to thee of.

And Jacob awaked out of his sleep, and he said, Surely the Lord is in this place; and I knew it not. And he was afraid, and said, How dreadful is this place! this is none other but the house of God, and this is the gate of heaven.

And Jacob rose up early in the morning, and took the stone that he had put for his pillows, and set it up for a pillar, and poured oil upon the top of it. And he called the name of that place Bethel: but the name of that city was called Luz at the first. And Jacob vowed a vow, saying, If God will be with me, and will keep me in this way that I go, and will give me bread to eat, and raiment to put on, so that I come again to my father's house in peace; then shall the Lord be my God: And this stone, which I have

set for a pillar, shall be God's house: and of all that thou
shalt give me I will surely give the tenth unto thee."
— Genesis 28:10-22

Let's really think about that story. Jacob saw angels ascending and
descending from heaven on a ladder.

Do you think that was the only ladder on earth to heaven?

It is my opinion that it was not the only ladder on earth to heaven. I
can just imagine, (like an airport), there are interactions every day with
thousands and ten thousand, millions of angels ascending back to heaven
and descending to earth to accomplish God's work here. The extraordinary
event was that a mere mortal was allowed to see it.

Note in the story, the Bible records, *"And the LORD God stood above it?"*
My next question, why didn't Jacob see it before?

What changed in Jacob's life that made him susceptible or sensitive to that
world of heavenly host? Jacob was a born thief, (or a heel-grabber). Genesis
25 - Jacob is born. He was also a fraternal twin, but he would be the second
child born. In Israel's time that meant something! Jacob was the 2nd; and
he desired that which was only given to the 1st. He wanted his position as
head of the family. He wanted the blessings of riches that accompanied
inherited his father's substance. But there was something else Jacob, (heel
grabber) wanted. He wanted the Abraham blessing!

The Bible records that the babies wrestled in Rebekah's womb for position.
Do you understand that thought?! They wrestled for position inside of the
womb. Esau, his older brother, is born and the infant, Jacob, still attempts
to usurp the authority by grabbing his infant brother's heel - from the
womb! (Genesis 27).

These boys were destined to have it out! They grow into men and Jacob
intently watches for an opportunity. A series of events take place, a delicious
bowl of red lentil soup is made while Esau is out hunting. It would be ready
for Esau to be tempted when he returned from his hunt. Esau arrives home

with game in hand, but smells the savory meat. In fact, I would imagine that the entire encampment smells of wild game and lentils. Esau is carnal man; a fleshy nature. His hunger for a meal outweighs his common sense and Esau falls. The offer is extended, *sell me your birthright!* The deal is struck and the transfer takes place. Now, through the transaction of a bowl of soup, Jacob has just become head of the family after his father passes away. He bought title! Jacob's mother, Rebekah knew the promise that God had said. "*Two nations are in thy womb, and two manner of people shall be separated from thy bowels; and the one people shall be stronger than the other people; and the elder shall serve the younger.*" (Genesis 25:243). She had a word from God. She knew who God designed to lead the family. It would not be a carnal man who could possibly sell out her family for food. This leader would have to have respect and full understanding of the importance of what he possessed. No, Rebekah would conspire with Jacob, for the first-born blessing as well. Not just conspire, but actually orchestrate the whole thing. End result: Jacob is running for his life, because Esau is going to kill him after his father dies!

So, I ask again, why did Jacob see the ladder this time?

Why did he see the angels ascending and descending from heaven? Because God is going to introduce himself to the young man and open his revelation to what that first-born rite was; what it meant to have that blessing. It was a spiritual world that both he and his brother Esau knew nothing about. It's called growing up and having spiritual responsibility.

> "And, behold, the Lord stood above it, and said, I am the Lord God of Abraham thy father, and the God of Isaac: the land whereon thou liest, to thee will I give it, and to thy seed; and thy seed shall be as the dust of the earth, and thou shalt spread abroad to the west, and to the east, and to the north, and to the south: and in thee and in thy seed shall all the families of the earth be blessed.
>
> And, behold, I am with thee, and will keep thee in all places whither thou goest, and will bring thee again into

this land; for I will not leave thee, until I have done that which I have spoken to thee of.

And Jacob awaked out of his sleep, and he said, Surely the Lord is in this place; and I knew it not. And he was afraid, and said, How dreadful is this place! this is none other but the house of God, and this is the gate of heaven.

And Jacob rose up early in the morning, and took the stone that he had put for his pillows, and set it up for a pillar, and poured oil upon the top of it. And he called the name of that place Bethel: but the name of that city was called Luz at the first. And Jacob vowed a vow, saying, If God will be with me, and will keep me in this way that I go, and will give me bread to eat, and raiment to put on, so that I come again to my father's house in peace; then shall the Lord be my God: and this stone, which I have set for a pillar, shall be God's house: and of all that thou shalt give me I will surely give the tenth unto thee."
— Genesis 28:13-22

I feel like sharing here. We need to access our faith to see our heavenly host. We need to remember the story of the angels ascending and descending from it. Obviously, they were doing the LORD's work on earth.

"Bless the LORD, all His angels mighty in strength who carry out His word, who hearken to the voice of His command."
— Psalm 103:20

Angels were even sent to shut the mouths of the lions. (Daniel 6:22). Look what Daniel 7 says,

"A river of fire was flowing, coming out from His presence. Thousands upon thousands attended Him, and myriads upon myriads stood before Him. The court was convened, and the books were opened."

— Daniel 7:10

Look around you. You may not be aware, but either standing right next to you, side by side; in front of you or behind you, is God's angel.

Psalm 34:6-9 Angels Encamp Around God's Elect

"This poor man cried, and the Lord heard him, and saved him out of all his troubles. The angel of the Lord encampeth round about them that fear him, and delivereth them. O taste and see that the Lord is good: blessed is the man that trusteth in him. O fear the Lord, ye his saints: for there is no want to them that fear him."

— Psalm 34:6-9

There are angels in this room. They come into any room that you walk into. They have been commissioned to be set around you - as a security task force. **Ask God to allow you to feel God's presence and His angelic angels around you so you will not be fearful.** Angels have a divine responsibility (found in scripture) to minister, help, and aid humanity.

Adam and Eve were thrust out of the garden by the LORD, and an angel stood guard with a flaming sword in hand. (Genesis 3:24).

Genesis 28:11-16 Young Jacob fled from Esau, slept in the desert and had a dream - of angels ascending to heaven and descending to earth doing the LORD's will.

Daniel 9:21; Gabriel is the messenger angel; speaking to young Daniel to give him an answer to his prayer and fasting.

In Daniel 10:13, Daniel 12:1, Michael, is the warring angel. He battles principalities so that Gabriel can go forward to proclaim the message of God.

In Luke 1:26-38, Gabriel announced to young Mary the promise of the LORD through her own womb.

Gabriel came to Joseph in a dream not to put away Mary; expounding on the miracle down to the virgin through the Holy Ghost in fulfillment of scripture. (Matthew 1:18-25).

Gabriel announced to Zacharias the name of his son before he was conceived in Elisabeth's womb. (Luke 1:5-21).

In Hebrews 13:2, we are warned to be sensitive to strangers ("forget not to show hospitality to strangers") for they may be angels, sent from God.

Jude1 1:6, warns the Early Church of the example the fallen angels gave to humanity of their disgrace, ("those who did not keep their positions of authority, but abandoned their proper dwelling... reserved for the day of judgment.")

Luke 16:22, Jesus tells a story of the beggar Lazarus who died and was carried to Abraham's bosom.

In Matthew 18:10, Jesus warns humanity to be kind to little children, for their angels will come before the LORD God and declare their unkind works.

Psalm 91 boldly says, that God Himself will command His angels concerning you - to guard you in all of your ways!

Revelation 5:11, shares that we shall hear the voice of many angels, numbering thousands and ten thousand times ten thousand which encircle the throne of God.

The Book of Zechariah, 5:9 tells of two winged creatures resembling women, with wind in their wings.

Joshua 5:13 saw a man over against him with his sword drawn in his hand. Joshua asked the man, "Are you for us?" The angel answered, "Nay, but as captain of the host of the LORD, am I now come!"

Numbers 22:25, Balaam's donkey saw the angel of the LORD with a sword in hand and tried to turn aside to protect her master.

"Are they not all ministering spirits, sent forth to minister for them who shall be heirs of salvation?"
— Hebrews 1:14

THE STRUCTURE OF THE ANGELS IN HEAVEN

From Father Vincent Lampert sermon series Entries and Remedies for Evil. The Necessity of Exorcist, #3 of 5 videos. January 2020.

Categories:
Seraphim's (fiery ones)
Cherubim's
Dominions
Powers
Principalities
Archangels
Angels

"Angels are intellectual creatures who received knowledge from the moment they were created. Fallen angels are diabolical; they oppose the sovereign will of God and the redemptive work of Christ. Lucifer was once called the son of the morning. After his fall becomes complete darkness, all of his glorious light has gone out. God's children radiate the glory of God. For example Moses on Mount Zion. His face shined in the presence of God.

God did not create demons. God created good angels. They exercised their own free will to rebel against God; in doing so they morphed or physically changed into evil. After their fall they do not lose their own intellectual quality, but now they are deprived of the Light of God. Their minds are darkened, they lose all goodness and are consumed with the depth of depravity.

Humans have the capacity to grow and to learn; to be converted. Human beings can change; that is a part of our nature. Unlike humans, whose free will and change, an angel by reason of their purely intellectual nature is situated from the start in the presence of all that he can know. Angels don't constantly learn. They knew everything from the beginning with this infused, (God-given) divine knowledge."

— Father Vincent Lampert
Retreat Center, Bloomington, Indiana
Series Entries & Remedies for Evil.
The Necessity of Exorcist #3 of 5 video
January 17-19, 2020

FOUR LEVELS OF DEMONIC ENERGY

5. Infestation
6. Vexation
7. Oppression
8. And demon possession

God's reconquest was to free humanity of our servitude to Satan and to restore us to God. The Love, Mercy, and Patience of God Jesus Christ answers their one question with three parables: 1.) The Faithful Shepherd, 2.) The Persistent Woman, and 3.) The Loving Father that never gave up! Read Luke 15.

Satan is always about divide and conquer. The Good News is that all this maleficent activity will come to an end. With an infinitive banishment of Satan into eternal fire.

> "And the devil that deceived them was cast into the lake of fire and brimstone, where the beast and the false prophet are and shall be tormented day and night forever and ever."
>
> — Revelation 20:10

Satan is a reality on earth. His demonic angels are also a reality, they exist. The Church is the means whereby we can fight against these realities and demonstrate our love and commitment to God.

PART SEVEN

PART SEVEN

CHAPTER TWENTY-TWO
BLESSINGS OUR ENEMIES

"But I say unto you which hear, Love your enemies, do good to them which hate you, Bless them that curse you, and pray for them which despitefully use you."
— Jesus Christ, (Luke 6:27-28)

This book was about successfully defeating Satan. This area is a big one!

Luke 6 was the best gift of knowledge that Jesus Christ gave to us. It is also one of the most difficult to accomplish on our own. No, we need a Savior.

The ministry of blessing our enemies might even take years to cultivate; through it all, the LORD God is maturing you. It accompanies the act of forgiveness. Many spiritual things happen when we obey Jesus Christ, (literally take him at his Word), and do what he has instructed us to do.

God is so close when one of his children is in an overwhelming situation. Our LORD acts as a buckler or a shield of defense. I know, during these types of very personal trials, we may feel alone, but I assure you, we are not. Jesus said this in the sermon on the Mount, Matthew 5:43-46.

"Ye have heard that it hath been said, Thou shalt love thy neighbor, and hate thine enemy. But I say unto you, Love your enemies, bless them that curse you, do good to them that hate you, and pray for them which despitefully use

you, and persecute you; that ye may be the children of
your Father which is in heaven: for he maketh his sun to
rise on the evil and on the good, and sendeth rain on the
just and on the unjust.

For if ye love them which love you, what reward have ye?
do not even the publicans the same? And if ye salute your
brethren only, what do ye more than others? do not even
the publicans so?

Be ye therefore perfect, even as your Father which is in
heaven is perfect."
— Jesus Christ, (Matthew 5:43-46)

This was said to all 12 Disciples of Jesus Christ and to the thousands of
people who were there on that day! Stop hating each other!

SPIRITUAL MATURATION

There comes a time in every Christian believer's life when we must walk
through facing an enemy. The test: ***will you apply the word of God?
Will you have the victory? Will you leave your emotions and feelings
at the feet of Jesus? Will you have the right attitude during the trial?***
Blessing our enemies is the mark of spiritual maturity. It demonstrates to
those around us our spiritual development, depth, and experience. The
process is grueling; it is where a believer must stay on the Potter's wheel,
(so to speak), until our Heavenly Father tells us it's finished. ***The goal: to
be like Jesus Christ.***

The Truth: We can all quote our favorite scriptures. We can even boldly
proclaim, *Amen!* to God's triumphant battles against Satan, but it is a
whole another thing when we are facing hardships day after day, month
after month, and year after year.

Why, blessing our enemies?

First, because it goes against human nature.

I have said this before earlier in the book, but the flesh is not tamed, (or subdued), no, it's crucified! Death is an element of this life that most human beings fear. Crucifying our flesh can be a scary thing. Blessing your enemy truly benefits you as a believer and your enemy. And that, well, feels unfair. Inside, we don't want God to bless them. We want God to avenge us; defeat them, make them pay for what they have done. That is called, fleshy, lower level thinking. It's carnal. It's knowledge descends from hell. Let's enter a conversation between Jesus and His disciples in Luke 9.

> "And sent messengers before his face: and they went, and entered into a village of the Samaritans, to make ready for him. And they did not receive him, because his face was as though he would go to Jerusalem. And when his disciples James and John saw this, they said, Lord, wilt thou that we command fire to come down from heaven, and consume them, even as Elias did? But he turned, and rebuked them, and said, *Ye know not what manner of spirit ye are of. For the Son of man is not come to destroy men's lives, but to save them. And they went to another village.*"
>
> — Jesus Christ (Luke 9:52-56)

Jesus points out – *don't let Satanic influences cause you to have the wrong attitude!*

It's called growing up, proving the word of God, and learning to let the LORD, fight your battles, defend your personal or professional reputation, or save your fate. Blessing those who hate you, despitefully use, and say all manner of evil against you falsely, places you in the hands of Jesus Christ, our LORD, our real Savior, and our King. It is the safest place to be. Applying the teachings of Jesus Christ, to *"bless our enemies,"* also helps you not to open a door for Satan to enter into your life, and especially your heart and mental wellbeing. The door is secure when you obey the scriptures. Remember that! I'm going to write it again: The door into your life, your mind, your heart, your emotions is secure from the attacks of Satan, when you obey the Word of God and do things God's way! Blessing your enemies prevents a fiery dart from hitting you and bursting your into flames.

Unforgiveness is a sin. Unchecked, it opens the door to something else, the human emotion called *Bitterness*. Have you ever read the definition of that word?

Merriam Webster: Bitterness. Adjective.

> **1a**: being, inducing, or marked by the one of the five basic taste sensations that is peculiarly acrid, astringent, and often disagreeable and characteristic of citrus peels, unsweetened cocoa, black coffee, mature leafy greens (such as kale or mustard), or ale
>
> **b**: distasteful or distressing to the mind.
>
> **2**: marked by intensity or severity:
>
> **a**: accompanied by severe pain or suffering
>
> **b**: being relentlessly determined : VEHEMENT
>
> **c**: exhibiting intense animosity - *bitter* enemies
>
> **d(1)** : harshly reproachful
>
> **(2)**: marked by cynicism and rancor - *bitter* contempt
>
> **e**: intensely unpleasant especially in coldness or rawness
>
> **3**: caused by or expressive of severe pain, grief, or regret

If you do not bless your enemy there is a chance that bitterness can spring up in your life; especially your heart. Bitterness ruins your life because it steals your joy. It can be visibly seen by others, your family, your friends, and those closest to you. Yes, bitterness even comes out in our speech. In Matthew 15, Jesus is speaking to His disciples about what truly *"defiles"* a person. There was some debate with the Pharisee's over *"unwashed hands."* Look what Jesus says,

> "And Jesus said, Are ye also yet without understanding? Do not yet understand, that whatsoever entereth in at the mouth goeth into the belly, and is cast out into the draught? But those things which proceed out of the mouth come forth from the heart; and they defile the man. For out of the heart proceed evil thoughts, murders, adulteries, fornications, thefts, false witness, blasphemies: These are the things which defile a man: but to eat with unwashed hands defileth not a man." (Matthew 15:16-20)

Bitterness gives way to evil thoughts; even thoughts of killing someone, even if it's killing them academically. Have you ever seen at work when people try to sabotage another person's promotion, recognition, or professional reputation? It stems from jealousy and fear. It stems from that person's insecurities. It's a miserable place to be or work alongside someone like that.

For twelve years I had a lead person shut down every idea I had for our UBT Unit Based Team projects; talk about me behind my back, laugh and mock me, (sometimes in front of others and in my face), she sabotage my reputation to higher management and staff, ganged up on me, inspired others to be unkind to me, day after day, year after year, until finally I asked the LORD in 2020, how long will you allow this person to have their foot on my neck?

During the pandemic her cruelty became more frequent; she was bolder. I would drive to work and ask the LORD, Help me not to hate her; forgive her, hold not her sins against her; bless her; let her hear the voice of the Good Shepherd and flee the voice of the stranger, (Satan). I knew this person was miserable and she truly disliked me. I took it. Have you ever just had to take the abuse; day after day because that person has authority over you. It will be the hardest trial of your Christian experience.

My family needed me to have this job. We needed the benefits: it clothed, fed, and sheltered my family. My love for them, would help to suffer the emotional and psychological abuse. Bullying on the job is real. Hostile work environments exists.

One day it dawned on me – pray against the source! You have to spiritual pull up the root. I knew the problem in our Radiology department began before she was even hired; it had manifested through another strong personality. So, I began to pray against the spirit of Jezebel, her children, her religion and her prophets. You cannot have a Jezebel, unless you have an Ahab (leader). An Ahab is weak management that allows the abuse. I wanted the spirit of Jezebel out of our department! 2020, I wept before the LORD, just like Hannah, asking God to remove her foot from my neck. I had a Peninnah in my life and I had reached the point of ENOUGH! Being hurt and broken at the feet of Jesus is a sacred place. It's a holy place, because it is God who comforts us.

In mid 2021, God moved on the situation. Peninnah put in for a transfer. As she came to me and said she was leaving, I blessed her and wished her well. I will say this, that's not me, that's Jesus inside of me. I thanked the LORD for His goodness. But then I thought to myself, *I could have prayed about this much sooner? Why did I wait?*

Spiritual fact: We have no authority to hate another person. We have no authority or permission to wish them evil. *Vengeance belongs to God!* Do not covet that which belongs to God, but trust that everything we say or do will be weighed in the balances of God's righteousness and Law – in light of that, pray for mercy and truth.

I want to say here, I am NOT Mother Teresa. I have times when I wrestle with fairness. I shared with a friend at work, *You know if I heard she stepped off a curb and got run over by a bus, I would say, Wow that's sad. But I have to admit, inside I might just quietly utter to God, "thank you."* That tells me

I still have more to go. Just keep working to lining your behavior up with Christ, and He will complete the work in you.

Let's look at some scripture:

"Do not seek revenge or bear a grudge against any of your people, but love your neighbor as yourself. I am the LORD."
— Leviticus 19:18

"To me *belongeth* vengeance, and recompense; their foot shall slide in *due time*: for the day of their calamity *is* at hand, and the things that shall come upon them make haste."
— Deuteronomy 32:35

"Do not say, "I will avenge this evil!" Wait on the LORD, and He will save you."
— Proverbs 20:22

"Do not say, "I will do to him as he has done to me; I will repay the man according to his work."
— Proverbs 24:29

"Dearly beloved, avenge not yourselves, but *rather* give place unto wrath: for it is written, Vengeance *is* mine; I will repay, saith the Lord."
— Romans 12:9

"Do not repay anyone evil for evil. Carefully consider what is right in the eyes of everybody."
— Romans 12:17

"...and do not give the devil a foothold."
— Ephesians 4:29

"And the Lord turned the captivity of Job, when he prayed for his friends: also the Lord gave Job twice as much as he had before."

— Job 42:10

AS WE GO THROUGH OUR TRIALS, WE MUST BLESS OUR ENEMIES AND DO GOOD TO THEM THAT HATE US FOR THE SAKE OF JESUS CHRIST.

Let our love for Him, restrain us! God is a diligent recorder of everything that has happened to you. God will reward gracefully and abundantly. Let go of lower-level thinking – REVENGE! It's not worth the results it will bring.

God will vindicate in time, but in His way. Our ultimate goal is truly to be a child of God, and not a child of Satan, or darkness. Satan will always work through offense, or perceived offense, but the Word breaks down the offense, and makes us stronger in the Spirit and develops our character. Yes, we are better people: kinder, more loving, compassionate, and patient with one another. The Apostle Paul wrote this to the Corinthians church, (2nd Letter),

"For to this end also did I write, that I might know the proof of you, whether ye be obedient in all things. To whom ye forgive anything, I forgive also: for if I forgave anything, to whom I forgave it, for your sakes forgave I it in the person of Christ; Lest Satan should get an advantage of us: for we are not ignorant of his devices."

— The Apostle Paul, (II Corinthians 2:9-11)

He brings up an excellent point: *"Let us forgive, unless Satan should get an advantage over us – we are NOT ignorant of Satan's devices."*

Then the Apostle Paul says this in verse 14,

"Now thanks be unto God, which always causeth us to triumph in Christ, and maketh manifest the savour of his knowledge by us in every place."
— The Apostle Paul, (II Corinthians 2:14)

Yes, God causes us to triumph in Jesus Christ; He gives us the wisdom of His kingdom mysteries. So, let us willingly forgive as Jesus Christ forgave!

LET GOD BE GOD

Be His beloved child, seek the LORD's guidance, hide under the shadow of His wings, and He will help you through blessing your enemy. His way really works.

"What shall we say then? Is there unrighteousness with God? God forbid.

For he saith to Moses, I will have mercy on whom I will have mercy, and I will have compassion on whom I will have compassion.

So then it is not of him that willeth, nor of him that runneth, but of God that sheweth mercy. For the scripture saith unto Pharaoh, Even for this same purpose have I raised thee up, that I might shew my power in thee, and that my name might be declared throughout all the earth.

Therefore hath he mercy on whom he will have mercy, and whom he will he hardeneth. Thou wilt say then unto me, Why doth he yet find fault? For who hath resisted his will?

Nay but, O man, who art thou that repliest against God? Shall the thing formed say to him that formed it, Why hast thou made me thus?

Hath not the potter power over the clay, of the same lump to make one vessel unto honour, and another unto dishonour?

What if God, willing to shew his wrath, and to make his power known, endured with much longsuffering the vessels of wrath fitted to destruction:

And that he might make known the riches of his glory on the vessels of mercy, which he had afore prepared unto glory, even us, whom he hath called, not of the Jews only, but also of the Gentiles?"

— Romans 9:14-24

CHAPTER TWENTY-THREE
WHAT HAPPENED IN 2020?

Why create such a book? This book had to be written. It will one of many that spoke of the Global Pandemic of 2020. I have to admit, that as I read over it and relived what we all just went through, I find myself really upset, even apprehensive; angry! But history has to be recorded: what I experienced, how I felt; just the uncertainty of it all.

> *"A healthy democracy requires a decent society; it requires that we are honorable, generous, tolerant, and respectful."*
> — *Charles W. Pickering*
> *Judge of the U.S. Court of Appeals*
> *for the 5ᵗʰ Circuit*

A PATHETIC YEAR IN HUMAN EXISTENCE THAT WILL LIVE IN INFAMY – TRULY IT WILL!

By November 2020, I was tired of Satan winning.

I was sickened by the images on the T.V. screen; I was saddened by the race wars that were burning in our nation. Our national historical monuments were toppling over one after another weekly. Whether they had anything to do with slavery or not. The 2020 Summer months of May, June, July, August, September were some kind of twilight show experiment. There was a brutal, non-stop attack on the traditional American culture. It was disturbing; frightening. The generation of Y & Z ideology was a new world – foreign to adults, grown-ups and especially parents. The inmates (or kids) were running the place! The place was our country. It was like a daycare center went full anarchy. *But who were these key players? Who were the kids? Who was calling the shots?* The Caucasian culture and history was under direct assault. In May, a police station in Seattle Washington was held captive by specialty groups. Several of the demands: Chap stick, water, and snacks. I read their list and just shook my head; my thoughts, *"Where are their parents?"*

HISTORY REWRITTEN

Marxists were rewriting our American history and calling for the dismantling of our Western democracy as we had known it. The twenty-somethings were DEMANDING eccentric whims and the Democrats party, (left liberals) gave them everything they wanted. The American people, especially anyone over the age 35, with any reasonable common sense, had to ask, *why?* According to this new world, what was once considered good, wholesome or pure was now evil, offensive or racially motivated. What was once known as mental disease, was now considered an alternative lifestyle choice and *"politically correct"* or *"untouchable or non-negotiable!"* It was going to happen, without the consent of all the people.

The American Government was crushing the middle class; they were destroying free enterprise and dismantling the heartbeat of American businesses. Our nation saw our United States Constitution and our Bill of Rights violated, completely taken away without any dialogue and without any of our opinion.

Everything our American Founding Fathers: George Washington, Thomas Jefferson, James Madison, Benjamin Franklin, Alexander Hamilton, and the other 56 signers wrote in both our Declaration of Independence from Great Britain or our United States Constitution was being discarded.

THE CANCEL CULTURE

The Cancel culture removed books from our public libraries; they removed old films from the screen. They removed household products, children's toys, musical band names, sports teams, and American food products which had always been part of the American tradition: Monopoly, Mr. Potato Head, Barbie dolls, Uncle Ben's rice. Aunt Jemima brand pancake mix. Cream of Wheat was to remove the black chef. The native American woman on the package of Land O' Lakes butter was canceled. Eskimo Pie was termed derogatory against indigenous people. The Dixie Chicks are now the Chicks. Because the word Dixie was too close to Confederate flag. WWF wrestling, was now WWE, World Wrestling Entertainment. *Gone With the Wind*, was gone! Comcast became Xfinity. Victoria Secret was to now include plus size, transgender models. Books were beginning to censured. Six Dr. Seuss books were removed from the shelf. The Berenstain Bears were censured. The cancel culture attempted to removed normal stereotypes of Papa Bear, Mama Bear, or anything that had to do with natural foundation of family was considered a threat; stating gender: boys or girls forbidden! The Washington Redskins, Companies were forced to rebrand! It really was like Nazi Germany had rolled their tanks into our free nation. But who was the 21st Century Adolph Hitler? He hid in the shadows and only gave sound bites to our local stations to address to us.

ABUSE OF POWERS

All I could assuredly say was that our elected Democratic governors had lost their minds! They overnight morphed into little *King George* tyrannical dictators taking full advantage of the Coronal virus. One by one, we saw our natural God-given rights taken away. Our Nation had established early on that our freedom was a right given to humanity by God, not man; and now we had lowered ourselves to hoarding toilet paper and Clorox cleaning wipes? Fights broke out in our grocery stores as consumers were hording household goods and commodities. Panic had brought out a side of humanity that we only watch in historical movies on wars.

Our trucking unions threatened strikes amongst the chaos; they wanted protection for their drivers. I was concerned about the welfare of our police officers, who were being ambushed on the streets. Democratic leaders, Antifa, and BLM were calling for local and state agencies to DEFUND the police departments and law enforcement agencies. I was astonished at the people getting caught up in that mindset. Innocent lives, people, families would be hurt without the protection of the police.

A SUMMER OF PROTESTS

The youth (20's and 30's) were escalating anarchy, lawlessness, and disorder. The Democratic leaders in Congress were silent to condemn any of the attacks we were seeing across the nation. They didn't just march in protest for one weekend, but it continued for over six to seven, to eight and nine months. think about that: what working class person could financially afford to protest for eight months? It was said that George Soros was funding the riots. Someone was footing the bill – and the unlawful, unregulated, violent protests continued. It was the push of the mobs. The ones who would be hurt, would the vulnerable and innocent law-bidding citizens: the middleclass that actually worked every day.

It was the Summer that Washington D.C. almost completely burned down; rioting, looting, and protests were anything but *"peaceable assemblies."* The American news media painted the violent protestors as heroes. I was disgusted by the lack of perspective of the basics of journalist ethics or any type of thorough fair reporting; I was revolted by all the cover-ups; the upper elite of America was literally getting away with murder and walking away from very serious crimes. The left, liberal-leaning, news media resemble third-world country propaganda machines such as in North Korea, China, or the Middle East.

Christian assemblies were the first to be shut down by the government! yet, liquor stores were allowed to remain open. It didn't make sense.

> *"America. The greatest losses to our freedom have come not from someone attacking us but from the government ignoring*

*the United States Constitution and the majority letting them
get away with it."*
— *Andrew Napolitano*

I live in California. Gavin Newson actually banned Church singing and
worship to God. How dare he? How could they write such ordnance
which completely stood against our First Amendment right to Freedom
of Religious practices of our United States Constitution?

THE AMERICAN CHRISTIAN CHURCH

So, the American Church improvised. We developed outreach and services
through the high-tech social media platforms: YouTube, Zoom, Facebook
Live, etc. For the first time, Churches and their congregations held their
entire services outdoors! All of this was fine in March, April, May, June,
July, August, September, October, but come November and December, it
started getting cold outside. Instead of midweek Bible studies and Sunday
services, they were happening now seven days a week. By trying to squash
it, it seemed to have the opposite effect; the services multiplied under the
attempts. Our little home mission's work never stopped. We were so small
and insignificant no one noticed we were still praying, still singing, and
still having a full service, including good old-fashioned altar calls.

In May 2021, Harvest Church in California, just won a 1.5-million-dollar
lawsuit against the state of California. We celebrated, until one saint asked
the Question: Is that also going to come out of our taxes? I shook my head. I
didn't have the answer to that, nor had I considered that California would
pass the bill again over to the American working class.

ESSENTIAL VERSES NONESSENTIAL

During this time of Covid, the population of American citizens were
divided up into two groups: *Essential vs. Nonessential* - it was based on
what the government said you were. Thousands lost their jobs and some
businesses had to close. A group of *Essential Workers*, were working

frantically to hold it all together, while our brothers and sisters were on lockdown; or standing in long lines that appeared as the old Soviet Union bread lines.

The governors/mayors instituted unconstitutional curfews at night. (A small form of martial law). Thanksgiving and Christmas were supposed to be canceled, *by elected officials? What on earth?* It was just insanity. And the American people asked: *When did the government get involved with who I invite into my home?* And if that wasn't bad enough, they were encouraging its citizens to report their neighbors for non-compliance. A hotline was set up! Can you imagine? It truly resemble Nazi Germany during WWII.

The question was, *would the American people actually comply?* Would they call the authorities on their neighbors? Most 800 hotlines were shut down because those that did call had some choice words for their new protocols.

AMERICAN EDUCATION

Schools and classrooms, (from elementary to university) were shut down. Only virtual learning would be allowed. Our kids were being homeschooled through the public school's virtual learning Zoom classes. It was creating depression, fear, and increased anxiety in our homes. Our children were weeping in utter frustration; and parents, well, we were trying to figure it all out, while working full-time. Parents were getting frantic phone calls while at work with internet IT problems at home and then having to carefully navigate (7, 8, 9, 10, 11-year-olds) on how to get their internet connection up and running to see their class.

Children's playground was surrounded by yellow restrictive tape forbidden access due to COVID. How would they exercise? Emotionally, children needed to run around and play to burn off their energy. It was healthy for them to be active. We were being forced to have sedentary lifestyles. Weight gain was inevitable. Families gained weight. Humanity was meant to congregate, (they needed to be around their family and friends,) and when kept inside for too long, began to show the signs of an emotional breakdown. It was truly psychological warfare.

BANKING INDUSTRY

Funny things began to happen at the banks: No more coins?

Overnight the local news began to report that there was a coin shortage? Which was absurd, absolutely preposterous! With the COVID concerns, people were afraid to touch money, coins, even debit cards. Hand gel was offered at cash registers to sanitize their hands after each transaction. In 2020, the invisible tanks of Chinese Marxism had rolled into America and it came through dirty politicians, the indoctrination from the movies we watched, and over our news channels. A bad feeling was looming in the air and the uncertainty of *"how long is this going to continue?"* We had flattened the curve, but our restrictions worsened.

Someone posted on Facebook, *"Do you remember when the 2nd plane hit the Twin Towers in New York, and you realized America really had been attacked - it was an act of war against the United States, not an accident? Let that sink in."*

2020 PRESIDENTIAL ELECTION

The 2020 United States Presidential election was highway robbery; (a true Presidential Heist). It utterly lacked any civil credibility; it certainly had no voting integrity! Voter tampering and voter fraud were obvious - and we all knew it. I was offered a sharpie to fill out my Presidential ballot, only to later find out that those ballots, (using sharpies) didn't count?!

When difficult and unreasonable state policies become more stringent and then continue on for months the mind begins to fear the worst. It reminded me of the 1959-1964 T.V. series by Rod Sterling: *Twilight Zone.* I wanted to shut it off and wake up in the morning to a new day; I wanted the America I knew, back!

A CALL TO TURN BACK TO GOD!

The world around me was changing too quickly, too violently, and I feared for my Nation. Yes, 2020, had me tapping out, and saying, *"What is happening to my nation, and where are our United States Constitutional freedoms!?* The frightening question was where would we all go from here? Where would we live in America the Great was gone? What would seriously happen if the Nation's Christian historical influence was destroyed from within? Benjamin Franklin said,

> *"I have lived, Sir, a long time, and the longer I live, the more convincing proof I see of this truth: that God Governs in the affairs of men. And if a sparrow cannot fall to the ground without his notice, is it probable that an empire can rise without his aid?" He continued: "I therefore beg leave to move—that henceforth prayers imploring the assistance of Heaven, and its blessings on our deliberations, be held in this Assembly every morning before we proceed to business, and that one or more of the Clergy of this City be requested to officiate in that Service." And so it has been, and is, in the new government to this day."*
> *— Benjamin Franklin. (U.S. Constitutional Conventions)*
> *Wallbuilders.org.*

The problem with that solution is that most American's were not practicing Christians!

The 21st Century American had lost their identity in Christ and the mind of God. A majority of Americans had lost the understanding of why God was important in our lives. They had redacted their Savior from public houses, court systems, schools, their children's early education, from everything. In doing that they forfeited their protection, power, and defense (that came from God). The American atheist and agnostics did it in such a way that was insulting, and absolutely disrespectful to a holy God. The Christians knew it was a matter of time before the God of Abraham, Isaac, and Jacob came to reckon with the American people. If God would deal with a backslidden Israel (before Christ), then He would certainly deal with us. (Isaiah 24:1-13; Romans 8:8-15; Genesis 4:10, and the entire book of Jeremiah and Lamentations). Judeo-Christian ideals, practices, and principles were organically interwoven in our Founding Father's documents: Declaration of Independence, our United States Constitution, the Federalist Papers, and our Bill of Rights. These documents only truly made sense when applied with sound Biblical principles and moral people, but they were one with the God of the Christian Holy Bible - He was our Divine, Great Creator.

There were really five principles established from our Declaration of Independence:

1. All men are created equal.
2. Our Rights come from God alone.
3. Every individual has the God-given Right to live, be free, and own property. (In essence also run their own business.)
4. The Purpose of our Government is to Protect our God-given Rights.
5. When Governments fail to protect our Rights, (instead infringe upon them), the People have the responsibility and duty to altar, or abolish that Government and to institute a New Government that actually fulfills its Rightful purpose.

There are two problems with the above bullet points: First, we are no longer one, or in unison with our God in heaven. And two, our mass populations were divided in thought, in concepts, in doctrines, in purpose, in culture, in everything.

So, what happens when citizens begin to live for themselves? We lose compassion and empathy for one another.

When no one is stopping to hear the voice of the Spirit of God, what happens when a free society pulls on the string from their fabric that holds it all together? The year 2020 was that moment in human history. We were not the first nation to come to this end.

ISRAEL'S HISTORY AND OUR OWN

In the book of Jeremiah, Israel also had done the same thing. In their freedoms and their wealth they forgot him. How did He respond? *God allowed His people to get sacked! He allowed their natural enemies to rise up and encroach their borders. Oppression began to seep into their lives and life wasn't as easy as it once had been.*

Israel's wickedness was so bad, that the Bible records the very earth under their feet cried out to God to dispel them. Read the book of Jeremiah. Particularly, chapter nine. God instructs Jeremiah to call for prayer warriors. What was God's purpose of allowing that? To bring them to repentance! To turn that nation from its wicked ways!

When Judgement finally comes,

> "And the Lord saith, Because they have forsaken my law which I set before them, and have not obeyed my voice, neither walked therein; but have walked after the imagination of their own heart, and after Baalim, which their fathers taught them:
>
> Therefore thus saith the Lord of hosts, the God of Israel; Behold, I will feed them, even this people, with wormwood, and give them water of gall to drink. I will scatter them also among the heathen, whom neither they nor their fathers have known: and I will send a sword after them, till I have consumed them.
>
> Thus saith the Lord of hosts, Consider ye, and call for the mourning women, that they may come; and send for cunning women, that they may come: And let them make haste, and take up a wailing for us, that our eyes may run down with tears, and our eyelids gush out with waters. For a voice of wailing is heard out of Zion, How are we spoiled! we are greatly confounded because we have forsaken the land because our dwellings have cast us out.

Yet hear the word of the Lord, O ye women, and let your ear receive the word of his mouth, and teach your daughters wailing, and everyone her neighbor lamentation. For death is come up into our windows, and is entered into our palaces, to cut off the children from without, and the young men from the streets.

Speak, Thus saith the Lord, Even the carcasses of men shall fall as dung upon the open field, and as the handful after the harvestman, and none shall gather them.

Thus saith the Lord, Let not the wise man glory in his wisdom, neither let the mighty man glory in his might, let not the rich man glory in his riches: But let him that glorieth glory in this, that he understandeth and knoweth me, that I am the Lord which exercise lovingkindness, judgment, and righteousness, in the earth: for in these things I delight, saith the Lord."

— Jeremiah 9:13-24

Today in America, another factor was our population and landmass. In 1776, the 13 Colonies were thought to have 2.5 million people, total. They were all situated along the East Coast. According to the 2020 US Census, we are looking at around 329.5 million people. That does not include undocumented souls living here. We now have fifty states today which spread from sea to sea. Yes, from the East Coast all the way to the Pacific Coast. Our people are not just Angelo Sazon and native American Indians, but masses, multitudes from all over the world. There were so many languages, religions, and culture in America and we didn't understand one another very well. So, how do you unite that many people?

SOCIAL MEDIA – THE NEW PUBLIC SQUARE

The American people could no longer trust the nightly news; rightfully branded, FAKE NEWS! Believe me, it was a title they earned and fairly deserved, they were FAKE!

American families looked for Conservative watch groups to for honest reporting or to help us understand what was really going on in Washington D.C. Our United States President could freely talk to us through those accounts. America bypassed ABC, NBC, MSNBC, and most certainly, CNN!

Literally anything from the US local stations was questionable.

Now, what happened after January 6, 2021?

Knowing the threat that Antifa would come to Washington D.C. and mingle amongst the MAGA protestors to cause problems was high. (Actually inevitable!) Everyone knew there was a potential for riots – it was in the air, palpable. Not amongst TRUMP supporters, but those posing as them. We would later learn that it is the House Speaker that approves the police around the Capitol. Nancy Pelosi saw no threat, and would side against the President, Donald Trump. She would not approve the United States military or reserves to come in.

What we feared most, happened. People died and TRUMP supporters were blamed for the damage and the President was tried for inciting the riot.

After January 6, 2021, the Democratic party and the United States Tech world shut down the Conservatives' voices and their platform. The President of the United States was silenced off of Twitter, Facebook, and most Social Media apps. A high wire fence was put around our U.S. Capitol building. Yes, the People's House was inaccessible!

It wasn't only our United States President that was banned from social media outlets and the news, but all conservative voices! Don Bongino, General Flynn, Rush Limbaugh, Sidney Powell, Lin Woods, Tom Fitton's Judicial Watch, Brandon Straka, (WalkAway Movement), and thousands of other Patriotic citizens, and watch groups (especially those with a large group following.) Essentially, High Tech was shutting down Christian Conservative Voices in America. The Democratic party was on the verge of unchecked powers.

On January 8, 2021, 10:30 A.M The Dan Bongino show said this:

"If you were going to implement a 4-point strategy on destroying our republic and decimate the conservative movement, and the freedom-loving patriots with it, how would you do it?

What would be the first step? The first step would be to make sure that your political opposition, (not necessarily big corporations), but working-class people, (dirt under the fingernails) people on the ground. You make them go bankrupt. They are not going to think much about politics if you can't feed your family. We are kind of witnessing that now, aren't we?

You bankrupt your opponents because if you are thinking about eating, you are really not thinking about voting. And while you bankrupting your opponents through lockdowns, endless attacks, destroying their credibility, sending in health inspectors; but you would want to enrich your friends. (Fantastically richer.) Amazon's Basio alone saw his net worth by more than 70 billion dollars. So that's step one.

Step two would be to eliminate and decimate election integrity, as well, right? You certainly can't have elections where you might lose because the working-class folks who you angered, may actually vote. In fact, in 2020, many of them did; with the highest turnout. So, the bad guys would want to make sure that they have an insurance policy in the election too. I'm mean just in case the election was free and fair and you the bad guys lost.

Step three, of course, you would want to use the U.S. Government to weaponize and attack and destroy your opposition. (That hasn't happened? Has it?) It's not like they haven't spied on a Presidential candidate and started fake/bogus investigations on Trump? Or maybe using people with law enforcement powers to target groups like the NRA (National Rifle Association).

And step four, shut down any political speech by monopolizing the new Public Square. What's the new public square? It's the social media outlets, Google, Facebook, Twitter, etc.

Tucker Carlson, (Fox News), summed these four points up beautifully, (January 7th, 2021). He made the point that the election was rigged through these four points.

THE CALL AND MISSION TO WITHSTAND SATAN!

As a Christian woman, I wanted Satan and his influence out of my life; out of the life of my family, out of my nation, and out of our world around me! After 2020, the American people wanted America free again! It was time to petition the LORD for His counsel and help from above! Immediately!

If you are waiting for the *"Liberty"* bell to sound the alarm, this is it!

It is time to stand up for yourself, for your family, and your country. It is time to shove back hard with a force that will knock this enemy on his butt. I'm sorry, but bullies will not just go away. They thrive on the energy they create through fear and intimidation. Bullies don't shrink in time, (if left unchecked); no, they grow in power. Yes, Believer, we shall have our crosses to bear, but not everything is your cross! This was a true satanic attack against humanity! Know this: We do not have to live in fear or live beneath God's best for our life.

2020 was my breaking point! When I declared, *"ENOUGH!"*

Tongues and Interpretation
Pentecostals of Alexandria Louisiana January 2020

Posted by Rick and Elizabeth Wright. 73k views.
YouTube Song: *"I'm going to see a victory"* – Pentecostals of Alexandria 9.44 song. At the 7.50 mark:

> *"You see lots of changes around you. These changes are Me trying to bring My People unto Me. I need you to come closer to Me. I need you to walk the way that My instructions have commanded you to walk. Come walk with Me. And when you come and walk with Me, the others will see and will follow. Come and walk the old path, the old way with Me. My instructions are clear. I am calling, I am calling. I am calling."*
>
> *— Tongues and Interpretations*
> *Pentecostals of Alexandria*
> *January 2020*

CHAPTER TWENTY-FOUR

ABOUT THE AUTHOR

My name is Kari Quijas, RT (R) (M). I am a Christian author and teacher. I have been a pastors wife for 14 years and woman's leader. I am also a licensed Radiology Technologist and Mammographer, with 22 years of experience in my field.

MY BOOKS

This is not my first book that I have written. It will be my 3rd published book with Westbow Press: *What is our Christian Purpose? Unplugging from the world wide web and Developing Christ within us.* (1st and 2nd edition), *I Do, A Christian Guide to Marriage,* and now this one, *And the Devil is Defeated! Winning the War Against Satan.*

INSPIRATION

What's my inspiration for my books? I will share with you, that each book was literally birthed through frustrations in my life. Things that bothered me, bugged me, perplexed me, and yes, even hurt me or tried to destroy me as a person. There is an old saying, by Friedrich Nietzsche, (1888 German philosopher), *"Out of life's school of war – what doesn't kill me, makes me stronger."* (Editorial on Friedrich Nietzsche's saying: https://thejns.org).

My books were birthed, (forged) through the personal fires of adversity. I laugh at that thought, because what the devil meant to destroy me, is actually what spring-boarded me to accomplish things I didn't know that I could. It then helped me to reach to more people just like me! That is why the Christian's conversion story is so powerful!

Life's *"hard road"* naturally develops personal experience and knowledge; and those traits can be shared. When I come across a problem, or problems – what the Church metaphorically calls *"mountains"* I tend to naturally look for a way around it or a better solution. I learned this process through my ADHD and dyslexia – work outside the box and the solution will be there! You just have to find it and then channel the negative into a positive.

THE POTTER'S WHEEL OF BOOK WRITING

I may write a book in two months, but it takes over a year to edit them; over and over rewriting them. For me, it is just like shaping and forming a clay vessel upon a potter's wheel. Can you see the image? The Potter uses water, the texture of the clay, and the movement of the wheel to form the vessel. For each page you glanced over or read once, was reread by me at least six, to seven times. Chapters were placed in different sections; or removed all together. Yes, even sometimes, destroying the manuscript to rebuild it again. Sometimes, I walked away from it for months. Then return to it and re-read it with the idea asking myself: *Is that what you wanted to say? Did you convey your message?*

Next, I spend a lot of time listening to my books with some audio software programs; that is the biggest help. It's tedious, takes hours. The hope is that there is flow and rhythm to the manuscript. In the end, you want to expound the full thought of your point.

All in all, it's really God working through the vessel, (me); to get the message out. During this time, I am still performing the duties of wife, mother, pastor's wife, and my secular employment. I gauge myself, *"do what is in front of you first, very well. Be patient, you will have time to go back to your project."* Having all these thoughts come to you, brainstorming in your mind, and then telling the creative side, *you have to wait – there are other responsibilities ahead of you* – is the most difficult for me. Remember, you will always find the time to do that which is important to you and anything we do for Jesus matters in eternity.

BIBLE STUDIES

I have learned that my studies help me to grow as a person, and even more, to learn the beauty of my Holy Bible. Many times, sermons heard over the pulpit catch only small fragment of the full story. Know this, a great sermon will inspire the listener to explore the whole story for themselves. Of course, the important part of the sermon is the message from God – *What is God saying to the Church?*

Increasing our depth of understanding the Bible story, the history behind it, or the very nature of mankind – enriches us as people. There is something about going step by step and reading the entire passage of scripture; carefully studying all the characters in the story – their conduct, their choices, and even so, their outcomes that benefits us.

EVEN IF ONLY YOUR FAMILY SEES IT – WRITE IT!

Fourteen years ago, I wrote and designed a children's book, *Children, How Must a Man be Saved?* I illustrated through pictures the salvation method. The book was solely for my three daughters. It is our *Family Tradition and Values* that I wanted passed on to my lineage – *Above all we are Christ's.* Each child received my book and I wanted them to remember in our Nation, there used to be Christian families who served God with their whole heart.

WHO AM I

For me, there is no greater honor than being a child of God. The late Rev. Billy Cole once said, *"That's not arrogance, that's knowledge!"* Oh, how I love and cherish the voice of our elders. And if you really are God's beloved child, then you will have a heart open to receive and will be full of good works! But not just in church service, but outside the four walls of your local assembly: to your neighbors, to your place of employment; to the general public. Jesus said,

> "Rejoice, and be exceeding glad: for great is your reward in heaven: for so persecuted they the prophets which were before you. Ye are the salt of the earth: but if the salt have lost his savor, wherewith shall it be salted? it is thenceforth good for nothing, but to be cast out, and to be trodden under foot of men.
>
> Ye are the light of the world. A city that is set on an hill cannot be hid. Neither do men light a candle, and put it under a bushel, but on a candlestick; and it giveth light unto all that are in the house.
>
> Let your light so shine before men, that they may see your good works, and glorify your Father which is in heaven."
> — Jesus Christ, (Matthew 5:12-16)

MY CHRISTIAN TESTIMONY OF FAITH

My Christian conversion was the greatest event that ever took place in my life!

During my Christian conversion, Jesus Christ never left my bedside. *He is amazing, astounding, and ferociously protective over His new babies in Christ.* His hands rocked me and stilled my aching heart! It took months and years to heal the world out of me. Some work was quick; but some was a struggle. I know the ways of the LORD from my own experience. If you are a sinner, you'll understand this concept: It was like being pulled out of the Matrix, in the 1999 movie with Keanu Reeves. *"Your reality is about to change - what you thought was real is actually just a dream."* Yes, the LORD captured my heart, I was His. I wanted my life to line up with Jesus Christ; I wanted my thoughts to be His thoughts. The word of God taught me how to boldly renounced all evil and wickedness. I have personally felt the weight of sin taken off my shoulders and I was free! That's what Christians offer to the world around them.

MY WORK IN THE HOSPITAL – MY HEALING MINISTRY

I love the creativity, (in problem solving radiology positioning through different body habitus), and continually developing my imaging skills. I truly enjoy medicine and patient care. This is the truth: In Radiology each day is a new day? Each week I meet, speak with, and assist hundreds of patients. I am a fierce patient advocate. I am an educator. I am a firm believer in the patient's Bill of Rights. The LORD gave me this gift in 1998 and I never regretted the four years it took to obtain my career as a Licensed Radiology Technologist, RT, R, F, M, (ARRT). I read a meme on Facebook just last week: *You travel back in time to talk to your 18-year-old self and you only have three words you can say, what do you say?* My response: *Stay in school!*

2020 ESSENTIAL HEALTHCARE WORKER

In 2020, I was an *"Essential Health Care worker."*

I realized how and why God placed me in my current profession of medicine – it was all in God's timing. I was able to work with patients who were so fearful. I have the Living God of Abraham inside of me; and the LORD was desperate to touch them through my voice. I prayed with patients, almost daily; I encouraged them and listened to their stories. I laughed with them – you laughter really is good medicine. Joy is contagious. I often heard them say, *"You're an angel."* I became an angel, (so to speak), in that I wanted to ministry and bless each patient I saw, (yet, work within the restrictions of secular employment and human resource policies), and Yes, there are ways around them – that satisfy all parties. My goal: *When they leave Radiology, they will be lifted up – I will be a light in their darkness. I will be loving and kind.*

I purposely dressed in bright colors and wore flowers in my hair. I made the decision, *I will change the atmosphere with goodness! I will laugh and be cheerful. I will enjoy them; and I will allow them to have a little piece of me in a sweet memory.*

I prayed in Jesus name that fear will be destroyed and that my patients would be stronger – bolder, yes, strengthened! My Bible tells me in Proverbs 17:22a, *"A merry heart does good like medicine..."* And I know it to be true. Not that I am so spiritual, I was just sensitive and obedient to God - I was willing to step up, I was willing to speak up. I was available for Him to use. That is all He's really looking for.

Will you be His hands, His feet, His heart, His mouth, His mind, His eyes to a dying world? Will you go and touch others around you? Will you become Jesus' Essential Worker?

WE ARE ALL ESSENTIAL!

"They may forget your name,
but they will never forget how you made them feel."
—*Maya Angelou*

"Kind words can be short and easy to speak,
but their echoes are truly endless."
—*Mother Teresa*

"If you want to lift yourself up, lift up someone else."
—*Booker T. Washington*

"A merry heart doeth good like a medicine:
but a broken spirit drieth the bones."
—Proverbs 17:22

NOTES AND BIBLIOGRAPHY - LIST OF BOOK REFERENCES

- Holy Bible, King James Version, Apostolic Study Bible
- Bunyan, John: *the Pilgrim's Progress* (Illustrated), Life Sentence Publishing books, P.O. Box 652, Abbotsford, WI 54404
- Mangun, Vesta Layne: *Vesta Mangun Continues.* Published by the Pentecostals of Alexandria, 2817 Rapides Avenue, Alexandria, LA 71303
- Quijas, Kari: *What is Our Christian Purpose? Unplugging from the World Wide Web and Developing Christ Within us.* West bow Press, A Division of Thomas Nelson & Zondervan, 1663 Liberty Drive, Bloomington, IN 47403
- Meyers, Joyce: The Battlefield of the Mind, Winning the Battle in Your Mind. Life in the Word, Inc. P.O. Box 655, Fenton, Missouri 63026. Faith Words, Hachette Book Group USA, 237 Park Avenue. New York, NY 10017
- Butterfield, Rosaria Champagne: *The Secret Thoughts of an Unlikely Convert; An English Professor's journey into Christian Faith.* Expanded Edition. Crown & Covenant publications. 7408 Penn Avenue, Pittsburgh, PA 15208
- Strobel, Lee: *The Case for Christ; A Journalist's Personal Investigation of the evidence for Jesus.* Zondervan, 3900 Sparks Drive, SE, Grand Rapids, Michigan 49546.
- Neal, Mary C. MD: *To Heaven and Back, A Doctor's Extraordinary Account of Her Death, Heaven, Angels, and Life Again. A True Story.* Waterbrook Press. 12265 Oracle Blvd., Suite 200. Colorado Springs, Colorado. 80921

- Graves, R. Brent: *The God of Two Testaments*. World Aflame Press, 8855 Dunne Road, Hazelwood, MO 63042. Pentecostals Publishing.com.
- Graham, Billy: Angels, Angels, Angels, God's Secret Agents. Guideposts Associates, Inc. Carmel, New York. Guideposts edition published by arrangement with Doubleday & Company Inc, 1975.
- Mangun, Anthony: *Heaven to Earth*; Made in the USA; Columbia, SC, January 2019.
- Wilberforce, William: *A Practical View of Christianity;* Hendrickson Christian Classics; Hendrickson Publishers, Inc. P.O. ox 3473, Peabody, Massachusetts 01961-3473
- Cann, Jonathan: The Harbinger; published by Frontline, Charisma Media/Charisma House Book Group, 600 Rinehart Road, Lake Mary, Florida 32746
- *5 Principles of opposition to Tyranny. Understanding the Declaration of Independence.* (Freedomist show, episode 5). YouTube channel.
- Skousen, Paul B: *How to Read the Constitution & the Declaration of Independence;* Izzard Ink Publishing, P.O. Box 522251, Salt Lake City, UT 84152.
- Wehle, Kim: *How to Read the Constitution and Why;* HarperCollins Publishers, 195 Broadway, New York, NY 10007.

Printed in the United States
by Baker & Taylor Publisher Services